SOCIETY AND POLITICS IN INDIA
Understanding Political Sociology

SHEFALI ROY

Associate Professor and Head
Department of Political Science
Patna Women's College
Patna University, Patna

PHI Learning Private Limited

Delhi-110092
2025

In fond memory of ***Shri Asoke K. Ghosh*** *(October 1942 – February 2024), Founder Chairman and Managing Director of PHI Learning, whose vision endlessly inspires.*

The Legacy Continues....

Published by Pushpita Ghosh, PHI Learning Private Limited, Rimjhim House, 111, Patparganj Industrial Estate, Delhi-110092 and Printed by Syndicate Binders, A-20, Hosiery Complex, Noida, Phase-II Extension, Noida-201305 (N.C.R. Delhi).

₹595.00

SOCIETY AND POLITICS IN INDIA: Understanding Political Sociology
Shefali Roy

ISBN-978-81-203-4992-6 (Print Book)
ISBN-978-93-90669-39-4 (e-Book)

Realizing the dreams of my father (Late Biswanath Roy)
who has always inspired me to be a true academician.

I owe it to you 'Baba'.

Contents

List of Figures

List of Tables

Preface

The growth of empirical study as a result of behavioural movement in United States of America, after the termination of Second World War, gave birth to Political Sociology. As a branch of Political Science, this subject shifted its focus from traditional and descriptive approach to modern and analytical methodology. The meaning of Political Science has been changed often with the passage of time. In ancient period, political science dealt with the affairs of State and Government, medieval age regarded the subject as the study of ethical governance and omnipotence, and modern definition of Political Science gives attention to the process of seeking, retaining and demonstrating power. Of late, in contemporary political scenario, the thrust of study has shifted to conflict and conflict resolution. It meddles functions of bureaucrats, ministers, people, policy makers and judicial system with social norms, values and behavioural patterns.

The emergence of Political Sociology widened the frontiers of political science. The nature of study became interdisciplinary. Political scientists noticed that the nature and scope of polity and society are interdependent. The absence of one makes the other meaningless. Politics cannot survive without social base and society cannot prosper without political will. This complementary relationship enriched the contents of Political Sociology. A relatively young subject, Political Sociology strives to seek research excellence, in its process of evolution.

The book tries to highlight certain issues which have developed a bond between society and polity. This book is my maiden venture, though I have specialized in this subject, still its flexibility demands keen observation. The book comprises sixteen chapters. The concepts like political socialization, culture and participation makes the subject more representative. Human error is inevitable and this work is no exception. Hope readers will benefit from this book and will also provide suggestions for its improvement in the next edition.

I am thankful to one and all for lending me a helping hand in one way or the other in conceptualizing the book. My sincere thanks goes to PHI Learning's Editorial and Production team for willingly supporting me.

Shefali Roy

Acknowledgements

I did it because I had a child like faith in you 'Maa'.

I am indebted to my student Shilpi, who became my right hand in typing some of the chapters selflessly when I underwent my wrist surgery.

My deep sense of gratitude to my husband Anand Madhab, who played a crucial role, in spite of his busy schedule in giving final shape to this book. His critical appreciation and suggestions enriched the contents of this book.

My love and blessings to my daughter, Shatakshi Anand, who never let me procrastinate my writing work.

I am also thankful to Vatsala Shrivastava for her persuasion to pen down my knowledge in a form of a book.

Sincere thanks goes to my brother-in-law, Arun Kumar Verma (Mukhiyaji), for relieving me from house hold chores.

I am sincerely thankful to the Principal, Patna Women's College, Dr. Sister Doris D'souza, A.C. for being my inspiration, and to my colleague Dr. Prabha Kumar for her constant support.

Last but not the least, my thanks goes to Vinod Kumar, DTP operator of Patna Women's College, for his dexterity.

Shefali Roy

1

Political Sociology
Origin, Nature and Scope

CRUX

More than one person, in any age, creates power activity; which we call 'political.' The activity may be political but the 'actor' is essentially an individual who is a basic unit of the society. So the realization that polity and society has inherent linkages which needs to be articulated and assessed. This process lead to the emergence of a relatively young discipline known as 'Political Sociology.

EMERGENCE OF POLITICAL SOCIOLOGY

'Politics' was the title of the famous work of Aristotle, which indicated that politics is derived from the Greek term *Polis* which means city-states; that which is concerned with the affairs of state, government and administration. Political Science, as a discipline, emerged out of this philosophy. It was more a philosophy, than a science, if we at all believe that science is a systematic study of facts. As originated in Greek theory, political science was actually political philosophy based on theoretical interpretations, descriptive ideas, speculative notions, abstract and value-laden thoughts, or in other words, a 'normative study'. Idealism remained the core idea, be it Plato's Ideal State ruled by Philosopher Guardian or Aristotle's Best State ruled by the middle class community. Tocqueville's analysis of pre-revolutionary and post-revolutionary France in his work entitled "The Old Regime and The French Revolution", (1856) has largely contributed to the study of relationship between social-economic development and political institutions.

With the growing complexities, the latter half of nineteenth century witnessed emergence of political science. Charles E. Merriam and Barbara Leigh Smith divided political science into four general phases:

(i) The Classical Period upto 1850;

(ii) The Institutional Period upto 1850–1900;

(iii) The Transitional Period, upto 1900–1923, and
(iv) The Behavioural Period from 1923 to the present.[1]

The classical period stressed on 'ought to be' situation of polity, strived to create a 'Utopian State', which could not be actually realized on the earth. The Institutional period, however made political science a distinct branch of study. Though being descriptive in nature, it tried to provide an explanation to political structures, constitution and organs of government. There was a paradigm shift in the transitional phase. During this phase, political science was concerned with particular type of human activity, the activity to seek power, even by adopting wrong, unethical and illegitimate methods. This was a stage of turmoil, finally reaching to the stage of behavioural movement. This was also a phase of protest against traditional or classical period of political science. Charles Merriam's quest for scientific politics sprang from his concern with social policy.[2] The whole focus shifted from library resources to fieldwork, the journey from description to empirical study, from secondary to primary study. This movement known as pragmatism was a reaction against metaphysical philosophies. Catlin, Munro, Harold Lasswell and David Easton looked upon this model as both desirable and feasible for the present day politics. Political Science emerged as a study of conflict and conflict resolution, and of seeking, retaining and demonstrating power. Behavioural phase emphasized the relevance of inter-disciplinary approach, pragmatism was a philosophical co-relate of the psychological implications of the symbolic interactionist movement that became prominent in 1920s and 1930s. It redefined the scope of the discipline. This phase laid too much importance on methods and facts which was devoid of values and norms. Political Science was reduced to the extent of being a barren land. The vehement criticism was that political science, being a social science, cannot be absolutely value free, as it deals with animate objects. Thus, post behaviouralism made a striking balance between the two extremes of traditionalism and behaviouralism. This redirection implied by post behavioural development was future-oriented and was to perceive values in a scientific temperament.

The development of political science witnessed a marked change in its perspectives, which can be divided into five sections:

(a) From Idealism to Realism
(b) From Human Nature to Power Relations
(c) From Discussions to Empirical Analysis
(d) From Behaviouralism to Post Behaviouralism and
(e) From Sociology of Politics to Political Sociology to Political Economy

Political scientists down the ages were in accord that politics cannot grow without a social foundation. The origin of philosophy of science goes to Plato and Aristotle who talked about abductive, deductive and inductive inferences. Roger Bacon, an English thinker, started formally scientific method in understanding philosophy in 11th century.

In modern period, Francis Bacon outlined a new system of logic to improve upon the old philosophical process of syllogism. In the year, 1637 Rene Descartes came up with a new empirical framework in his work 'Discourse on Method' promoting rationalism. Then emerged the concept of logical positivism based on tenets of verified, meaningful interpretations. In late 1920's an organized attempt was made to prove the efficiency of cognitive meaning fullness.

Thomas Kuhn in his book *The Structure of Scientific Revolutions* talks about competing paradigms, which can never be measured by a yardstick of descriptive adequacy, Lakatos came up with his 'incorporation criterion' and the French philosopher August Comte elaborately discussed the perspective of positivism in his work entitled 'The Course in Positivist Philosophy.' His ideas became the basis of social research. His major contribution was in the field of quest for truth. He divided it into three stages (i) the theological (ii) the metaphysical (iii) the positive. Logic and probability are the two standard techniques of philosophy of science. Karl Popper was a believer of theory and practice compatibility. According to him, empirical method may reach to accuracy and precision, but a law or a theory is also determined by diversity and severity of tests it has passed.

Thus, philosophy of science is concerned with the methods and implications of science, a rational fact finding process. Philosophy is a hard discipline to be defined precisely and so is science.

Plato and Aristotle did not find any distinction between state and society, however, during middle ages, Church dominated the State as priests were regarded as representatives of God on earth. They were not made to commit any error, if ever they did, they were never subjected to corporal punishment by mundane people. This was a Dark Age where the State was made subservient to the city of God. Hegel's statement that 'State is a march of God on Earth' glorified state supported by Thomas Hobbes, in his monumental work 'Leviathan'. But this absolutism was challenged in the works of J.S. Mill, Locke and Rousseau. Nicollo Machiavelli stepped into the world of realism. Graham Wallas studied human nature in politics culminating into Harold Lasswell's "Politics: who gets what, when and how?" Power relations became the focal point of analysis.

The age of discussion was over. Empirical analysis of David Easton was recognized and appreciated. Over emphasis on scientific approach led to a new beginning of post behavioural era. Value fact dichotomy was not rigidly followed. American scientists, unlike Marx, did not agree to the fact that society precedes polity. They failed to identify social determinants or bases of political behaviour. They generalized that State and Society are the two sides of the same coin. A significant concern for political sociology is the analysis of socio-political factors in economic development. Karl Marx and Max Weber laid the foundation of sociology of politics and political sociology, as the former made study of political sociology equivalent to the study of social structure, whereas latter gave autonomous and institutional approach to the study of political sociology. Weber was a leading critic of Marx and substantially contributed to the field of political sociology in terms of some vital concepts and methods. This trend towards empirical methods dominated the works of American thinkers in the latter part of nineteenth century. Political science entered into the age of political process and political behaviour.

There were certain reasons, which motivated American social scientists to undertake studies in political sociology. In the years, following World War I, they grew conscious of the pathologies and shortcomings of the democratic framework of their country.[3] Their vision however was limited, confined to the practices and lacunae of European-American models and perceived Communist or Fascist model as an aberration. However, post Second World War witnessed studies of political process and behaviour of the third world countries of Asia, Africa or Latin America. These newly liberated states were at the take-off stage with their specific indigenous problems. Thus, political sociology emerged as an evolving discipline to grapple with specific social problems of developed and developing countries.

DEFINITION

> S.M. Lipset defines political sociology as "the study of the inter-relationship between society and polity, between social structures and political institutions."
>
> In the words of R. Bendix, "Political sociology starts with the society and examines how it affects the State".
>
> Michael Rush and Philip Althoff say "we have defined political sociology as being a subject area which examines the link between politics and society, between social structures and political structures and between social behaviour and political behaviour".
>
> Giovanni Sartori defines "Political Sociology as an interdisciplinary hybrid." Robert E. Dowse and John A. Hughes define political sociology "as the study of political behaviour within a sociological perspective framework".
>
> A.K. Mukhopadhaya remarks, "Political Sociology is a child from the marriage between sociology and political science and, as in human issues, cannot be solely characterized by its parental qualities alone."

NATURE

As an outcome of behavioural and developmental analysis, political sociology emerged as a separate field of study. The sociological perspective in political science is as old as political science itself. However, in recent years, focus shifted from sociological interpretation of politics to politiological and sociological approaches interacting with each other. The term sociology was first coined by

August Comte. Von Stein studied society an as autonomous subject. Karl Marx felt that study of society as an independent subject is important, but becomes more important as a study of society, preceding and determining the nature and functioning of polity. He gets the credit of finding 'sociology of politics'. But actually speaking, an Arab scholar Ibn Khaldun has been the earliest exponent of economic conception of history.[4] Politics was made a handmaid of sociology, which was later challenged to make politics autonomous. This traditionally started with realist thinkers like Chanakya and Machiavelli, followed by neo-machiavellians, such as Pareto, Mosca and Michels. Marxist interpretation of politics made it subservient to society, whereas Machiavellians gave politics an independent stature; however an element of realism and scientific temperament dominated both the thinking. This kind of political realism recognizes the utility of political management of conflict through compromise and adjustment among various social forces and interests. Political sociology aims at understanding the sources and the social bases of conflict, as well as process of management of conflict.[5] Sartori rightly claims that political sociology gives equal attention to any kind of conflict and cleavage, race and ethnicity, region and locality culture and tradition, religion and ideology, caste or class. It also translates conflicts into politics as a strategy of conflict management. Political science has tended to concentrate on the visible part of the political iceberg. In contrast, political sociology has paid greater attention to the submerged portions.[6]

This was the era when political science has been seen as more than the study of power, than managing social affairs. It was the time when political science came out of the classroom and reached to the community.

Political sociology is very closely related to political science. It is very technical approach to study political science. Everyone knows that politics cannot grow in isolation—society provides the foundation or in other words, social economy provides the infrastructure on which stands the superstructure of polity. Power is the key concept in political sociology. It deals with power in the social context. It also deals with organization and exercise of political power in hands of different social classes. The nature of political sociology in 1950's and early 1960s were different from contemporary political sociology. Earlier it was institutionalized, now the thrust area is individual's political belief, behaviour and its implication on the political process. Here politics invaded social psychology, because even personal belief is influenced by the social beliefs, and it changes with the social environment and surroundings.

SCOPE

Political sociology is a discipline, which is mainly concerned with the analysis of the interaction between politics and society.

Duverger considers political sociology as a science of power and authority relationship. He believes that the scope of political sociology revolves around two ingredients—power and authority. To him scope comprises (a) political structure and phenomena (b) the existence of antagonism or to say inherent dialectics and (c) conflict resolution and integration. Charles Merriam and Harold Lasswell supports Duverger and further adds that the scope of political sociology consists of inherent aspects of influence, force and power, especially in the struggle and conflict among groups or classes in the given society under the influence of political relationship.

Greer and Orleans explain political sociology as "being mainly concerned with the description, analysis and sociological explanation of the peculiar social structure called the state".[7]

Two groups of scholars have discussed the scope of political sociology in two different manners. According to Greer and Orleans, "Political Sociology is concerned with structure of the State; the nature and conditions of legitimacy; the nature of the monopoly of force and its use by the State; and the nature of the sub-units and their relation with the State".[8]

Andrew Effrat another thinker believed that political sociology has a broader perspective as it is also concerned with "causes patterns and consequences of the distribution and process of power and authority in all social system".[9] Social system has definitely a broader framework for political study as it includes family, educational institutions, peer groups and political institutions.

Richard Braungart claims that political sociology is concerned with (a) social origin of politics (b) the structure of politics or the political process (c) the effects of politics on the surrounding society and culture.[10]

It is therefore understood that the main concern for political sociologists is to investigate the problem of social order and political obedience. It covers following areas for specific study:

1. Social structure—Role of caste, class, community, regional language in determining polity, and rural-urban divide.
2. Political structure—Three organs of the government, political parties, pressure groups, interest groups, etc.
3. Political life—Power, authority, legitimacy, political development, political modernization, political socialization, political culture, political participation and political communication all play a crucial role in providing insight into the political life.
4. Political leadership—Recruitment policy so as to create elites or political leaders or bureaucracy for an efficient functioning of leaders within the prescribed social base.

Political sociology in India has been greatly influenced by events that have taken place in the country. The tradition, social structure and the norms formulate political ideologies on their own terms. The umbrella character of the Congress party in India is due to the fact that it emerged as a movement for the liberation of India than a mere party, hence it engulfs all prevalent ideologies of the country.

POLITICAL SOCIOLOGY AND SOCIOLOGY OF POLITICS

Political science can be defined as a discipline, which regards political structural conditions as explanatory variables or in other words determinants. Sociology can be regarded as a study that tends to opt for social structural condition as explanatory variables. Having drawn the dividing line between political science and sociology, the pertinent question now arises as how to bridge the gap between them, and moreover how to study them at their points of interaction. While doing so, two disciplines emerged—'sociology of politics' and 'political sociology'. Political sociology should not be considered as a synonym for sociology of politics. Apparently, both seem alike but meticulous study reveals their deep-rooted differences. The sociology of politics is sociological reduction of politics and takes political phenomenon as a dependable variable and the underlying social phenomenon as an explanatory variable. Thus, it teaches one to look politics sociologically. Political sociology instead, is an inter-disciplinary hybrid attempting to combine social and political explanatory variables on the same platform.

Karl Marx is regarded as the pioneer of 'sociology of politics'. He regarded polity as a dependent variable. Ibn Khaldun and some others had talked about the importance of socio-economic factors, but some of them epitomized to the extent of making the point a classical one. Politics to Max represented the super-structure; the character of which was totally conditioned by the character of social order on which it grew. Marx therefore rejects synthesis between social and political approaches as have been meticulously done by political sociologists.

A group of thinkers, viz. Bendix, Lipset, Coser following almost the Marxian approach are in accord, that political sociology is basically a branch of sociology, because for these scholars, sociological variables, such as society, class and status are independent variables and political variables, such as State, law and political parties are dependent on them. Bendix defines political sociology as "the study of how society affects the State".[11] Lipset claims that main area of interest of political sociology is concentration of economic power and political decision-making, political parties, voluntary associations, ideologies of interest groups and problems of oligarchy and bureaucracy.[12] Coser says that political sociology is that branch of sociology which is concerned with social causes and consequences of given power distribution within or between societies and with the social and political conflict that leads to changes in allocation of power.[13]

This view was challenged by an Italian political scientist, Giovanni Sartori, who seeks to emphasize the autonomy of politics and the impact of politics on the moulding of social and economic structure or behaviour.[14] He claims that political sociology is only born when the sociological and 'politological' approaches are combined at their point of intersection. Sartori selected a major stream in the sociology of politics, namely the stream that investigates the imprint of social class and stratification upon political behaviour. While investigation may be carried out at various levels—the electoral level, the party level and the elite level. Various threads are amenable to the general heading of 'sociology of parties'.

Since the study of parties is equally a concern of political scientists, first the boundary should be drawn. Political scientists consider party system as an explanatory variable, whereas sociologists tend to perceive party system as a dependable variable. The distinctive contribution of sociologists to the study of parties is to investigate to what extent party system is in response to and a reflection of social stratification, the solidarity structure of society, its socio-economic and socio-cultural cleavages, its degree of heterogeneity and of integration, its level of economic growth and the like.

The classical formulation of this approach is presented in Lipset's 'Political Man'. In this work, he claims that in any form of democracy, conflict is inevitable, and is expressed through different political parties. Their role is basically to represent democratic translation of class struggle. Politics is the study of conflicts and conflict resolution.

He discusses about two types of conflict—Marxist and Pluralist. Former is a temporary necessity and it ends with the victory of proletariat ever bourgeoisie class, whereas latter is an ongoing process which results from variety and variety is per-se-seminal.

Sociology of politics talks about Marxist (class) conflict and muddles it with pluralist conflict, and does not believe in any other form of conflict. Political sociology, on the other hand, gives equal attention to any kind of conflict—race, caste, ethnicity region, locality, tradition, ideology, religion, sex—which are all important dimensions of conflict as its class dimension.

Sociology of politics heavily concentrate on 'class voting' and they rely on the assumption that party system can operate within the framework of socio-economic cleavage and conflict of the society, whereas political sociology has a very different point to emphasize. Political sociologists very strongly believe that 'class voting' is not sufficient enough for the functioning of political parties, because they cannot translate all socio-economic cleavages into party cleavage. It also needs, 'leaders' or in other words 'elites' bent on attaching rewards and deprivations to class divisions. Political leadership, thus, redirects attitudes and calls values into question. Even if one was to believe that social cleavages and conflicts translate themselves into party competition, the roles played by the leaders of the translation process must be property appreciated.

Sociology of politics illustrates conflict, its origin, growth and domestic causes responsible for it, and seeks to find an amicable solution. It never makes on effort to probe into the non-domestic or to say political causes playing vital role in either aggravating the tension or minimizing it to the lowest ebb as per the power game requirement. Political sociology explains lucidly why many of the conflicts and cleavages existing in the society may not be 'translated' into party politics—the reason being the absence of a translator. Translation calls for translator (leader) thereby focusing the attention on handling or mishandling. The mishandling may intensify the conflict, instead of deviating it. In India, leaders as compared to regional diversity do not seriously address the problem of poverty. The obvious reason is electoral interest of politicians.

The issue of autonomy of politics is indeed of profound significance so far as the distinction is concerned. Sociological variables are identified as determinants of political behaviour by sociology of politics. The traits of the political actor's personality are not highlighted. Here the approach of sociology of politics is criticized. Political sociology believes that it is equally, if not more, important to know how and with what consequences, political factors influence social and personal aspects of a public leader. It is more so important to analyze the role played by the leader to handle a particular situation, which is conditioned by the social order.

Thus, we see that political sociology no doubt incorporates much of sociology of politics within itself yet representing two different worlds.

Questions for Discussion

1. Define political sociology. Discuss its nature and scope.
2. Examine the emergence and relevance of political sociology.
3. Discuss the difference between political sociology and sociology of politics.
4. Political sociology is an inter-disciplinary hybrid, Elucidate.

References

1. Smith, Barbara Leigh, et al. (1976), *Political Research Methods, Foundation and Techniques*, Boston, Houghton Mifflin Company, pp. 2–6.
2. Somit, Albert and Tannenhaus, Joseph (1967), *The Development of American Political Science: From Burgess to Behaviouralism*, Boston, Allyn and Bacon, Inc., p. 111.
3. Almond, Grabiel A. and Bingham Powell Jr., G. (1972), *Comparative Politics: A Developmental Approach*, Delhi, American Publishing Company (Indian edition), p. 5.
4. Michels, Robert (1949), *First Lectures in Political Sociology*, New York, Harper and Row, p. 10.
5. Sharma, L.N. and Ashraf, Ali (1983), *Political Sociology: A New Grammar of Politics*, Universities Press, Madras, p. 3.
6. Coser, Lewis A. (Ed.) (1967), *Political Sociology: Selected Essays*, New York, Harper and Row, pp. 3–4.

7. Greer, S. and Orleans, P. (1964), *Political Sociology* in Faris, R.L. (Ed.) *Handbook of Modern Sociology*, Chicago, Rand McNally, p. 810.

8. *Ibid.*

9. Effrat, Andrew (Ed.) (1973), *Perspectives in Political Sociology*, New York, Bobbs-Merrill Company, p. 3.

10. Richard Braungart, G. (Ed.) (1976), *Society and Politics: Readings in Political Sociology*, New Jersey, Prentice Hall, Introductory Essay, p. 2.

11. Bendix, R. and Lipset, S.M. (1964), *Political Sociology* in Faris R.L. (Ed.), *Handbook of Modern Sociology*, Chicago, Rand McNally, p. 810.

12. Lispet, S.M. (1960), *Political Man: The Social Bases of Politics*, New York, Doubleday and Company.

13. Coser, Lewis A. (Ed.) (1967), *Political Sociology: Selected Essays*, *op. cit.*, p. 1.

14. Sartori, G. (1972), *From Sociology of Politics to Political Sociology* in S.M. Lipset (Ed.), *Politics and Social Science*, Delhi, Wiley Eastern.

Suggested Reading

Amal Kumar Mukhopadhyaya, *Approaching Political Sociology*

L.N. Sharma and Ali Ashraf, *Political Sociology: A New Grammar of Politics*

R.A. Dahl, *Modern Political Analysis*

Rush and Althoff, *An Introduction to Political Sociology*

Web Link

www.wisegeek.com/what-is-politicalsociology.htm

2

Approaches and Methods to the Study of Political Sociology

CRUX

The emergence of political sociology provided socio-political scientists conditions to offer well-researched methods and approaches for the study of growing discipline. A phase of transition came where the focus was shifted from abstract notions to concrete reality. However, difference in approaches made the study more interesting and enriching and provided magnified dimensions to study political sociology. The striking difference of opinion of political scientists added abundance to the content of this relatively young discipline.

STUDYING POLITICAL SOCIOLOGY

Approaches and Methods

An approach "consists of criteria of selection—criteria employed in selecting the problems or questions to consider and in selecting the data to bring to bear; it consists of standards governing the inclusion and exclusion of questions and data."[1] In simple terms, it is a point of view in explaining a particular phenomenon. Very close to it is method almost inter-related, but Van Dyke draws distinction by following words, "approaches consist of criteria for selecting problems and relevant data, whereas methods are procedures for getting and utilizing data."[2] An approach is subjective, therefore varies from person to person resulting in numerous approaches. There is no single approach universally accepted. Broadly speaking, an approach is divided into two parts—traditional, scientific/modern (see Table 2.1). Former laid emphasis on values and latter is fact oriented, also known as modern approach. Behavioural approach can be distinguished from traditional approach in nature, goals and methods.

Value fact dichotomy became the basis of the two approaches. While traditional approach comprised philosophical, descriptive (historical), institutional

Table 2.1 Specifications of the Two Approaches

S. No.	*Traditional*	*Scientific/Modern*
1.	Descriptive	Analytical
2.	Normative	Real
3.	Value laden	Fact laden
4.	Speculative	Empirical
5.	Ought to be	What it is
6	Rational	Pragmatic

and legal approach; modern approaches talked of psychological, sociological, quantitative, behavioural, system analysis and structural-functional approach.

MODERN APPROACHES

Political sociology, as a young discipline, is the result of operating modern approaches, particularly behavioural, system analysis and structural-functional approach.

Behavioural Approach

Behavioural approach was a challenge to traditionalism. American political scientists reacted sharply to traditional norms and focused on the behaviour of individual as a political actor in a given society. This approach received formal recognition after the termination of Second World War, though it's origin goes back to the work of Graham Wallas entitled 'Human Nature in Politics' in 1908. Charles E. Merriam of the Chicago University gets the credit of being the father of this movement. His ideas drew attention of Gabriel A. Almond, Robert A. Dahl, Harold Lasswell and David Easton. They all evolved behavioural movement to build up an empirical theory. According to Robert Dahl behaviouralism is a protest movement within political science.... associated with a number of political scientists, mainly American's, who shared (a) "a strong sense of dissatisfaction with the achievements of conventional political science particularly through historical, philosophical and the descriptive—institutional approaches", and (b) "a belief that additional methods and approaches either existed or could be developed that would help political science with empirical propositions and theories of systematic sort tested by closer, more direct and more rigorously controlled observations of political events."

David Easton writes, "Behavioural research seeks to elevate the actual human being to the centre of attention. Its premise is that the traditionalists have been reifying institutions virtually looking at them as entities apart from their component individuals."

David Easton laid down the features of behaviouralism and called them as "intellectual foundation stones". The assumptions are as follows:

Regularities

Behaviouralists claim that there are certain discernible uniformities in political behaviour, which can be expressed in generalization and theories in order to explain and predict political phenomena. Electoral behaviour study can be cited as its example. Psephologist found that there are certain uniform features guiding the voting behaviour and behaviouralism suggested political scientists to do analytical treatment of voting behaviour, and give up descriptive studies for explanation.

Verification

Behaviouralists strongly believe that knowledge or data collected must be subject to empirical investigations for proving its validity. It was further stressed that all evidence must be based on observation of five senses.

Techniques

The collection of data is an art supported by scientific techniques. Techniques adopted should depend on the subject matter of study. For example, study of historical events should rely on content analysis, whereas study of a particular event will be best understood by the case study method. A researcher must make use of sophisticated tools, such as multi-variable analysis, sample surveys, mathematical models, etc. This will neutralize researcher's personal bias and values and the report finding will be fact laden.

Quantification

Behaviouralists further argue that data itself is not sufficient; it should be quantified and measured. The data should be revalidated and the hypothesis must be tested in the light of new situations and evidences so that the findings remain correct, reliable and relevant.

Values

Social science cannot be value free as it deals with human beings. Behaviouralists, however believe that researchers should make a value fact dichotomy. While doing research, ethical or moral orientations must be discarded. In acquiring and interpreting data, researcher must make scientific inquiry and do empirical explanation. While doing so, the values and biases of the researcher will be neutralized and the generalization drawn will be scientific. This is the major bone of contention between traditionalists and behaviouralists.

Systematization

Research should be systematic claims behaviouralists. It simply means that research should be theory oriented and theory directed. It should form as "closely inter-related part of a coherent body of knowledge" the theory will have nothing to do with speculation or idealism; rather it will rely on analysis, explanation and prediction.

Pure Science

Research should be pure, emphasize behaviouralists, and they call it as 'pure science approach'. Researcher must mingle theory and its application in such a harmony that it becomes difficult for others to filter out. Knowledge should be scientific enough to find solutions to the problem and help in reshaping the society. Though it cannot be a pure type as of natural science and cannot be applied to all problems alike, even then, it can form the basis of utilizing knowledge in solution of urgent political problems of the society.

Integration

Behaviouralists very strongly believe that political science as a discipline does not grow in an isolation rather it is one of the sister social sciences. They favour inter-disciplinary approach. The understanding of political science can be drawn from sociology, history, economics, so on and so forth. A political man is very much an economic man, a social man and a cultural man so an interdisciplinary study is useful.[3]

As a result of this approach the scope of political science widened, but it was subject to vehement criticisms on the following grounds:

- Traditionalists retorted that in search of facts, behaviouralists committed serious mistakes.

  Firstly, political science is a branch of social science, and cannot be value free as natural science. It deals with animate objects which cannot be completely sterilized of values. Thus, fixity and definiteness of a natural science cannot be infused in the discipline of social science.[4]

  Secondly, the traditionalists contend that quantification of political phenomena is not possible, because most of them are immeasurable.

  Thirdly, an overemphasis on the interdependence of political phenomena may prove dangerous as it would make political science hand-maid of sister social sciences.

  Fourthly, no conscious experiment can be carried out on the political phenomena. They are beyond any experiment.[5]

- In fine, we can say that too much stress on objectivity has made political science a barren land with no output. This was the greatest loss for social scientists. There was a demand to alter behaviouralism with more pragmatic approach, though it made remarkable achievements in field of research and introduced empirical method of enquiry.

In the late 1960s, David Easton, the pioneer propounder of behavioural revolution, criticized the behavioural position on several counts.[6] He introduced a new approach 'post behaviouralism' based on seven principles, which he called as 'Credo of Relevance' working on two innovations—relevance and action.

Post behaviouralism was not going back to traditionalism, but it was an effort to strike a balance between the extreme views of traditionalism and behaviouralism. In other words, it was a task of preserving traditional values with more scientific temperament.

The ingredients of post behaviouralism are the following:

1. Substance must precede the technique.
2. Post behaviouralists focused on social change rather on status quo as championed by behaviourlists.
3. Post behaviouralists' main objective was to use knowledge for reshaping the society.
4. They argued that knowledge should be used in the right direction to solve social problems.
5. They further believed that there cannot be value-fact dichotomy in absolute terms. Their logic was that all knowledge stood on value premises.
6. Behavioural enquiry must reach out to real needs of mankind in the times of crisis.
7. Political scientists have to make society move in the direction of these goals, the politicization of profession would become inevitable.[7]

The post behaviouralism do not deny the importance of technical proficiency in search of reliable knowledge. But they would accept that to achieve this end, the political scientist should not isolate himself from the practical concerns of the society.

Thus, it served as an important ideological weapon in defense of established social and political order.

System Analysis Approach

This is a modern approach which emerged after Second World War, but its origin is found in the work of Ludwig Von Bertallanfy in 1920's. It started with an assumption that all elements in the system are organically linked together and there is a mutual interdependence among the elements. Works of sociologists Durkheim, Talcott Parson, Almond and Deutsch show that they have used this approach.

The primary question is what is a system? David Easton defines a system as "any set of variables selected for description and explanation".[8]

Almond writes "a system implies the interdependence of parts and a boundary of some kind between it and its environment".[9]

To some writers "it is a set of elements standing in interaction".[10]

While to others, system, is "a set of objects together with relationships between the objects and their attributes".[11]

David Easton has been the first to apply the system approach to political analysis. If David Easton and Gabriel Almond made significant contribution in the field of national politics, Morton A. Kaplan has enriched the area of international politics through system analysis. He regarded system analysis as the study of interrelated variables as distinguished from the environment of the set and of the ways in which this set is maintained under the impact of environment disturbances. Several writers were writing on this theory, however general system research, in 1956, made a monumental rise in its graph. It gave insights to political thinkers and the concept became an asset for political science.

David Apter laid down three features of system theory:

1. Systems have boundaries within which there are functional relationships mainly based on some of the communications;
2. Systems are divided into sub systems;
3. Systems have a capacity for coding—that is, they take information inputs; are able to learn from inputs, and translate inputs into some kind of output.[12]

The most important name in this field is of David Easton who in his two classical works—*A System Analysis of Political Life* and *A Framework for Political Analysis*, published in 1965, gave an original interpretation of the system analysis theory, with following salient features:

1. A political system is a set of interactions abstracted from the totality of social behaviour, through which values are allocated for a society.[13]
2. There are certain properties common to both natural and social systems like both the systems possess the capacity to cope with the worse type of situation.
3. Political system is not static, but a dynamic affair. It can maintain itself, yet keep its identity. This is possible with the feedback mechanism which can be of positive or negative character.
4. Political system is an open system amenable to the influence of environmental factors. It means that system has both internal and external environment viz. physical, social, economic, etc., which may exert influence on the functioning of the system.
5. The environment may be intra-societal or extra-societal. Intra societal forces operate within the system and extra-societal, outside the

system. However, both have an impact on decision-making process that results in 'authoritative allocation of values'.

6. A political system is subject to challenges from forces operating in the environment. Easton calls forces as 'stresses' that constitute response mechanism of political system. The stresses are of two kinds—demand stress and support stress; former is input load and latter is the support given by the members of the system itself.
7. Political systems may remain steady, if there is a balance between input and output, i.e. between demand and support system.
8. A political system may have critical condition, if inputs have overload and output fails to provide sufficient support leading to break down.
9. The survival of political system requires certain structural bases in forms of both institutional and non-institutional arrangements, former being political parties and latter political beliefs.
10. The objects of the support of political system are—political community, regime and authorities, i.e. common people, Constitution and decision-making people.
11. The political system consists of sub systems which help in the decision-making process besides, there are certain organizations which also a play vital role in influencing decisions which Easton calls para political system.

Thus, political system (see Figure 2.1) can be seen basically as input-output mechanism dealing with political decisions and the activities associated with these conditions. In fine, political system is just a means whereby certain kinds of inputs are converted into output.[14]

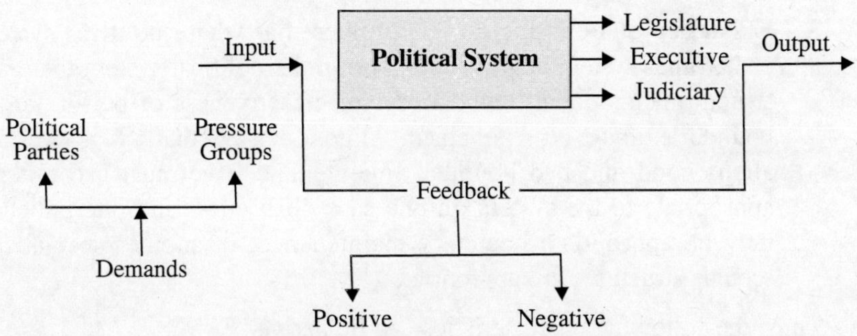

Figure 2.1 Model of political system.
Source: Mitchell's *Model of Political System*, J.C. Johari, *Comparative Politics*, p. 74.

Criticism of Easton's approach

His approach has been subject to vehement criticisms.

Firstly, it is very difficult to set the boundary of the political system, and is equally difficult to apply abstract concepts in empirical studies.

Secondly, Easton has failed to give a precise definition of 'political' and how it can be distinguished from 'social interaction'.

Thirdly, Easton does not create a theory in terms of explanation, rather offers a conceptual framework. He also fails to identify political systems with national system. He is not at all concerned with individual interest or behaviour; rather he only discusses occurrences making his concept empirically useless. Therefore, some critics regard his theory as 'empty vision of politics'.

Fourthly, his overemphasis on the survival of the political system minimizes the scope of ideology, which in actual practice, provide direction to the political system, despite all these criticisms, it can be safely asserted that David Easton made serious contribution in the field of political enquiry. He was the first to introduce this theory in the analysis of politics. Talcott parson applied it to Sociology. His methodology is highly useful for conservative analysis of two different political systems or of both national and international political systems. His analysis goes beyond equilibrium approach and accepts that the system is dynamic and creative.

Gabriel Almond gives three properties of political system. These are comprehensiveness, interdependence and existence of boundaries.

1. **Comprehensiveness:** He talks of political system which includes input, output and feedback process. He discussed not only structures like legislature, executive but also informal organizations like political parties, interest groups which affect the functioning of the political system.
2. **Interdependence:** He very strongly believes that change in one subset produces change in all other subsets, for e.g., change in science and technology brings a change in the electoral process.
3. **Existence of boundaries:** It implies that where political system ends, other system begins. Even within the political system there are structural functional boundaries. For effectiveness of performance, boundaries must be maintained. Almond speaks that when "we talk about good and bad boundary maintenance, we must use criteria appropriate to the system. In one case diffuseness and intermittency may be appropriate boundary maintenance; in another specialized secular structures are appropriate".[15]

Thus, the following characteristics can be derived:

1. **Universality of political system:** It means all political systems, whether primitive or modern, developing or developed have well-defined structure, same functions to be performed, no matter how specialized and multi-functional they be, and that all political systems are mixed in the cultural sense.
2. **Universality of political structure:** This implies that all political systems have political structures. Be it primitive or modern, developed

or under developed, even political systems in its transition phase possess a political structure.

3. **Universality of political functions:** All political systems perform same functions, though there may be different frequencies, but the kind of the function is the same.
4. **Multi-functionality of political structure:** Political structure does not perform single function. A structure performs numerous functions at the same time. For example, an executive implements laws, but at the same time can frame law under delegated legislation or ordinance making power of the President.
5. **Culturally mixed character of political system:** Almond regards all political systems as 'mixed' because there are not "all primitive" or 'all modern' structures or culture. Political systems differ in the relative dominance of the one as against the other, and in pattern of mixture of the two components.

Certain disadvantages of system analysis approach have been drawn.

1. It has certain methodological weakness, which is not suitable for empirical analysis.
2. It may prove useful in macro analysis but not in micro analysis. Young rightly says that it does not offer very much for studies dealing with the political aspects of such matters as 'perception, expectation cognition'.[16]
3. System analysis may fail to answer questions, such as depth and scope of power.
4. System analysis discusses various concepts which are not practically relevant.
5. A proper application of this theory is very difficult, because it require high level of theoretical insight and research orientation.
6. Kaplan argues that use of systems analysis in social sciences can be made with certain reservations and awareness of its limitations.[17]

In spite of criticisms, the system theory has helped in broadening the frontiers of political science.

It has lucidly explained the complex realities of political life in a broad social setting. It also creates new tools of investigation into the political process and help to find out remedial measures from disintegration of the system. Most importantly, it facilitates inter-disciplinary approach and helps social scientists to go for empirical study.

Structural-Functional Approach

Structural Functional approach is an offshoot of system analysis approach. "It is a means of explaining what political structures perform what basic functions in the political system and it is a tool of investigation".[18]

Concept of Structure and Functions

Structure is an arrangement in the political system with its definite traits. For example, political party is a structure where ideological commitment is the dominating feature. Functions are activities of the arrangement to achieve set goals. Political party as a structure has a typical function of contesting election and seeking power, besides many other subsidiary functions.

This concept became quite dominant in mid 60s in the world of social science. The credit of adopting this approach in political enquiry goes to American political scientists.

Gabriel Almond provides a proper framework of structural-functional approach, which looks at political system as a coherent whole.

Almond in his classical work, "The politics of developing areas" with his co-author Coleman gives four characteristics of political system as follows:

1. All political systems have structures. The more specialized structures perform more functions than the simple structures which perform less function.
2. Similar functions are performed in all political systems.
3. All political systems, whether primitive or modern are multi-functional.
4. All political systems are mixed systems in the cultural sense.

Almond suggests a classification scheme of structures that is based upon basic following dimensions of political systems;

- Degree of differentiation,
- The extent to which system is manifested,
- The stability of the functions of various roles and
- The distribution of power.

He identifies two types of functions of a political system—Input and Output functions. He further discusses four input functions of a political system:

1. **Political socialization and recruitment:** Political socialization is a learning process through which individuals develop an attitude towards their political system and political events. The political recruitment function begins where the general political socialization ends. It recruits members into specialized roles into the political system, and train in the appropriate skills.
2. **Interest articulation:** Every political system has a machinery for articulating interests of the citizens towards achieving the goal of the political system, for example, institutional groups, attitude groups, anomic groups, etc.
3. **Interest aggregation:** After the interests are articulated, the next major function of a political system is to aggregate the interests by formulation of general policies, in which interests are combined, accommodated or otherwise taken account of.

4. **Political communication:** All the above three mentioned functions are performed in the political system by means of communication.

It means flow of information from society to polity, from one political structure to another political structure, to get the output from the political system and also facilitates the feedback from output to input and to enable them to move in an uninterrupted cycle.

Output functions, according to Almond can be divided into three parts:

1. **Rule making:** This refers to the legislative function. This is usually performed by legislators in accordance with the demand put into the political systems by common people. This is present in all political systems.
2. **Rule application:** Once laws are enacted, their application becomes the major function of the political systems. The ministers and the bureaucrats in the modern political systems are mainly responsible for rule application. They not only enforce legislation but also create new rules under its power of delegated legislation.
3. **Rule adjudication:** This essentially is the function of judiciary to see that there is no case of rules violation. It is a specialized structure of conflict resolution and administration of justice. It also involves imposition of authoritative restraints or obligations on individuals. Output functions are called conversion functions because inputs are converted into outputs by the political process.

The structural functional approach of Almond has been criticized from different perspectives.

Firstly, there is no universal acceptance of what comprises 'functions' to be performed by the political system. Secondly, his definition of political systems is faulty; he does not clarify what he means by 'independent'. Thirdly, Almond's understanding of political system is based on the western political system, mainly American political system. Fourthly, the seven variables list of functional categories has certain apparent weaknesses. It becomes difficult to draw boundary line between various interest groups. Finally, Almond does not attach much importance to output functions or even to the role of feedback process. Despite these criticisms, Almond's structures work together to keep the society in operation. It also enables social scientist to compare different societies as well as different stages of same society. This approach has been accepted as one of the most important techniques of empirical investigation in modern political science and its strength lies in the area of pattern maintenance of the political system.

The next important thinker in this approach is Talcott Parsons. According to him, parts can be understood in the context of whole. He wants to analyze society and system of functionally interrelated variables, and a system as an ongoing set of recurrent and interrelated social actions.[19]

In his system he talks about four problems:

1. **Adaptation:** This is the capacity of any system to meet the demands of the 'actors', which must be increased. It is concerned with the relationship between social systems and its non-human environment–relationship that lead to the supplying of disposable resources which can be used as means to realize the goals of the system as a whole or the goals of any of its subunits.[20]
2. **Goal attainment:** It means the coordinated effort to achieve the goal as one of the most desired one. It is the preservation of the society itself, the defense of the realm involves a set of activities that contribute to the satisfaction of the goal attainment functional requisite. In society this function is performed by the state of polity.[21]
3. **Pattern maintenance and tension management:** Goal attainment is concerned with cultural components of a system and pattern maintenance with its social components.[22] Three major premises are involved here
   (i) The major values must be passed on from one generation to another and it may be called acculturation process.
   (ii) A social control process is concerned with application of sanctions for violations of the prescriptions of the value system.
   (iii) Attention management process attempts to prevent the development of situations that increase the probability that large number of actors will violate basic norms.[23]
4. **Integration:** It is concerned with establishing relationship between and among the units of a system, in order to create a conducive environment for effective functioning and growth. It involves features of socio-controlled process. Parson admits that in every social system there may be some behaviour that is not prohibited by norms, but is nevertheless mal-integrative. The integrative function is performed both by coercive mechanism[24] (state) and non-coercive mechanisms (social institutions).

There are five pattern variables which are known as "five dichotomous choices of action that actors must take in every situation—tools for analyzing conscious processes—fundamental problem of orienting oneself to the situation".[25] The five patterns variables are as follows:

1. **Affectivity:** It is also known as affective neutrality. By this Parson claims that either the actors are compromising or they prefer discipline.
2. **Specificity:** It is opposed to diffuseness. It refers to the scope of the relationship.

3. **Universalism:** Contrasted with particularism, it is a way to judge an object. It may be judged in terms of some universal reference or a particular reference in which ego is personally involved.
4. **Ascription:** It may be called achievement too. The dilemma is whether the primary consideration in defining the relationship is given to the ascriptive quality of the object or to some particular complex of performances.
5. **Self-orientation:** It also may be known as collectivity orientation. It means whether the relationship is disinterested or self-interested. Parson admits that factor of change is never at rest, it is always been pushed, prodded, keel-hauled, it is always subject to stresses and strains though he desires an orderly change which is gradual and peaceful.[26]

Robert K. Merton's contribution towards structural functional analysis is commendable. He talks about 'functions', which he classifies, into latent and manifest. The 'manifest functions' are these whose consequences are covert, unintended and unrecognized. Merton also brings out the difference between 'functions' and 'dysfunctions' on the basis of survival and disintegration of the system. While 'functions' are those observed consequences which facilitate the process of adaption, 'dysfunctions' are those observed consequences which lessen the adaptation.[27] He gets the credit of saving structural functional approach from the charge of being implicitly conservative and biased towards social change.

David Apter in his book entitled *Politics of Modernization*, in 1965 tried to place the functional model to the comparative study of modernizing countries. He was highly influenced by Marion Levy and Talcott Parson.

Apter believes that structural functional analysis is concerned with the limits by which particular choices take place in a political system. He not only studied political systems but also dealt with the classification of government. He studied some African countries like Uganda and Ghana and tries to interpret the concept of modernization from the stand, point of structural functional approach. In doing so he analyzed political system in three respects:

1. **Nature and purpose of government:** Apter believed that during the period of transition from a traditional to a modern form, the business of government is to get popular support and thereby become legitimate.
2. **Models of government:** He termed political system as pre-democratic and presented three models namely: (i) Mobilization system; (ii) Reconciliation System and (iii) Modernizing Autocracy System.
3. **Functions of government:** All political systems perform four functions:

(a) The logic of sanctions in the society
(b) The provider of symbols linking the people's past and future
(c) The responsible agents for the orderly arrangement and performance of roles in a system
(d) The providers of criteria for deciding on membership and participation in society.[28]

As per him each system has three kinds of structure, viz.:

(i) Structure of authoritative decision-making
(ii) A structure of accountability
(iii) Contingent structures and sub-structures.

Marion Levy Jr., a renowned sociologist analyzed structural functionalism, and was basically concerned with the problem of the survival of the system. His interpretation was in conformity with general system theory. He laid emphasis on environment of the system and its boundary conditions. In addition, his analysis is concerned with questions focusing on differences between relevant system levels, the reciprocal influences of various system levels on one another, and the implications of these factors for the levels of generalization and abstraction at which particular analyses are formulated.[29]

William C. Mitchell in his work on 'American Political System' provides four essential functions for the survival of a polity which are the following:

1. The authoritative decisions of any modern polity,
2. The authoritative mobilization of resources to implement the goals,
3. The integration of the system,
4. The allocation of values and costs.

Finally, we make a critical analysis of Mortan A. Kaplan who used this subject in International Politics. He described system as 'states' and further claimed that the behaviour of the system depends on the changes in the variables which are called outputs. Inputs lead to radical changes in the system. They alter the characteristics, behaviour and even the structure of the system. He regards equilibrium and stability as two major requisites of a progressive system. He explained the effects of the equilibrium change in three broad terms:[30]

1. A system remains in equilibrium until it is disturbed and the main disturbance comes from the environment. However, it is the strength of the system to meet disturbance without change.
2. If the disturbance has a great force then the equilibrium changes.
3. If disturbance appears and nothing else changes and the system fails to return to its earlier stage, a system change has occurred.

So, Kaplan's concept is to change the essential rules of the political system.

Critical Estimate

The structural-functional analysis has been criticized on various grounds.

1. The structural functional analysis tends to focus primarily on static relationships rather than on dynamics. Therefore this approach is accused of being promoting anti-change. Marxist criticizes it as a promoter of bourgeoisie imperialist order. He further adds that there can never be an equilibrium and harmony in the society, if two opposing classes exist within the same political system. Critics claim that this approach has a serious flaw of being 'concerned with the present' and having 'no perspective of the future'.[31]
2. This approach was called 'Ivory Tower Approach' which cannot be applied to the poor, backward and developing countries of Africa, Asia or Latin America. The problem of disintegration is rampant in third world countries, and therefore, they cannot apply the tools of empirical politics of the western world.
3. This approach also suffers from, what is termed by Merion Levy, 'The fallacy of functional teleology' which means functional necessity for the survival of the system. This approach has a parochial view of the system as it is not concerned with the breakdown of the structure and how to stop from such political decay.

Leonard Binder criticizes the seven function approach of Almond. According to him, Almond has simply generalized the broad classes of political activity found in the western political system.

Jean Blondel criticize that Almond's approach has certain difficulties:

- It is difficult to achieve complete objectivity
- It does not make us aware of functions
- It depends on what we expect of functions
- Lastly, this approach is primarily culture bound and reflects only the characteristics of the western political systems.

Criticisms left aside, this approach is useful for following reasons:

Firstly, it reduces the risk of ethnocentricism. Secondly, it is quite relevant for the comparative analysis of different political systems of the world. Thirdly, it provides a vital method in the area of pattern maintenance of the system. Fourthly, Marxian attack on this approach holds no value because pluralists contend that there are many conflicts other than class conflict and therefore the conflict resolution mechanism of Marx is itself faulty. And most importantly it has made a giant stride in the area of empirical analysis in modern political science.

Structural-functional approach therefore should not be known for its weaknesses rather for its realist analysis of widely diverse political systems. The existence of this approach becomes more so relevant in the context of understanding political sociology.

Questions for Discussion

1. Analyze Almond's structural-functional approach.
2. Examine David Easton's system approach.
3. Critically examine behaviouralism.
4. Analyze application of system approach to the study of political sociology.
5. What do you mean by post behaviouralism? Is it against scientific research? Give reasons.

References

1. Van Dyke, Vernon (1962), *Political Science: A Philosophical Analysis*, Stanford, Stanford University Press, p. 114.
2. *Ibid.*
3. Varma, S.P. (1983), *Modern Political Theory*, Vikas Publishing House, New Delhi, p. 54.
4. Young, O.R. (1968), *Systems of Political Science*, Englewood Cliffs, New Jersey, Prentice Hall, p. 26.
5. Varma, S.P., *op. cit.*, p. 56.
6. Hass and Becker (1970), *The Behavioural Revolution and After*, Introduction by Hass and Kariel, Chandler Publishing, pp. 66–69.
7. Excerpts from David Easton's Presidential Address in 1969, Annual Session of the American Political Science Association.
8. Easton, David (1956–1957), *An Approach to the Analysis of Political Systems*, World Politics, Vol. 9, p. 1.
9. Almond, Grabiel A. and Powell Jr., G. Bingham (1972), *Comparative Politics: A Developmental Approach*, Delhi, American Publishing Company, Indian Edition, p. 19.
10. Von Bertallanfy, Ludwig (1956), *General Systems*, Vol. I , pp. 1–10.
11. Hall, A. and Fagen, R. (1956), *Definition of a System*, Vol. I, p. 18.
12. Apter, David (1978), *Introduction to Political Analysis*, New Delhi, Prentice Hall, pp. 257–258.
13. Easton, David (1965), *A Framework for Political Analysis*, Englewood Cliffs, N.J., Prentice Hall Inc., p. 112.
14. *Ibid.*
15. Almond (1960), *Introduction in Almond and Coleman* (Eds.): *The Politics of the Developing Areas*, Princeton, Princeton University Press, pp. 8–9.
16. Young, Oran (1968), *Systems of Political Science*, New Jersey, Prentice Hall, p. 24.

17. Kaplan, Morton (1957), *Systems Theory* in Charles Worth James C. (Ed.) John Wiley and Sons, New York, p. 156.

18. Ball, A.R. (1971), *Modern Politics and Government*, London, Macmillan, p. 14.

19. Bhambhari, C.P. (October–December 1973), *Functionalism in Politics in Indian Journal of Political Science*, Delhi, Vol. XXXIV, No. 4, p. 455.

20. Holt, Robert T. (1967), *A Proposed Structural Functional Framework* in Charles-Worth (Ed.), *Contemporary Political Analysis*, New York, Free Press, p. 94.

21. Parson, Talcott (1949), *Essays in Sociological Theory: Pure and Applied*, New York, Free Press of Glencoe, pp. 93–94.

22. Johari, J.C. (1982), *Comparative Politics*, New Delhi, Sterling Publishers, p. 96.

23. *Ibid.*, p. 93.

24. *Ibid.*, pp. 94–95.

25. See Ritzer, *Classical Sociological Theory*, p. 467.

26. Bhambhari, C.P. (October–December 1973), *op. cit.*, p. 459.

27. *Ibid.*, pp. 109–110.

28. Rathod, P.B. (2005), *Fundamentals of Political Sociology*, Jaipur, ABD Publishers, pp. 140–141.

29. Young, Oran R. (1968), *Systems of Political Science*, Englewood Cliffs, New Jersey, Prentice Hall, p. 28.

30. Eugene, J. Meehan (1967), *Contemporary Political Thought*, Homewood, Illinois, The Dorsey Press, p. 183.

31. Bhambhari, *op. cit.*, p. 462.

Suggested Reading

David Easton, *The Political System: An Enquiry into the State of Political Science*

Hari Hara Das and B.C. Choudhury, *Introduction to Political Sociology*

J.C. Johari, *Comparative Politics*

S.P. Varma, *Modern Political Theory*

Web Link

www.jstor.org/stable/588779

3
Political Socialization

CRUX

From womb to the tomb, socialization is the continuous process of learning irrespective of any divide—class, caste or gender. The outcome of the process is varied as it is affected by variables viz. environment, education and personality traits. The pre-dominance of any one variable creates a new personality. Thus, each one is a product of ongoing socialization (learning process). However, its impact also differs with the change in the nature of political system, say that of authoritative as contrasted with democratic system.

MEANING AND DEFINITION

Socialization is a learning process, which is ongoing from infancy to adulthood. It refers to the process of social interaction through which an individual acquires the norms, values, beliefs, attitudes and language characteristics of a specific society or social group.[1]

Political socialization is an earlier phase of opinion formation—a phase in which individuals acquire knowledge, information, values and attitudes towards the political system.[2]

Rush and Althoff describe it as 'the process, by which an individual becomes acquainted with the political system, and which determines his perception of politics and his reactions to political phenomena.'[3]

Easton and Dennis define it as 'those developing processes through which persons acquire political orientations and pattern of behaviour.'[4]

The end product of political socialization is a set of attributes—cognitions, value standards, and feelings towards the political system, its' various roles and role incumbents. It also includes knowledge of values and feelings affecting the inputs of demands and claims, and the authoritative outputs.[5]

Political socialization therefore is the process of transmitting life thought process and practices from one generation to the other. It is known as a means whose end product is 'culture.' Almond rightly claims that 'socialization is induction into the political culture'. The main function of political socialization is to sustain and enhance cultural norms through individuals who are oriented by their life experiences and environment.

This ongoing process ceases only at a senile stage where human mind stops to respond to a given stimulus.

Herbert Hyman published a book in 1959 entitled *Political Socialization* and gave the concept which was in practice with the emergence of human race, but not focused or analyzed. The life cycle demands fitting new individuals into on organized way of life and established cultural tradition. The learning process involving an internalization of the existing cultural pattern is called socialization, and whenever this process exhibits political connotation it enlarges its scope into political socialization.

As it is both overt and covert, its implications and output sometimes become negative. As socialization continues until death, at a particular stage of life, an individual or system can react sharply against the prevalent norms and can spearhead new social movement to overthrow the existing cultural product as an outcome of age old-socialization process. The dismantling of USSR in 1990s is a glaring example of it. A dining table discussion on Gandhian ideology from day one can develop, in a child, an inherent feeling of challenging ideologies to make more pragmatic demands in the society. Younger generations are prompted to do so, but this process of de-socialization mostly is followed by re-socialization, which ultimately aims at the inculcation of new values, attitudes and knowledge and transmission of new information, in a way, a process of new indoctrination.

Socialization → De-socialization → Re-socialization → A Socialization

Thus, socialization is an evolving concept. Flexibility gives it continuity otherwise future generations would feel tempted to break it, that which we term in our day-to-day life as 'generation gap.' Therefore, if political socialization is accepted as a development process, desocialization and resocialization are to be accepted as its integral parts. However, growing concept of a socialization among youth is also distressing issue which should be tackled with care and precaution.

KEY VARIABLES

There are four key variables in political socialization process. These are: environment, experience, education and personality.

The surroundings always exert an impact on the thinking process of an individual. Location and food habits also have a major role to play in changing nature of political socialization from person to person. For example, people from hilly region are more hard working, the reason being climate and lifestyle.

A negative wave creates a passive and pessimistic personality; on the contrary, positivity enhances optimism and cooperative attitude.

Man is the product of his experiences. His knowledge, values and attitudes are contributory to his experience and are in due course affected by it. Thus, an individual's politically relevant experience arises out of, and is contributory to, the process of political socialization. Group experiences re-enforce commonly held values and attitudes, while experiences often assume considerable political significance.[6]

Education is undoubtedly the most forceful variable in understanding political socialization. Different levels of education possess different levels of knowledge. The difference of knowledge is translated into different political actions. The caliber to distinguish between right and wrong can be developed only through education. Educated man becomes a noble person and can make polity democratic. However, it is not beyond doubt, as the life experiences reveal a contrasting picture at times.

Individual trait differs from person to person. It has been found that sometimes basic instinct predominates over environment and experience. On the basis of personality trait, a person's perception is guided. Up-bringing in the same family may also create two diametrically opposed personalities. For example, Father practising Gandhian values has two children, former follower of communism and the latter propagating Jan Sangh philosophy. Individual traits are very much influenced by rest of the other factors mentioned above.

STYLES

The nature of political system determines the process of socialization. The ideology of the state becomes the official bases of the actions and pervades all activities. The totalitarian societies differ from democratic systems in the degree of control they exercise over the process of political socialization.[7] Table 3.1 explains political socialization process in an open society versus a closed society. As former allows dissent and opposition, latter condemns and controls it.

Table 3.1 Contrasting Styles of Political Socialization

Liberal Open Society	*Totalitarian Closed Society*
Manifest	Latent
Direct	Indirect
Universal	Particular
Diffused	Specific
Affective	Prescribed
Active	Passive

Totalitarian societies differ from democratic system in the degree of control they exercise over the people. The ideologies of a totalitarian state become the official basis of the actions, and pervade all human activities. Such a system has full authority over mechanisms of political socialization. This was abundant in Nazi Germany under Hitler or Fascist Italy under Mussolini or Communist Russia under Stalin. The liberal society (Democracy) on the other hand allows dissent and opposition. Thus, the style of political socialization differs in different political systems.

In a totalitarian political system the state controls all aspects of life. The educational institutions prescribe books based on government ideology. Any political dissent is dealt with stringent action. In the name of information, the state uses tool of propaganda based on distortion of facts. Opposition is outlawed. Political socialization converts into political indoctrination. A closed society of ruling elite prescribes suppressed thinking process. The demagogues in such a political system are subjected to coercive and manouvered political orientations of the ruling class. Effort is not on opening the brain rather on washing the brain with dogmatic notions. Political socialization can never happen in a closed mind. Openness to an idea is the starting point of learning which culminates into a socialization process. Liberal democracy promotes competition and transparency. It allows opposition to function and accept protest participation as a legitimate mode of political action. Political parties and pressure groups play a vital role in putting forth the demands of demagogue into the political system. The three organs of the government perform their universally prescribed functions. Electorate is educated by the good governance notion. Welfare state primarily concedes on the process of deliberations, tolerance and accountability. The period between two elections is also very crucial for electorate. They are continuously kept abreast of political actions and public policies. The formation of government, its assessment, anti-incumbency policy determines the functioning of democracy. The systematization does not prevent the government from adopting humane approach in handling socio-political issues. While totalitarian system depends on coercive strategies, liberal state creates conducive environment for the natural growth of the personality. Recent international and national movements have depicted that autocratic or despotic rules are strongly condemn, whether it is Syria or Lebanon or any other Middle East country Thailand is facing the same situation. Even in India the emergence of Aam Admi Party (AAP) is the natural outcome of the desperate desire of masses to do away with corruption and criminalization. With the passage of time the movement may fizzle out, but public outburst was phenomenal, and will always provide a lesson to the future leaders.

Democracy demands participation of all and more particularly representative culture. Good governance is the outcome of awakened citizenry. The delivery of democratic edifice depends on demagogue. Therefore, polity should identify styles of political socialization or public opinion formation. Liberal philosophy promotes openness in public opinion and even regimented society cannot gain stability without popular support. New theories of psychology emphasize the importance of learning (political consciousness) in regulating impulse and promoting rationale of mass, information and toppling the government.

STAGES

Theories of political socialization emerged in an inevitable thinking process of human beings. Erick Erickson a Neo-Freudian covers eight stages of life (see Table 3.2):[8]

1. Infancy — 0–1 year of age
2. Early childhood — 1–3 years old
3. Pre-school — 3–6 years
4. School age — 6–11 years
5. Adolescent — 12 years till 18
6. Adulthood — 18–35 years
7. Second stage of adulthood — 35–64 years
8. Last stage of adulthood — 65 and above

Table 3.2 Traits and Characteristics of Different Stages

1st stage	Basic Trust vs. Basic Mistrust
2nd stage	Autonomy vs. Shame
3rd stage	Initiative vs. Guilt
4th stage	Industry vs. Inferiority
5th stage	Identity vs. Role Confusion
6th stage	Intimacy vs. Isolation
7th stage	Creativity vs. Stagnation
8th stage	Ego Integrity vs. Despair

Source: Lawrence Kohlberg (1971), p. 108.

Lawrence Kohlberg's theory of political socialization holds that moral reasoning has six identifiable developmental stages which can be grouped into three levels of two stages each: pre-conventional, conventional and post-conventional.[9]

Level 1: Pre-conventional Morality

Stage 1. Obedience and Punishment

This is the earliest stage of moral development, commonly found among young children, but even adults are capable of expressing this type of reasoning. At this stage, children obey the rules to avoid the punishment.

Stage 2. Individualism and Exchange

At this stage, children account for individual points of view and judge actions based on how they serve individual needs.

Level 2: Conventional Morality

Stage 3. Interpersonal Relationships

Interpersonal relationships are often referred to as the "good boy-good girl" orientation, this stage of moral development is focused on living up to social expectations and roles.

Stage 4. Maintaining Social Order

At this stage of moral development, people begin to consider society as a whole, when making judgements. The focus is on maintaining law and order by following the rules, doing one's duty and respecting authority.

Level 3: Post-conventional Morality

Stage 5. Social Contracts and Individual Rights

At this stage people begin to account for the differing values, opinions and beliefs of other people.

Stage 6. Universal Principles

This is based upon universal ethical principles and abstract reasoning. At this stage, people follow those internalized principles of justice and equity which they have gained through socialization process, even if they conflict with laws and rules.

Man is an animal, selfish and violent by basic instinct, but the rules and norms of society gradually makes man a social animal. An individual gets closer to the mundane world from the womb of a mother (0 to 1 years of age). The five sense organs of the human body play a crucial role in making an empirical analysis of the society, thereby socializing a creature (1 to 3 years of age). The smell and the touch of a mother lay down the foundation of the socialization process. Political learning begins from the age of three. During pre-school age (3 to 6 years of age) child start forming an opinion or attitude. This is the very inquisitive stage where one needs patience to carefully answer the queries of a child. He gets primary knowledge of the world around him. During the school age (6 to 11 years of age), children identify themselves with their country, state and community. A feeling of belongingness, oneness, patriotism and nationalism entails the child's personality. At the adolescent stage (12 to 18 years of age), children get aware of the political notions, like liberty, democracy, elections, power, etc. and they also start playing a role in the political process. This is the stage when a person imbibes varied ideological notions. Young child forms early loyalties towards political system as they are more emotional than being intellectual. The adulthood stage (18 to 35 years of age), is the stage where human beings hold their own distinct personality, attitude and culture. No change can usually take place in the perception of a person after the adulthood stage. However in a very rare case, certain eventuality can change the personality. As children mature, their level of political information and analysis increases. They tend to become critical towards politics and sharply criticize the policies of the government. In the second adulthood stage (35 to 64 years of age), a person internalizes the values and becomes the product of the long socialization journey he undertakes. Their affection for the country, gained at an early age is difficult to be challenged or changed. Only when there is a conflict, radical changes in the political behaviour may occur. Such conflicts may have its roots either in early socialization or may also be attributed to the experiences of later socialization.[10] At this stage a very rigid personality emerges who is unable to compromise with value change, which at times leads to generation gap. From 65 years onwards one takes a step towards the ultimate destination. In late sixties, individual almost fulfill their major responsibilities and lead a retired life and remains closer to political activities. The leisure is fully utilized by the old generation in political dialogues, discussions and deliberations. Truly speaking, the end part of life is more oriented towards political activities and in the words of Aristotle, man becomes a political animal. It can be safely asserted that political socialization continues till the last breath.

AGENCIES

Political socialization is an earlier phase of opinion formation, and its transmission from generation to generation and from one part of the globe to another, this process helps societies to gain cohesion through a shared understanding of values, norms and symbols. Since it is a continuous process, it requires different agencies at different stages of life. Various agents transmit the elements of political socialization through three ways or mechanism: imitation, instruction and motivation.[11] Robert Le Vine suggests that these are the mechanisms of political socialization in childhood, but Rush and Althoff point out that these mechanisms are applicable to the whole socialization process.[12] Imitation is generally found among children, but in the case of adolescents and adults, imitation is mixed up with both instruction and motivation.

Family

Family opens the first door of knowledge and people develop their political attitudes unconsciously in the family.[13] Environment is an important factor in socialization which is quite evident from difference of attitudes between urban and rural; educated and uneducated; high class, middle class or low class. A child learns both lesser or higher values from family because family generates values not norms or set standards. A street child of slum dweller fluently uses abusive language, while a child from value-laden family gets a cultural shock. The difference is because of the family environment and upbringing. There are two major styles of socialization at family level. These are overt and covert socialization.

Former, results from direct oral preaching, given by old and senior members of the family, in form of moral tales. Latter is formed by observing actions and behaviour of the elderly family members which has a more striking impact. For example, if there is a difference in the preaching and actions of the family, then the child is often seen to opt the wrong practices. "The family provides the major means for transforming the mentally naked infant organism into adult, fully clothed in its own personality. And most of the individual's political personality—his tendencies to think and act politically in particular ways—has been determined at home several years before he could take part in politics as an ordinary adult citizen and politically prominent."[14] Herbert H. Hyman observed that "the individual's political orientation is a product of socialization essentially within the family."[15] David Easton and Robert Hess suggest that in United States political learning begins at the age of three and is well-established by the age of seven. It's a formative stage and the impression given at this stage is carried throughout the life. Robert Lane has suggested that there are three ways in which the foundation of political beliefs may be laid through the family. These are: by overt and covert indoctrination, by placing the child in a particular social context and by moulding the child's personality.[16]

Easton and Dennis refers to four stages in the process of political socialization at the childhood stages:

(i) Recognition of authority through particular individuals such as parents, policemen and the President of the country;
(ii) Distinction between public and private authority;
(iii) Recognition of impersonal political institutions like national legislature, judiciary and voting behaviour; and
(iv) Distinction between political institutions and persons engaged in activities associated with those institutions so that idealized images of particular person such as the President or the Congressmen are transferred from the Presidency and the Congress (USA).[17]

Educational Institutions

Starting from the primary school to colleges and universities, educational institutions play a catalyst in the process of political socialization of an individual. Formal education and the higher intelligence of the child reduce the extent of parental influence.[18] Plato, Aristotle, Rousseau and Locke have also emphasized education as an important variable for training both the rulers and the ruled. School as a center of primary education is regarded as an explanatory variable of political action. Almond and Verba have pointed out that the more extensive and individual's education, the more likely he is to be aware of the impact of government, to follow politics, to have more political information, to possess a wider range of opinions on political matters, to engage in political discussions with a wider range of people, to feel a greater ability to influence political affairs, to be a member of and to be active in voluntary organizations, and to express confidence in his social environment and exhibit feelings of trust.[19] At college and university level, political socialization becomes wide, extensive and mature. At the school level, child undergoes dialectics if family and school preaches diametrically opposed views. But at university level mind becomes mature, and therefore, student unions are formed, elections are held and political ideology is developed. Textbooks, syllabus and the courses of study should be well-directed so as to infuse spirit of belongingness and patriotism for the nation. For example, textbooks must prescribe roles of freedom fighters and makers of constitution. With the growing consumerism, greed is overpowering man's life. So value education should be included in the study course and be made mandatory. Educational institutions provide a platform where students gain varied experiences along with peer groups outside the family. This experience can be either positive or negative, depending on the nature of company.

Peer Groups

At adolescent stage, peer group has a major role to play in orienting political socialization. Peer group of friends and work associates also involve close personal contact. Their influence increases with growing distance between parents and children. It becomes quite evident with entering into new job or circumstances of life. He or she develops care for his fellow beings, develops modesty and group spirit which ultimately makes a man harmonizing creature, but it has also been observed that too much influence of peer groups at this stage may sometimes take a person to a path of aberration. This is the most delicate stage of life, where decisions are mostly guided by impulses without analyzing consequences. Hasty decisions are taken which sometimes become dangerous. Parents need to be alert, but not coercive or dominating and nagging their children every now or then. Tender, love, care and friendly approach can definitely evolve a pleasing personality.

Religious Institutions

In an indirect manner, religious institutions and leaders play a major role in guiding political socialization. Ideally speaking, politics and religion are the two sides of the same coin and one becomes meaningless in absence of the other. Gandhi was the protagonist of this view, because he felt that religion has close association with morality and ethics. He further added that a religious man cannot escape himself from political activities. But today, the values given by Mahatma Gandhi hold no relevance. Religion has become an instrument of vote bank. Politicians serve their vested interests by creating community cleavage in the society. This has led to the growth of religious fanaticism and separatist tendencies. The 'mandal' and the 'kamandal' issues have virtually tarnished the image of our statesmen. Political leaders are openly capitalizing the religious sentiments of the common man whether it is *Ram Mandir* or *Babari Maszid*, or *Golden Temple*, whether it is Jain dharma or Buddha dharma. Today, religious institutions and leaders do not preach love and service and rather are looking for opportunities to promotes violence, riots, thereby, weakening the bond of human spirit. It can be asserted that religious institutions can play a harmonizing role, but unfortunately it is fostering conflicts. Therefore, it is often said that there must be a divorce between religion and politics, and religious institutions should keep themselves away from power politics.

Mass Media

Media not only creates awareness, it plays a more responsible role beyond mere readership or viewership. It controls the thinking process and the behaviour of human beings, and converts them into action, deeds and shapes public opinion. Communication revolution has created a global village. Any incident happening in any part of the world is circulated all over within no time. The mass media of communication, be it print media or electronic media, helps the individual to gain reliable information at the right time which definitely bears an impact on the personality of an individual. In early days, even in a democratic set-up, news channel was owned by government so the news was censored. In communist societies, the situation was still worse. The privatization of electronic media has created ripples in the sea of information. Information percolates at the grassroots level and this dissemination of information has educated the electorate regarding the issues, manifestos, efficacy and the performance of different political parties. Audio-visual aids are very effective means of political socialization. For example, corruption is the relic of the past, but media has made it a burning issue, affecting each and every strata of the society, in India. Media hype at times flare up the issue to an extent of mass movement, ex Anna Hazare's movement for the enactment of Jan Lokapal Bill since 2011. On the contrary, it may blow an issue out of proportion to create social disintegration, for example, Godhra riot case.

Political Institutions

Political parties, pressure groups, interest groups, attitude groups and party workers lobbying are also some of the important factors in determining political socialization. Political speeches and manifestos enable citizens to know the goals and the objectives of the government. Opposition parties also make people aware of the weaknesses of the government by its propaganda. The support and the protest participation of the mass is the result of political cognition of the people. The more the people are informed, the less the chances of government being inefficient. In a democracy, representative participation is a must because legitimacy of the government is proved through popular support. Electorates are educated to exhibit matured voting behaviour, in other words, to cast votes on the basis of efficacy of the government and not on caste, religion or personality. During elections and in between two elections people must be well-informed, because no democracy can flourish without the participation of the majority, if not all. The selection of Narendra Modi as the BJP's head of election campaign and prime ministerial candidate for the parliamentary election 2014, has led to much hue and cry. It has given a jerk to the Indian politics, and has made people of India more politically conscious as it had earlier happened in 1975 against Indira Gandhi, when she proved to be a dictator with Maintenance of Internal Security Act (MISA) and force full emergency. Jayprakash Narayan wave came, though it died its natural death with its internal bickering surfaced by some Janta parties power mongors.

In addition to all these agencies, the experiences that a man gather during the course of his employment brings a great deal of insight into human nature by the way employer, colleagues and juniors behave towards an employee. If a child is brought up in the family along democratic lines, i.e. caring and sharing, he/she may initially protest against the unruly behaviour of his surroundings. In the due process realizing the fact that the values propagated by him fell on the deaf ear and that he remained isolated, creates a depressive note within. In such a case, his early socialization either crumbles and he succumbs to the pressure else he becomes a rebellion. "No matter how positive the view of political system which has been included by family and school, when a citizen is ignored by his party, cheated by his police, starved in the bread line, and finally conscripted into the army, his views on the political realm are likely to be altered. Direct formal and informal relationships with specific elite in the political system are inevitably a powerful force in shaping orientations of individuals to the system."[20]

Goals of Political Socialization

The values established by the political socialization process need neither be coherent nor consciously held to contribute to the stabilization of the political system. Some processes of socialization are more homogeneous, and the various agencies will complement each other rather than conflict; yet this does not preclude change, nor does it stifle variety. Political socialization is a continuous process, and as such is not completely static. The test for a stable political system is whether the socializing agencies are sufficiently flexible and interdependent to allow change without violent disruption.[21]

There are two schools of thought. One believing that political socialization is essentially a conservative concept, regardless of the case of democratic and totalitarian society and its real concern is survival and maintenance of the political system whether it is a free and open society like that of United States or Britain, or it is opposite as we find in the Soviet Union (yester years) or China, the net overall effect of political socialization "is in the direction of supporting the status quo, or at least the major aspects of the existing political regime.[22] The other school claims that political socialization as a matter of fact, strives to emphasize the point that the test for a stable political system is whether the socializing agencies are sufficiently flexible and inter-dependent to allow change without violent destruction.[23]

Political socialization has two features: homogeneous and heterogeneous. Former is the continuous process, in which individuals cooperate with each other. There is a mutual trust and rectitude towards their political system. On the contrary, heterogeneous process signifies an element of doubt, suspicion and despise towards their political system and political process. It needs to be mentioned here that the ultimate goal of political socialization is to bring about political stability. This is however, nowhere to suggest that it is a static concept maintaining status quo-ism. It only seeks to maintain equilibrium and to bring about gradual constitutional changes, if and when required, without dismantling the basic structure of the polity. In other words, it condemns radical, rapid or violent change.

As a result of political socialization, an individual adjusts himself/herself with his/her political system, and feels so comfortable in it that he/she is unlikely to rise in revolt against the existing order. Individuals form faith in the values and beliefs of the political system; they feel emotionally involved in the activities of the system and would make effort to keep the system alive. The survival of the political system leads to stability.[24] Political socialization saves a society from revolutionary uprising, chaos and anarchy. Without political socialization, a society would face strife, struggle or political turmoil leading to the decay of the political system. Political socialization is an evolving concept, because it infuses values and values invariably changes. So it cannot claim to be dogmatic. It varies according to time, situation and demand. It is closely related to the degree of change occurring in the political system. Thus in fine, political socialization is flexible and can never become anachronistic and at the same time, it also sustains and enhances the capacity of the political system.

CRITICAL ESTIMATE

Political socialization as a means develops political culture as an end which is translated into political action as a feedback. Therefore, even those who are very vocal in criticizing the concept of political socialization as a conservative one cannot ignore its relevance in a democratic, open society. As a matter of fact, political scientists have evolved this concept to save existing political system from their transformation into a form, i.e distinctly opposed to the world of free and open societies.

Marxists school openly declares that political socialization is the child of bourgeoisie mind, and cannot bring about scientific socialism rather it will promote stagnation. However, this criticism has been rejected by the open society as there was no logical reasoning associated with it. So the accusation of being conservative is a derivative of communist mind.

Despite criticisms, we cannot overlook the relevance of political socialization as it is the individual's learning of social patterns corresponding to his social positions as mediated through various agencies of society. It is the process whereby political attitudes and values are inculcated as children become adults and as adults are recruited in the different roles in a given political system. Therefore, it enables individual to introduce themselves to the society, and get acquainted with the system. To conclude, political socialization is a link between society and polity, and is therefore, inevitable for the political process.

Questions for Discussion

1. Define political socialization. Discuss its various agencies.
2. Discuss various stages of political socialization.
3. Examine the goal of political socialization in a political system.
4. Political socialization is a process of open society. Elucidate.
5. Discuss the role of political socialization in building democratic ethos.

References

1. Dawson, Richard E. (1966), *Political Socialization* in James A. Robinson (Ed.), *Political Science Annual: An International Review*, Vol. 1, Indian Polisny Bobbs, Merrill Co. Inc., p. 5.
2. Sharma, L.N. and Ashraf, Ali (1983), *Political Sociology: A New Grammar of Politics*, New Delhi, University Press, p. 171.
3. Rush and Athoff (1971), *An Introduction to Political Sociology*, London, Nelson, p. 1.
4. Easton, D. and Dennis (1969), *Children in the Political System: Origins of Political Legitimacy*, New York, McGraw-Hill, p. 7.
5. Almond, G.A. and Coleman, J.S. (1960), *The Politics of Developing Areas*, New Jersey, Princeton University Press, p. 16.
6. Sharma, L.N. and Ashraf, Ali (1983), *op. cit.*, p. 176.
7. Das, Hari Hara and Choudhury, B.C. (1997), *Introduction to Political Sociology*, New Delhi, Vikas Publishing, p. 62.
8. Erikson, Eric (1979), 'Resolutions of Psychological Tasks', *Journal of Nursing Care*, 12(5), 27–28 PMID.37478.

9. Kohlberg, Lawrence (1971), *From is to Ought: How to Commit the Naturalistic Fallacy and Get Away With it in the Study of Moral Development*, New York, Academic Press, p. 108.

10. Das, Hari Hara and Choudhury, B.C. (1997), *op. cit.*, p. 58.

11. Rush and Althoff (1971), *op. cit.*, p. 1.

12. *Ibid.*

13. Sharma, L.N. and Ashraf, Ali (1983), *op. cit.*, p. 172.

14. Davis, James C. (1965), *The Family's Roles in Political Socialization, The Annals of American Academy of Political and Social Sciences*, Vol. 361, September, p. 11.

15. Banerjee, Sunanda (2002), *An Introduction to Political Sociology*, New Delhi, Janaki Prakashan, p. 32.

16. Lane, R.E. (1959), *Fathers and Sons: The Foundations of Political Beliefs* in American Sociological Review, Vol. XXlV, pp. 502–511.

17. See Easton and Dennis (1969), *Children in Political Systems: Origins of Political Legitimacy*, New York, Part 3.

18. Ball, Alan R. (1971), *Modern Politics and Government*, London, The Macmillan Press, p. 65.

19. Almond and Verba (1963), *op. cit.*, pp. 315–324.

20. Almond, Gabriel A. and Powell, G.B. Jr. (1966), *Comparative Politics: A Developmental Approach*, Boston, Little Brown, p. 69.

21. Ball, Alan R. (1971), *op. cit.*, pp. 68–69.

22. Sigel, Roberta (September 1965), Assumptions about the learning of Political Values, *The Annals of the American Academy of American Social Science*, Philadelphia, Vol. 361, p. 1.

23. Ball, Alan R. (1971), *op. cit.*, p. 73.

24. Banerjee, Sunanda (2002), *op. cit.*, pp. 28–29.

Suggested Reading

Alan R. Ball, *Modern Politics and Government*

H.H. Hyman, *Political Socialization: A Study in the Psychology of Political Behaviour*

Hari Hara Das and B.C. Choudhury, *Introduction to Political Sociology*

Sunanda Banerjee, *An Introduction to Political Sociology*

L.N. Sharma and Ali Ashraf, *Political Sociology: A New Grammar of Politics*

Web Link

www.imej.wfu.edu/articles/1999/1/02/demo/glossary/p socialization.htm

4

Political Culture

CRUX

Every day is a new experience in life. The experiences create an attitude which is reflected in diversified action. The making and re-making of the thought process is called culture. It is a way of life, which is reflected in words, behaviours and deeds. Political system is a super structure based on its cultural and socio-economic foundation. Socio-economic culture reflects into political action and translates elite into a political actor. It has various degrees of cultural emulation, and is transmitted from one generation to the other.

MEANING AND DEFINITION

As an offshoot of behaviouralism and functionalism, political sociology emerged in the context of new theorem of power distribution. The decentralization of power and welfare schemes percolating at the grass-roots level makes democracy more representative and populous. This also requires better understanding of governance and its impact on citizenship and sovereignty. Government in isolation can never produce tangible result until and unless demagogue becomes aware and active. This awareness is generated by different agencies of political socialisation (means) culminating into political culture (end), which determines political participation.

Political culture is an evolving and heuristic concept, and is widely used today. It is a product of inter-disciplinary approach. Gabriel Almond and Sidney Verba can be regarded as protagonists of political culture. They defined political culture as "psychological orientation toward social object, cognitive, affective and evaluative orientations."[1] Lucian Pye defines political culture as a set of attitudes, beliefs and sentiments which give order and meaning to political process, and which provide the underlying assumptions and rules that govern behaviour in the political system.[2] According to Beer and Ulam "certain aspects of general culture of a society are especially concerned with how government ought to be conducted and what it shall try to do. This sector of culture is called political culture.[3] R.C. Macridis regards political culture as "the commonly shared goals and commonly accepted rules."[4] Dowse and Hughes point out that the focus of political culture studies is less on the formal and informal structure of politics, governments, parties, pressure groups and so on, or on the actual pattern of political behaviour observed within a society, but rather on what people believe about these structures and behaviours. It is these beliefs that give the behaviours of men meaning for them and others. These beliefs can be of several kinds, such as cognitive beliefs about what the state of political life is, or they can be values concerning the desirable ends of political life, or attitudes towards some perceived state of the system.[5]

A study of political culture enables us to understand the political ideals and standards of behaviour people have set for themselves in a polity. It constitutes an important link between the behaviour of individuals and political events. Lucian W. Pye has studied the meaning of political culture in the context of his concept of political development relating to the case of new states of the Third World and, for this reason; he has included three factors in his study:[6]

1. Scope of politics: how ends and means in politics are related?
2. Standards for the evaluation of political action: and
3. Values those are salient for political action.

Talcott Parson becomes little more specific when he says that political culture is concerned with orientations towards political objects. Orientations are pre-dispositions to, political action and are determined by such factors as traditions, historical memories, motives, norms, emotions and symbols.[7]

FOUNDATIONS

A political culture, whether diverse or homogeneous, is a product of many inter-related factors. To start with the History, it is the strongest pillar to comprehend political culture of a given political system. The fact has been earlier established by Professor Seeley that Political Science gives fruit to history, whereas history gives root to Political Science. For example, if we take three largest democracies of the world we can easily assess the importance of historical precedents. British political culture exists on the background of conservative relationships. Therefore, they have never tried to do away with House of Lords or Monarchy. They religiously believe in and follow the conventions until it poses a serious threat to the survival of the system. This definitely does not suggest that homogeneous political culture leads to political stability. It only means that diversity creates sub-culture as we find Irish sub-culture in Britain. France offers a glaring example of historical development in contrast with Britain. The Revolution of 1789 and the political conflicts of 19th and 20th centuries are largely determined by the radical political culture of French citizens. The American war of independence accompanied by certain social changes was based on democratic procedures as Americans never agreed upon non-constitutional methods. The impact of European colonial domination on many newly liberated states in Africa and Asia is an important factor explaining some aspects of the political culture of these states. The colonial influence is reflected in such states. India provides a classical example of carrying British legacy in its socio-political values, and also exhibits conducive tolerance level of its' people.

Besides historical influence, geographical conditions also play a vital role in designing a political culture. Britain's island insularity protected the country from foreign invasion, and therefore, they claimed to be the rulers. West Germany, because of its political structure, was sandwiched between the competing international alliances led by the Soviet Union, and America developed communist-capitalist political culture. However, unification of Germany resulted in political stability. India is a land of geographical variety. Running from plains to hilly regions, tribal and non-tribal living styles and the impact of ethnic differences greatly affect the homogeneity of Indian social system and stability of the political system. The instability caused by the ethnic groups becomes more magnified when government succumbs to the pressure of the agitating anomic groups, for example, North-South India cultural divide, Hindi and Non Hindi speaking belts, so on.

The socio-economic structure is another determinant of political culture. A predominantly urban, industrialized society is a more complex society, putting a premium on rapid communications. Educational standards are higher, groups proliferate and participation in the decision-making process is, of necessity, wider. Rural societies are not geared to change and innovate, and states with a predominantly peasant population tend to be more conservative.[8]

In European societies, the participation of the people in politics is higher than in Asian and African democracies. In Seymour M. Lipset's "Political Man", he writes that socio-economic condition determines the political culture of man.

SYMBOLS

Political culture in a society is reflected through various symbols such as:

1. The National Flag and National Anthem
2. National pride
3. Emotional adherence
4. Religion
5, Attire and food habits
6. Myth

Indian National Flag exhibits the colours of truth, prosperity and sacrifice, which is governed by our ancient culture. National Anthem depicts the high level of tolerance that the Indians possess, and it is also verified by 200 years of subjugation. Indian culture is a tolerant, dependent and less reactionary, whereas Britain's anthem claims that London waves can never be slaves. The rule of the monarchy is the testimony to the fact.

A feeling of belongingness and oneness strengthens the bond of political culture. Pluralist culturalism creates cleavage in the society, thereby weakening the democratic edifice. Indians express pride for their nation, but unfortunately such an attitude emerges after crossing the boundary of the nation. Within the country domestic strife dampens the spirit of nationalism and sectional interest overrides national security and integrity.

Democracy is a government run by the common people. Commoners are inherently emotional, and therefore, their action is usually swayed by emotions. Citing diametrically opposite examples we can refer to the political system of two giant democracies—USA and India. Former believes that sex is individual's choice, but remains intolerant towards President in such matters as they look upon them with high dignity. Some Presidents have gone to the extent of facing impeachment, viz. Nixon and Bill Clinton, whereas latter is conservative society yet multiple personal relationships of the elites are permissible. Emotional adherence in its varied forms is reflected in both the democracies.

Religious symbols may take the place of secular symbols in some political culture. Profound significance is attached to coronation ceremonies in the national church, national holidays are chosen from the church calendar in England, whereas in India Secularism blend with rationality, and harmony is reflected in religious performance by the government. State has no religion of its own, and levies no tax on religious ground (Article 27 of the Indian Constitution).

Myths play an important role in the political culture. The 'Elizabethan Age' is very important for Britishers. Mahatma Gandhi is regarded as the most important figure in the Indian Liberation Movement, and is acclaimed as Father of Nation and the Bolsheviks are portrayed as playing the major role in the 1917 Revolution. These facts are myths because they emphasise certain half-truths and therefore are distortions although politically important.

Attire symbolizes national political culture as well. The Gandhian cap for examples identify people having political inclination and desire to work for social welfare. Saffron colour is much closer to extreme rightist political ideology (Jansangh now BJP and Shiv Sena). AAP cap is also influencing to the latest political culture among the people who are against our system to a greater extent. Therefore, we can see a clear impact of apparel at least in Indian context of political culture.

The emotional intensity that embraces these symbols is a way of identifying political values and attitudes in the political system. They are sometimes used by Governments to gain popular support and foster national unity and integrity. The symbols are intensified by using them against foreign alien symbols in order to legitimize governance.

ORIENTATIONS TOWARD POLITICAL CULTURE

The concept of political culture finds place in the subjective realm. According to Almond and Powell, such individual orientations involve three components:

1. Cognitive orientations implying knowledge, accurate or otherwise, of the political system
2. Affective orientations implying feelings of attachment, involvement, rejection, and the like about political system, events and issues
3. Evaluative orientations implying judgements and opinions about the political objects, which usually involves applying value standards to political objects and events.[9]

Robert A. Dahl has singled out political culture as a factor explaining different patterns of political opposition whose salient elements are:

1. Orientations of problem-solving; are they pragmatic or rationalistic?
2. Orientations to collective action; are they co-operative or non-co-operative?
3. Orientations to political system; are they allegiant or alienated?
4. Orientations to other people; are they trustful or mistrustful?[10]

David Easton presents his input-output model as a component of system analysis which is known as Black-Box Model, and its features form different types of political culture. Input means all the 'demands' and 'supports' through which a wide range of activities in the environment can be channeled, mirrored, summarised, and brought to bear upon political life. It is exhibited through political parties, pressure groups and mass media. Outputs are the decisions of the authorities taken by the Legislature, Executive and Judiciary. Political culture is also determined by the self, i.e., his/her own assessment about the part he/she plays in the political sphere as a political actor and in between input and output process there is a feedback as a response to the output and can be either positive or negative see Figure 2.1 (Chapter 2).

TYPES

The citizen culture is based on participation, especially in the input functions; the subject culture is aware of the political system, but more as an object of the state activities, and the parochial is confined to the local and intimate world of his own family or group, hardly identifying himself with the larger political system.

1. **Parochial political culture:** When there is only cognition, no affection or evaluation either towards output or input process, it is regarded as parochial political culture. In this type of culture there are no specified roles by the mass. It may be that on account of

development, some of the individuals may become aware of the existence of central political authority, but their feelings for and evaluation of the system as a whole "have not crystallized sufficiently for them to establish for themselves norms and standards to regulate his relations with the system".[11]

2. **Subject political culture:** If the cognitive, affective and evaluative orientations are relatively high in so far as the outputs of the system are concerned it is called subject political culture. It occurs mostly in newly liberated colonies where people either accept the decisions of the rulers as legitimate or protest against them as state exploitation. The role of individual is limited and passive. People mainly react, but fails to initiate demands or put self effort.
3. **Participant political culture:** If the orientations are both toward input and output structures it is called participant political culture; and it is found usually in highly developed societies. Citizens are fully aware of their rights and duties. "Evaluation and criticism of the system exist at all levels, and it is generally accepted as discernible that political activity should be under the close scrutiny of individuals and groups within society."[12]

Apart from the three ideal types of political culture, Verba also refers to of the mixed variety political culture. The very purpose of political culture is to formulate classification of political systems. It was realized later that pure types of categorization is not sufficient to classify political system with accuracy (Table 4.1). Therefore, he puts three mixed types as follows:

Table 4.1 Biennial Graph of Political Culture

Political Culture	*Input*	*Output*	*Feedback*
Parochial	0	0	0
Subject	0	1	1
Participant	1	1	1

Source: Morton R. Davies and Vaughan A. Lewis (1971), p. 116.

1. **Parochial–subject political culture:** This combination of culture means orientation to the political system and output structures. Generally, people remain passive with a few actively criticizing the policy of the government. It believes in a transition from primitive tribal culture to modernized political system. For example, Asian and African states.
2. **Subject–participant political culture:** This represents a situation when the political system stands midway the active political actors and vocal citizens evaluating the outcome of the political system and the input orientation is sometimes limited and passive. For example, European and American states.

3. **Parochial–participant political culture:** This is the most peculiar type of culture, where one section is fully participant and involved in decision-making process and the other apathetic towards the political issues. For example, Regimental, Authoritative states.

On the basis of these ideas, Almond and Verba explain the concept of '**Civic Culture**'. According to them 'the civic culture is an allegiant participant culture. The civic culture is a participant political culture in which the political culture and political structure are congruent.[13] Civic culture combines all the three ideal type of cultures, i.e. parochial, subject and participant. It is in this sense that the authors assert that 'the civic culture is not a modern culture, but a mixed modernizing-traditional one.[14]

Civic culture is nothing else than an objective manifestation of what each society teaches its members by way of a certain religious conviction.

Civic culture was further classified into role culture and sub-culture. Role culture basically reflects the role model conceived by common people either in silver screen stars, sports giants or intellectual wizard. Countries with low literacy level are governed more by the role culture, for example, in India celebrities easily hold political posts. However, it is also found to some extent in developed societies, for example, Ronald Reagan, the superstar became the President of USA.

In a large country where population explodes and plural culture exists, there is always a possibility of the emergence of political sub-culture in addition to the national political culture. The glaring example is of India where citizens possess Indian culture and simultaneously exhibit regional cultures, for example, the political culture of Tamil Nadu is diametrically opposed to the culture of Bihar. However, such sub-cultures play a vital role in making of the Government. It is universally accepted norm as we find Blacks in USA or Irish in England. Sub culture as discussed by David Riesman is a minority style which challenges the passivity of majority style. Dick Hedige in 1979 came out with a book 'Sub-Culture, the Meaning of Style' in which he claims that sub culture bring like-minded individuals who feel neglected by societal standards, and allows them to develop a sense of identity. The study of sub-culture comprises the following:

- Dissent
- Assimilation
- Articulation
- Identification

The examples of this can be women's culture, Islamic culture, trans-gender, etc.

Prof. S.E. Finer classified political culture in relation to the possibility of military intervention, which, in his opinion, might be at four levels—that is influence, pressure or blackmail, displacement and supplement. He suggests three types of political culture as follows:[15]

1. **Mature political culture:** In this culture political consensus are very high and the need of the Government for counting on the support of the armed forces is at a minimum; and there is unquestioning belief in the principle of civil supremacy. Britain, America, Australia and the Netherlands are its classic examples.
2. **Developed political culture:** It refers to a society where the public is highly organised, though, from time to time, it becomes sharply polarised on either the legitimacy of its institutions and procedures or on the incumbents who hold office as a consequence of these. Here civilian Government are often threatened by military pressures and the people. Countries like Egypt, Algeria and Cuba can be put in this category.
3. **Low political culture:** It is found in countries having narrow minded publics divided on personal issues, and public opinion is too feeble to offer any sustained resistance to authoritarian rules. Countries like South Vietnam, Iraq, Syria, Burma and Indonesia can come in this category.

SOCIO-POLITICAL STRUCTURE

Almond gives an illustration of political system based on cultural orientations.

Anglo-American System

The Anglo-Americal system consists of highly developed western democratic countries, whose salient features are the following:

1. It has multi-valued political cultures which are homogeneous and are realized by making an agreement between political means and political ends.
2. Politics is like a game where there are several players though competitors, but they never take their differences to the extent of making playground a battlefield.
3. Politics also appears to be a market place where bargaining takes place between the ruler and the ruled. The efficacy of the Governments and the votes of the public interplay with each other.
4. Society has a plural character in which different political parties and interest groups operate together to create a democratic set-up.
5. There is decentralization of power along with checks and balances so that democratic norms are followed and good governance achieved.
6. Lastly, there is stability as old institutions perform their respective responsibilities and ultimately people's sovereignty.

Continental-European Political System

Continental-European political system is the second variety where a little less developed western democracies function, viz. France, Italy, Sweden, Norway, etc. It has following salient features:

1. Political culture is fragmented. Therefore, cultural development gives rise to political sub-culture. It reflects feudal mentality, but at the same time makes an effort to emulate the higher values of the advanced countries.
2. Each political sub-culture develops its distinct role which becomes the focal point of the whole system.
3. The process of political bargaining is virtually non-existent. Various sub-cultures fight with each-other, and try to impose its dogma on the others. So there is warfare for seeking power.

The features are quite similar to the political culture of Asian political system, in general, and India, in particular.

Pre-Industrialized or Partially Industrialized Political System

Pre-industrialized and partially industrialized political system category includes all those countries that have liberated themselves from long colonial domination. Here the political cultures of the elites are dominating over the masses. The main characteristics are the following:

1. Political masters dominate over the people and political cultures of the subjects are eroded as they are taken to be ignorant inferior lot.
2. Leaders try to strike a balance between legitimacy and force. Therefore the system becomes unstable as one charismatic leadership is exposed or replaced by another.
3. Here two or more political cultures function within a single social structure. For instance, a family remaining in power along with tradition and modernity.

Totalitarian Political System

Almond talks about totalitarian communist political systems having following characteristics:

1. Authority tends to be arbitrary and tries to create apathy among public by controlling means of communication and using instruments of violence and fear.
2. Coercion becomes the hallmark of the authority and state becomes all powerful where no opposition or rule of law is allowed to operate.

3. There is concentration of power and the authority works with the support of bureaucracy, police and army.

POLITICAL CHANGE AND STABILITY
Trait of Political Culture

Political culture as an end plays a crucial role in the sphere of political stability and change. As we have already discussed earlier that conservative political culture explains Britain, and radical political culture emphasize France. The conventional view in social as well as political relationships tries not to do away with an institution until and unless it does a positive harm. Political culture tries to strike a proper balance between the factors of continuity and change. The dynamism, however, does not mean erosion of values or beliefs of the people. It only implies that political experience gained by the history must be properly blended with modern ideas scientifically so that relevance of the political system continues. It does not become anachronistic, rather flexible enough to cater to the changing needs of the society. The objective is to bring equilibrium in the society along with an orderly change through constitutional methods as Fred. W. Riggs suggested while defining political development.

System of Parliamentary democracy is always changing and the control remains in the hand of common people. John Stuart Mill, a champion of individualism rightly said despotism was the best form of Government for the barbarians, while representative Government for the civilized society. For the stability of a political system along with innovative practices attitude of people must be positive and feeling of rectitude must be overwhelming. Legitimate Government flourish along with thc competence of people. There is a close relationship between dominant pattern of political culture and the final impact of political socialization process. The problems of continuity and change also require analysis of relation between political socialization and political culture. Various agencies of political socialization gives rise to stable political culture but at the same time culture vary from region to region, and it produces tensions as political socialization is not so dynamic. The problem becomes acute with sudden change in the international status of the society. However, political culture determines the success of the political system. Rapid industrialization, modernization, urbanization and secularization develop homogeneous political culture, which provides a strong support base to the political system having new attitudes with the existing value structure. Japan is the glaring example of a unique political culture.

For the stability of a political system, it is necessary to emphasize political culture of the people. Every political system is keen to use people's culture for seeking and retaining power. It has been observed that political culture is diverse and complex, at the same time, exhibits certain common patterns of support, expectation, demands and general character traits. All these have most profound impact on the political system and the way it makes decision. Political culture relate to the aggregate individual behaviour, represents blending of psychology and sociology of elite and commoners with the political system. Political culture sometimes remains consistent, and sometimes is reinforced by the attitudes and values imported from other countries. This gives rise to changing yet relatively stable political system. Political system can never be stagnant as it is the product of political process. For example, even in USA commitment to democracy sometimes is a step into the transitional phase. Political mobilization is the process by which people in any political system survive, sustain and enhance. Mobilization takes place with the aim of either changing the present structure or stabilizing for further improvement.

RELEVANCE

It's a novel concept and its relevance is increasing leaps and bounds and in contemporary political scenario it is used independently. It has acquired a heuristic device of analysis. It has indeed become an important parameter for the analysis of political systems. An example is furnished by a text on American Political institutions in the 1970's in which Part I is entitled American Political Culture.[16]

It underlines the close relationships between political actors and electorate. It helps in giving a proper understanding and analysis of countries histories and political goals. It also evolves political ideology and helps in bridging what has been called 'the micro-macro gaps by Almond and Powell.[17] This method of analysis involves both micro as well as macro analysis. It also helps us to understand the psychological aspect of political development. It helps us in testing the reality of belief and expectations. That is why some social scientists claim political culture to be a deep insight into the political reality. Political culture is the curious amalgam of various factors, which blend together to make a viable political method in the process of evaluating different political systems. The analytical tool provided by this concept makes comparative study more interesting and enriching.

Professor S.P. Varma in his book entitled '*Modern Political Theories*' discusses five major achievements of political culture:[18]

1. It has made political science a more complete social science.
2. It has focused our attention on the study of the political community, as a dynamic collective entity as distinct from individual, and thus, on the total political system.
3. It has encouraged political scientists to take up the study of social and cultural factors which are responsible for giving the political culture of a country its broad shape.
4. It has helped us in combining the study of rational factors which shape the actions of the individuals to a large extent.

5. It is the political culture which helped us understand why different political societies inevitably move in different directions of political development or political decay.

CRITICAL ESTIMATE

The utilities are numerous, but the shortcomings are also a part of political culture, as Almond and Powell said that this approach cannot be taken as correct barometer of individual behaviour. It has a great impact on the performance of the political system, but it is unlikely that any analysis of the political culture could be predicted with complete reliability.[19]

Political culture approach is an attempt to find one rubric to include what, in the past, have been variously described as attitudes to politics, political values, ideologies, national character and cultural ethos, etc. None of these terms are sufficiently broad to provide a basis of classifying political systems, though each of them separately is relevant to the study of comparative politics, but each one is vague and ambiguous, and as such serves only as the source of confusion for those attempting to compare political systems methodically.[20]

Sometimes fanatic or anomic groups emerge out of utter frustration and political turmoil, which eventually gives birth to a new type of political culture, which can be termed as desperation. This type of culture creates panic and may lead to even catastrophy. Growth of Talibani and LTTE culture are a glaring example of it. Naxalism and Maoism in India can be sighted offshoots of such desperate culture.

The political culture is basically a set of beliefs and understanding, which differs from person to person, and cannot be verified scientifically. This becomes an acute problem when there is a measure of difference between the political culture of the rulers and that of the ruled. In such a situation, the question would arise 'as to which of these different cultures may be considered more relevant to political development.[21] Lucian Pye has taken note of this fact that in no society there is a fundamental distinction between the culture of the rulers or power holders and that of the masses.[22]

Not only this, diversity of political culture may be seemed even in the community of the ruling class. One party may come into power after replacing the other with its own set of political notions, beliefs and commitments that leads to transitory political culture, which further develops into sub-culture and this plurality of culture sometimes makes the political system unstable.

Keeping all this in mind Kavangh has pointed out that describing subjective attitudes about the political system is 'not tantamount to a realistic description of the system itself', 'political culture approach has been used to cover so many different phenomena that it is easily used as a residual factor.'[23]

INDIAN POLITICAL CULTURE

The ancient culture of India is commonly known as traditional value-laden agriculture. The slavery of India in the hands of Mughal dynasty and East India Company evolved a mixed type of culture that was more or less depicted as a colonial culture following the British legacy. Indian political system witnessed its decay particularly in economic front, and gradually became prey to British divide and rule policy. Indian democracy faced a major challenge of economic emancipation and strived to enforce modernization along-with integration. Myron Weiner has made an elaborate study of Indian political culture.[24] He observed that the influence of western democratic institutions in India has created two distinct political cultures—elite culture and the mass culture. The administrative authorities promote elite culture and the mass culture is localized, subjugated and exploited. No doubt Indian Government cherished the goal of village republic as given by Mahatma Gandhi through decentralization of power and various rural development projects, but unfortunately the policies made in the ivory towers failed to percolate to the grassroots level. Reasons are many, but corruption being undoubtedly the most vital one. Therefore, political culture of lower strata is more characterized by social evils like casteism, communalism, lingual politics and regionalism. This big gap between the two elite and mass political culture is dangerous for a democratic political system.[25]

Though Weiner made a serious study even then to agree with his thesis is not beyond doubt. The reason being that any democratic system though being vocal in cherishing goals of liberty, equality and fraternity, but essentially develops into an elite culture. India is no exception. Even during the liberation period, a small group of upper middle class dominated the process of movement. They took major decisions which were followed by the nation. Harold Lasswell rightly said in his work "psycho-pathology of politics" that revolution is initiated by a few and the rest follow it swayed by emotions. The rationality of the few is sometimes used for the welfare of the nation, but at the same time it is misused for seeking power. Therefore elite culture is the natural outcome of all political system.

During 70's and late 80's the legitimacy of the Government has been established by enactment of affirmative action and popular support. This enhanced the political participation of the masses, but simultaneously created a new class of protestors. After making protest participation as an accepted norm of democracy, movements, marches, and demonstrations became a regular feature. It also fragmented the electorate who were divided on the basis of caste, class, gender, etc. The revolution in the means of communication has made the world a global village. The news spread like fire in no time. Therefore, Indian culture in 90's became tremendously alert and alive. Twenty-first century is an age of corruption, crime and conspiracy. The points where government failed to deliver, civil society, NGOs intervened, giving rise to new social movements and creating social capital for promoting good governance. Off late India is relishing the taste of civic culture.

Questions for Discussion

1. Define political culture and discuss its kinds.
2. Write an essay on political culture.
3. Discuss how political culture analyzes different political systems.
4. Political culture of a country is dynamic not static. Elucidate.
5. Analyze the role of political culture in bringing political stability and change.
6. Examine political culture as a component of political system.

References

1. Almond and Verba (1963), *The Civic Culture*, New Jersey, Princeton University Press, p. 14.
2. Pye, Lucian W. (1965), *Introduction: Political Culture and Political Development* in Pye and Sydney Verba (Eds.), *Political Culture and Political Development*, Princeton, Princeton University Press, p. 7.
3. Beer and Ulam (1962), *Patterns of Government*, New York, Random House, p. 32.
4. Macridis, R.C. (1961), *Interest Groups in Comparative Politics*, *Journal of Politics*, Vol. XXIII, p. 40.
5. Dowse, R. and Hughes, John A. (1972), *Political Sociology*, London, John Wiley and Sons, p. 227.
6. Pye, Lucian W. (1962), *Politics, Personality and Nation Building*, New Haven, Yale University Press, pp. 122–123.
7. Kavangh, Dennis (1972), *Political Culture*, London, Macmillan, p. 10.
8. Ball, Allan R. (1971), *Modern Politics and Government*, London, The Macmillan Press, p. 57.
9. Almond, G.A. and Powell (1966), *Comparative Politics: A Development Approach*, Little Brown University Press, p. 225.
10. Dahl, Robert A. (1966), *Political Opposition in Western Democracies*, New Haven, Yale University Press, pp. 352–353.
11. Davies, Morton R. and Vaughan, A. Lewis (1971), *Models of Political Systems*, Delhi, Vikas Publishing, p. 116.
12. *Ibid.*, p. 117.
13. Almond and Verba (1963), *op. cit.*, p. 31.
14. *Ibid.*, p. 32.
15. Finer, S.E. (1970), *Comparative Government*, London, Allen Lane, pp. 537–540.
16. See Cazaley, D. (Ed.), (1976), *American Political Institutions in the 1970's*, New York, Columbia University Press.

17. Varma, S.P. (1975), *Modern Political Theory*, Delhi, Vikas Publishing, p. 292.

18. *Ibid.*, pp. 296–297.

19. Almond and Powell (1966), *op. cit.*, p. 51.

20. Davies and Lewis (1971), *op. cit.*, p. 114.

21. Krishna, Daya (1979), *Political Development: A Critical Perspective*, New Delhi, Oxford University Press (1971), p. 151.

22. Pye, Lucian W. (1962), *op. cit.*, p. 13.

23. Kavangh, *op. cit.*, p. 65.

24. Weiner, Myron (1969), *India: Two Political Cultures* in Sidney and Verba (Ed.) *Political Culture and Political Development*, London, Princeton University Press, p. 200.

25. *Ibid.*

Suggested Reading

Alan R. Ball, *Modern Politics and Government.*

Hari Hara Das and B.C. Choudhury, *Introduction to Political Sociology.*

J.C. Johari, *Comparative Politics.*

Web Link

www.britannica.com/EB checked/topic/467721/political/political culture.

5
Political Participation

CRUX

Democracy flourishes in any part of the world with three cardinal principles of liberty, equality and fraternity. Liberty of an individual as a basic unit of society, equality in diversity to maintain equilibrium in the society and fraternity for resolving conflicts, competitions and marching towards integration of the society. This ideal form of democracy can be created, sustained and enhanced by voluntary mass involvement in the decision-making process. When the awareness and attitude of the electorate are translated into political action, the democratic structure gets strengthened, and operational deliverance penetrates till the grass-roots level.

MEANING AND DEFINITION

To begin with, participation is an ingredient of every polity large or small—whether the society is obligatory or a democracy, someone must make political decisions and appoint, uphold and remove leaders. Those who fail to participate whether out of neglect or exclusion are likely to enjoy less power. Although not all who participate possess effective power, but those who don't participate cannot exercise or share power.[1] Political participation as a concept has gained a key place in contemporary political science, in general, and political sociology, in particular. People perform the act of participation in different ways. Some individuals are highly active in politics; they may join political parties and take part in electoral canvassing and propaganda. Others may join pressure group with the aim of advancing particular demands; still others may choose to make politics their career and stand for public office. Some others, in contrast, may appear to abstain completely from political activity, refusing to vote.

Growth of democratic government, is in part, measured by the extension of suffrage. Whereas, traditional monarchies restricted power and participation largely to the nobility and their agents, democracies have transformed these prerogatives into rights enjoyed by every citizen.

This expansion of participation was stimulated by the desire to give meaning and force to the principles of consent, accountability and political opposition. Participation is the principal means by which consent is granted or withdrawn in a democracy and rulers are made accountable to the ruled.[2] To realize these democratic objects, it is essential to have equal participation of all irrespective of caste, class or gender divide.

Political philosophers, from the time of Aristotle, have regarded popular participation as a source of vitality and creative energy, a defense against tyranny and as a means of enacting the collective wisdom. By involving many in the affairs of the state, participation can promote representation in the light of equality and dignity. Philosophers have also claimed that political participation facilitates broader and wider understanding of the political system.

Political participation is the involvement of groups and individual at various levels in the political system. Involvement expresses itself in various kinds of overt or manifest activities. Nie and Verba define political participation as 'those legal activities by private citizens which are more or less directly aimed at influencing the selection of Governmental personnel and/or the actions they take'.[3]

Huntington and Nelson define political participation 'simply as activity by private citizens designed to influence Governmental decision-making'.[4] J.W. Protho defines political participation as 'all behaviour through which people directly express their political opinions.[5]

Myron Weiner restricts his definition of political participation to voluntary action. Mobilized participation refers to activity which is designed by someone other than the actor to influence Governmental decision-making. In other words political participation should not be influenced byelites and social leaders. It should be in a way of learning and influencing the authoritative allocation of values for a society. When citizens become socially aware then political events and issues acts like a stimuli and demogauge gives behavioural response to it. This sanguine participation of the mass is political participation in true sense of the term.

On the basis of the degree or extent of participation, political activities have been arranged by Rush and Althoff in the following manner:[6]

1. Holding political or administrative office;
2. Seeking political or administrative office;
3. Active membership in a political organization;
4. Passive membership in a political organization;
5. Active membership of a quasi-political organization (interest or pressure groups);
6. Passive membership of a quasi-political organization;
7. Participation in public meetings, demonstrations and so on;
8. Participation in informal political discussion;

9. General interest in politics;
10. Voting; and
11. Apathy.

Woodward and Roper suggest that five ways of behaving, taken together, constitute an operational definition of the term political activity.[7] In addition to voting at the polls, they include within their range supporting pressure groups through membership; participation in political party activity, and a subsequent claim on legislators; engaging in habitual dissemination of political opinions through word of mouth communications to other citizens and direct personal communication with legislators.

According to L. Milbrath, "The activities included in political participation may be divided into—gladiatorial activities, transitional activities and spectator activities." These activities are as follows:

1. **Gladiatorial activities:** This category includes the activities which are part of routine of the political parties, such as elections to political post, participation in election to legislature, gathering fund for the party, movements to increase membership and organization of meetings everywhere to form public opinion in its' favour, etc.
2. **Transitional activities:** These include activities of the helpers and well-wishers of the political parties, such as hearing the lectures of the leaders, donating to the fund of the party and maintaining contact with the leaders of the party.
3. **Spectator activity:** This category includes voting, influencing others vote, participating in political debate, being influenced by political stimuli, wearing badges of the political party and distributing leaflets, etc.

The analysis of Milbrath throw light upon the nature of political participation which is always changing from time to time, from place to place.

FOUNDATIONS OF POLITICAL PARTICIPATION

Huntington and Nelson identify and define the following common foundations of political participation:[8]

1. **Class:** Individuals of similar social status, income and occupation;
2. **Communal group:** Individuals of similar race, religion, language, or ethnicity;
3. **Neighbourhood:** Individuals residing in geographical proximity to each other;
4. **Party:** Individuals who identify with the same formal organization attempting to win over or maintain control of the executive and legislative branches of government; and

5. **Faction:** Individuals united by sustained or intense personal interaction with each other, one manifestation of which is the patron-client grouping which involves the reciprocal exchange of benefits between individuals of unequal status, wealth and influence.

According to Milbrath, political participation varies in relation to four major factors:

1. The extent to which the individual receives political stimuli;
2. The individuals' personal characteristics
3. The individuals social characteristics
4. The political setting or environment in which the individual finds himself.

Broadly speaking, political participation depends on psychological, social-economic and political environment. Lane makes a meticulous study to identify those socio-psychological and political variables to explain various forms of political participation in USA. His generalization could be easily taken into consideration for understanding the nature of political participation in general.

FACTORS AFFECTING POLITICAL PARTICIPATION

Psychological factors

The psychological factor emerges from individual personality traits and cognitive structures. Such structures involves political activities of man's need for power, competition, achievements, affiliation, aggression, money, prestige, status, recognition, approval, manipulation, sympathy and responsibility. Participation may also be classified in terms of goals.[9] These are: instrumental and consummatory.

Instrumental political activities are primarily oriented towards concrete goals, such as the party's victory in the election, the passage of a bill, or the enhancement of one's own status, influence or income. Consummatory or expressive activities are aimed at more immediate satisfaction. For example, common people who cast their vote and feel elated for being involved in the decision-making process. Self-esteemed or a feeling of pessimism have a major role to play in political participation.

Social factors

Political participation is determined to a great extent by social factors, such as sex, community, secularization, education, urban-rural divide, status, etc. Education acts as an important determinant in formulating reasonable thinking and voting. Educated persons can articulate their ideas more effectively. They naturally seek the fulfillment of their self-interest through active participation in politics.[10] Men take more interest in politics than women. It is a universal trend. Minority have a cumulative voting style which is used by politicians for their vested interest. High income group and low income group differs in their voting style. However, middle class families pass on politics from one generation to the other. Secular thinking enhances rationality in the voting behaviour, but their numbers are less in any given society. Urban culture is more exposed to information, therefore, voting assimilates. But recent studies contradicts the facts and claims that rural counterparts are easily mobilized and actively participate in political activities, and same is with low income groups. Vendors, hawkers, riksha pullers, auto drivers, etc. are now more politically vigilant than the middle class and their turnout in polls at times out number the middle class people.

Economic factors

Economy has an impact in formulating political participation. Affluent class of the society either controls political participation through muscle and money or tries to maintain the status-quo of the political system. As Aristotle suggested that middle class actively participates in politics and the educated lot belongs to this category. They rebel against the evils of the society and clamour for positive change. But the people at the lowest economic ebb do not rationalize their voting behaviour. They are swayed by emotions and mobilised by local area elites. Therefore, in a developed society the level of political participation is high as compared to the developing society.

Political factors

Political participation is no doubt a political activity, but it is highly influenced by non-political variables like caste, community, etc. as mentioned above. However, it is nowhere to suggest that political factors are of no use. They do play a crucial role in articulating political participation. The nature of political system (parliamentary vs. presidential, democracy vs. authoritative, capitalist vs. communist) have impact on the political participation. Constitutional structure, election procedure, party system, role of press and the functions of the organs of state decides the voting behaviour in any political system. Political orientations, affiliations, ideological commitments and cognition of issues and events determine political participation. When the electorate is educated, they understand the manifestos and parties also tries to gain popular support by debates, speeches, discussions on vital public issues. Opposition parties also generate a sense of belongingness and try to evoke passive citizens by their campaign and propaganda.

STYLES OF POLITICAL PARTICIPATION

Huntington and Nelson deals with different styles of political participation in contrasting modes.[11] These are:

1. Direct vs. Indirect
2. Voluntary vs. Hired or Involuntary
3. Professional vs. Non-Professional
4. Active vs. Passive

Direct participation is the involvement of people beyond the vote politics. It is a continuation and result of political culture. It also means active involvement of mass not only during election period, but even in between and above all comprises self-initiated activities. Indirect political participation is designed to appear in a little measure in the whole network of governmental activities. Such type remains active during election and sincerely takes voting both as a right and a duty of an awakened citizenry.

Voluntary political participation emerges out of personal interest of the citizen which is mobilized by interest groups, pressure groups, organized youth groups and government in power. Voting in favour of or against a particular candidate necessarily depends on the cognition and the interest of the voter. However, in involuntary participation people are hired for dharnas (protest) and demonstrations. Unaware of the issues, ideological commitments or general interest same faces can be seen raising slogans, demonstrating, marching for or against a political figure or a political party. Such involvements are dangerous for democratic edifice, and cannot be formulated as a design of political participation in strict sense of the term. India is beset with this vexing problem, because of illiteracy and poverty. Politicians mobilize masses by giving money or any other form of allurement or gratification.

A political professional is a one whose primary calling is politics or government. Holding political or administrative office, contesting elections, lobbying, performing tasks as a routine job in political circle turns into professional political participation. The activities of political leaders, therefore, cannot be regarded as a yardstick in assessing the political culture of demagogue. It is virtually mass political involvement which strengthens the democratic norms. Non-professional participation is intermittent political activity confining mainly to reading newspapers to casting vote. It becomes secondary role, giving primacy to family and community affairs. Active political participation is a type of public involvement not only during election period but also in between two election periods. As contrasted to it, is passive political participation which is mainly concerned with casting vote and evaluating verdict.

Off late two important, yet controversial styles of political participation were added. These are ceremonial or support participation and protest participation.

Former was the expression of the citizens in support of the government policies and projects. They are organized groups mobilising common people and preparing them for the next elections. Such a phenomenon is common in both developing and developed societies of the world. Later, Verba also added protest participation as a vital style of political participation though earlier they considered protest participation outside the ambit of political activities. They regarded the various forms of protest participation such as demonstrations, civil violence, riots, and assassinations as illegal activities. Sometimes, such activities may be 'illegal' according to the established norms of the political system. But they do not lose thereby their importance as a form of political participation, but on a contrary tends to enhance it.[12] After a lot of deliberations, political thinkers decided to include persuading or pressurizing government for the common welfare not only as legitimate, but also desirable for the successful functioning of democracy.

TYPES

There are different types of political participation, but the most overt and studied form is voting. But in between two elections, citizens should participate in political affairs in order to enhance the quality of democratic functioning. Participation is often the result of awareness and attitude towards political system, political events and political issues. Thus all activities of individual in influencing the decision-making process can be broadly classified into different types of political participation.

Voting

In a democracy, government is of the people, by the people and for the people as Lincoln claims. However in actual practice, it becomes an indirect democracy where leaders are the representatives of the people and they enjoy all the powers and people remain mute spectators. So, electorate in order to safeguard themselves from being cheated must always be critical in analysing government performance. Citizens must not be guided by social-psychological pressures rather should cast votes on the basis of political efficacy. So voting becomes not only a political right of a citizen but also a basic duty. Adult franchise is universally practiced where an adult citizen takes initiative to vote and to control the reigns of power holders. The scope of voting is very broad, but it varies from one political system to the other. In a communist society, there is intra-voting within the single political party, whereas in liberal society, there is vast choice for voters in a multi party scenario and therefore liberal society tends to become more democratic.

Campaigning

In this type of political participation, citizens actively involve themselves in canvassing. Citizens use their vehicles, money or manpower in canvassing for a particular political party or for a particular political candidate. They are usually workers of the party and with the close contact with the leaders; they create a space to seek power. Though they are not the main political actor, yet they seek and capture power as a reward of their loyalty towards a party or a person. Those persons who have keen interest in political affairs motivate masses to cast vote, and makes an effort to produce collective mobility.

Self-interest

The other two types of political participation (voting and campaigning) are mainly confined to the election period, but self-interest makes an individual an active citizen. They are continuously involved in political activities right from reading newspapers to taking processions they always assess and express the performance of the government through processions and debates and remain ready for forming interest groups or pressure groups or lobbying with the government officials to get his work or others work done with or without gratification.

Collective Activity

In such a type of political participation, citizens do not act on their own rather joins a group to influence the decision-making process. The citizens may even put pressure on the government and get certain policies framed. They work for the collective gain, but in most of the cases they promote a small group of interests. Such an activity is mainly the output of vested interests.

TYPES OF POLITICAL NON-PARTICIPATION

The outcome of democracy mainly depends on the activities of its citizens. If the level of participation is quite high democracy survives, if the level of participation is quite high and matured as well, then democracy flourishes, if participation level is low democracy struggles for existence. But most importantly, if citizens' level of participation is both low (turn out percentage) and parochial (narrow minded guided by caste, class alike variables) democracy is in shambles. Therefore, political participation becomes the yardstick to gauge the performance of a democratic edifice andit becomes very essential to understand the types of political non-participation and to examine the reasons behind it. Broadly speaking, there are four main types of political non-participation.

Apathy

Social scientists have shown interest in certain forms of political non-participation of which apathy is one of them. Apathy is a type of political passivity which provides support for the regime, but enables the individual to avoid the politicization of his whole being. There are different causes of apathy.

It happens with a person who has absence of information and lack of interest in political activities. For example, it is generally found that illiterate people or people coming from below poverty line are least concerned with political issues, and therefore, develop apathy towards the political system. At the same time there is another group of persons who are highly aware of the political changes and they are either frustrated and helpless or highly satisfied and wills no change whatsoever, to bring in the polity, and therefore, deliberately keeps themselves away from the political activities. This sense of political efficacy has been studied and measured by the authors of The Voter Decides.[13]

An individual can become a champion of change only if he/she performs his/her civic duties. Apathy leads to the decline of political vitality and vigilance. This might ultimately result in depriving this particular section of the society who need most to be represented for exercising the right to influence the decision-making process. Widespread apathy increases the chance of unscrupulous people to dominate the political structure.[14] Sometimes, political apathy becomes an ideology which is detrimental to the interests of the nation. Apathy results in the lack of capacity for forming viable political opposition. Political opposition is an essential ingredient of the defense against tyranny and abuse of political power. And above all apathy reveals the weakness of the political system.[15] Political apathy makes politics confused, complicated and contradictory, and political communication is mere propaganda. Personal reasons also may account for apathy. It develops certain degree of mental laziness to a phobia toward serious thought of political decay. Whatever be the cause or causes, political apathy remains a crucial problem. The necessity of reconciling apathy and democracy, supposedly based on the participation of the people is an important issue to be dealt with.[16] So, it can be said that apathy ruins the loyalty of people towards the political system and disillusions citizens. It is highly dangerous for democratic polity and can become explosive any moment.

Cynicism

Cynicism etymologically means complete distrust towards others. It is a psychological disorder where good deeds of others are always taken into suspicion and doubt. It is always felt that others goodness is due to some ulterior motive. This type of attitude damages social relations and an individual gets alienated from the society. Such a person grows a shell around him and becomes isolated. They also become pessimistic and regard political leaders as actors of oppression. Political cynicism if increases qualitatively or quantitatively, it weakens the foundation of democracy. Cynical person regards voting as a futile effort to control the government. They are fed-up with the existing political system and at the same time they are not optimistic towards bringing about change. Thus, cynicism leads to lack of legitimacy and popular support for the political system.

Alienation

Alienation as a concept was elucidated by Satre and Marx which is a stage of dilemma. The inherent conflict and the loss of judgement lead to it. In a political system, such a condition of a man divorces him from the day-to-day activities. People purposefully segregates themselves from the polity. Such a person has strong emotional and corporal bond with his family. He is never concerned about the rampant societal evils. His inaction in politics is a natural outcome of his self-centered attitude. Robert Lane defines political alienation as a person's sense of estrangement from the politics and the government of his society and the tendency to think of the government and politics of the nation as run by others for others according to a unfair set of rules. In one word, such a person is 'politically divorced.'[17] For a democratic political system, alienation is a serious problem because democracy hinges on popular support.

Anomie

Another psychological phenomenon is 'anomie' which refers to a sense of rootlessness, loss of values and lack of direction among individuals. Ever since Emile Durkheim identified the problem of social disintegration and the lack of international and external regulation on an individual, and gave it the term anomie,[18] the concept has captured the imagination of social scientists. Riesman makes the term 'anomie' synonymous with 'maladjusted'.[19] Erich Fromm suggests that anomic individuals may attempt to reintegrate with society, ideologically and socially through some totalitarian movement.[20] Anomie inhibits political participation because as in the case of apathy it implies a feeling of ineffectiveness, or a feeling that authorities do not care about the common people. However, there is also a difference between the two. While the former is passive in nature, latter involves fear, panic, violence and destruction. The implication of anomic attitude is reflected at the individual level—suicide; at the group level—riot; and at the country and cross-country level—terrorism. It is a very serious problem because it involves devaluation of norms and goals. The assassination of Mrs. Indira Gandhi, the then Prime minister of India in the year 1984, created an anomic situation, where unorganized sporadic riots took place all over India against the Sikh community. The penalizing of entire Sikh community for the crime of two Sikh bodyguards who killed Mrs. Gandhi can never be justified as it was based on the feeling of ruthless revenge.

VOTING BEHAVIOUR

Modern day democracies are indirect, representative democracies. To realize the goal of representative democracy, there is a need of institutional arrangement. The electoral system is one of them. It is the most essential function of political recruitment. Political scientists claim that electoral laws can have an impact upon the types of participation practiced by those who do not have the franchise. Political environment in which citizens live can stimulate or depress participation in elections and other political activities. The liberal democratic perspective particularly emphasizes the stability of the political system on the level of political participation. In recent development, civil society, NGO's and voluntary organizations are also projected as appropriate agencies for participatory development. In a true democracy, elections provide opportunities for the most overt forms of political participation. Charles Hickman Titus points out that because voting records are quantitative and show 'pragmatic recurrence of a situation', and because the large number of votes permit sound numerical summarizations, no other phenomenon seems to possess as many advantages for scientific analysis as the electoral process.[21]

The study of electoral process is done by Psephologists, and they also make predictions immediately before or after polls. Several studies in this field have been done all over the world. It appears that it interests political scientists, sociologists, psychologists and social anthropologists. Records of participation and the comparison of non-voting ratio have contributed to the understanding of the citizen's perception of political party and the voter's capacity to exercise power across the various ranges of political distance.[22]

In Indian democracy, there are two types of elections—direct and indirect. Direct is based on adult franchise, and the voting age at present is 18 years (as amended by late PM Mr. Rajiv Gandhi). In an indirect election, as in case of Rajya Sabha members, President and Vice-President; electorate is not the common people, but the MLA's and the MP's. However, by proportional representation vote theory and formula, common people are indirectly involved. In this case voting is not to be assessed. It is mainly in direct elections, where the electorate is educated by different political parties and mandate is usually fractured. We can see the trend since last 20 years with the formation of National Democratic Alliance and United Progressive Alliance. Initially after Independence, one party model was in vogue. The Congress hegemony was undisputed because people accepted Congress not as a party, but as a movement for liberation. With the passage of time, Congress saw its downfall and there was emergence of coalition politics. The year 1967 saw the beginning of actual era of choices and alliance. Aloo J. Dastur in her study of parliamentary elections (1967) in Bombay (based on interviews of 603 voters in three constituencies taken in three waves) found that Bombay voters had gained political consciousness and maturity through the passage of years. A high percentage of women, the illiterate, the backward and the scheduled castes, even in rural area, had become conscious of their power to vote. So, it can be said that the voting behaviour shifted from emotional bond to assessment of the political parties based on performance.

Broadly speaking, the factors responsible for voting behaviour can be classified into three categories—socio-economic, psychological and political. However, it is interesting to note that voting is a political activity, but is more influenced by non-political or domestic factors. This is found even in the western world. For example, the Columbia studies stressed social and environmental factors and the Michigan studies emphasized the psychological factors. Voting is not the product of any one factor; it is the result of multiple factors. At the same time, indigenous factors are diversified and specific to their own political system. The most crucial variable in the process of electoral choice in India has been the caste factor.

Socio-economic factors

The socio-economic factors are governed by the following:

1. **Caste:** The study of electoral behaviour claims that the main force behind voting is 'falia' and 'caste'. Rajani Kothari, the renowned psephologist had a firm belief that voting is an extended family affair usually guided by the choice of the head of the family or caste affiliation. He further added that caste and community are two easily identified social clusters, which are keenly and deliberately exploited by the politicians for the electoral gain. The most glaring example in India can be 'Mandal and Kamandal Politics'. The position that emerges is that caste appears to be important, but the degree differs from region to region and from centre to grassroots level. There are also instances of split voting within the same castes and of functional alignment between and across states. V.N. Sirsikar in 'Party Loyalties Versus Caste and Communal Polls: Poona Constituency' pointed out that voters are influenced by caste and religious loyalties. He finds that other residual factors, such as instructions of the family head, means of mass manipulation, minority fears also influenced the process of election.
2. **Class:** Class-cleavage in the society though being a sociological concept has a lasting political impact. Karl Marx rightly claims that there are only two class in the society—haves and have nots. The economically dominant class, he asserted, remains more authoritative than the middle income group. Politicians take help from capitalist class in contesting elections, and in return give them certain favours. For example, license, permits, etc. In a way, the producing class of the society easily influences plans and policies of the government, whereas the middle class remains value-laden and casts their vote on the basis of self-projected ideologies. People belonging to the lower strata of the society are easily cheated with quick delivery of goods and services immediately before elections. Memory of a man is short. Therefore they forget the pains of the past and gets allured with the immediate gains. Class factor remains important in orienting voting behaviour. The role of class in electoral politics has come in for critical review in a book edited by Geoffrey Evans which indicates

that class is still relevant as an important explanatory variable in voting behaviour. In India, there is a dynamic interaction between the class and the caste, but there are indications that the class factor in voting behaviour is weakening and the electoral behaviour is more volatile.[23]

3. **Community:** Religious affinity and race, if stretched too far, can turn into communal frenzy. The dictates of religious heads or priests in guiding voting behaviour should always be discouraged. As it is the sensitive issue, politicians try to gain optimum result out of it. Be it *Ram Janam Bhumi* versus *Babari Masjid* or making of Khalistan or issue of conversion, religious sentiments are aroused for vested interests. Unfortunately, it is the British legacy and is fully used by national leaders to foster divide and rule policy. The situation becomes more grin with the mushroom growth of fanatic organizations' disturbing communal harmony. Foreign hand is also playing a vital role in aggravating religious turmoil. Government remains apathetic towards communal riots, rather follows appeasement policy to woo the vote of minorities. The substance of ethics, values and morality are extracted from religion to make its blatant use for fear and destruction. The problem is becoming alarming with the growing lust for power of our politicians of today. Less educated and lower income groups are more vulnerable to religious pressures. The influence of religion is more pronounced in a developing country, like India where the pace of secularization is slow and the grip of tradition is strong.

4. **Region:** In a large country like India, geographical proximity also plays an important role in influencing the voting pattern. The north-south divide is the glaring example of opposed political behaviour. The autonomy of state within the federal structure is the result of regional imbalances and strikingly different political culture. The emergence of regional parties was mainly due to the fact that Congress as a party failed to serve the interests of the nation as a whole. It was alleged to be a party of North India and South Indians as a sharp reaction to it found their own regional parties for promoting their sectional interests. This, at times, disintegrates the society and the vote culture makes regions conflict with each-other on trivial issues which are fanned by political agendas. Since Independence, regionalism is posing a serious threat to national integrity and Jawahar Lal Nehru, the first Prime Minister of independent India claimed that India was to meet two basic challenges: modernization and integration. Vote bank politics leads to river disputes, boundary disputes or economic backwardness disputes. The more unaware are the common people, the easier it is for the politicians to widen the gulf based on regional disparities, as confirmed by Gaeteno Mosca in classification of elits.

5. **Language:** Linguistic loyalty sometimes forms the basis for the formation of political parties dedicated to meeting the needs of specific groups. Lingual affinity is a direct off-shoot of regional grievances, and is purposefully used by political leaders for seeking or holding power. Unfortunately, Hindi as a language has been a bone of contention between north and south India. A very dangerous slogan was raised in south '*English ever, Hindi never.*' Hindi was regarded as an alien language and people from South retorted that through Hindi language north India would establish its control and authority over south India, in other words, language would ultimately lead to north Indian imperialism. This lingual divide undermined the importance of national voting behaviour based on ideological appeals, and gave upper-hand to regional interests in the electoral process. It is rightly said that voters do not act as an individual, but as members of a class, caste, religion, sex or place of birth.
6. **Money:** In a large democracy of a developing country, food security, social security and adequate means of livelihood remains the most vexing problems. Welfare state functions on the principle of just and humane order. India is no doubt following this principle, but the non-delivery of services at the grass roots level aggravates the problem. Assessing the whole scenario, political representatives offer financial allurement during elections. The marginalized sections of the society get overwhelmed by their mesmerizing false promises, and they become easy prey to their ulterior motives. Votes are purchased, political participation is hired and the critical thinking of the electorates is thereby doomed. The pomp and show of rallies which has become the regular feature of today attracts voters who are later cheated on. For example, programmes like MANAREGA can amass votes of the poor, but people cannot repose their faith on such leaders for quite long if they realize that they are being duped by hollow words and flattery. Even then money safeguards heavy number of votes not only in a developing democracy. Inflation, rationing of cocking gas, petrol and diesel price hike, rate fixation of paddy crops and sugar cane, populist budget, etc. also influences the voting behaviour. Nearly in all countries of the world, money and muscle power have occupied an important place, and in some cases even play decisive role in elections. Criminalization of politics, scientific rigging, booth capturing, etc., have compromised the sanctity of elections, but even then there is no substitute to elections if we want democracy to survive.

Socio-psychological factors

Socio-psychological factors are as follows:

- Personality voting
- Sympathy voting
- Age and gender voting

D.N. Pathak, in his study of Gujarat (based on 698 interviews of voters in three constituencies in two waves), points out that male, young, highly educated and higher caste voters made their voting decisions easier, while females, old, less educated and lower caste voters delayed their voting decisions.[24] This voting behaviour reveals the fact that psychology also bears an impact on exercising of vote. Even in developed countries of the West, personality or sympathy voting cannot be denied. The sudden demise of any political leader pulls sympathy of the masses which are often reflected in their voting behaviour. For example, post Rajiv Gandhi assassination poll result is a testimony to the fact. Film stars or celebrities find easy to become representatives because of the popular support. Common political beliefs lay the groundwork for sharing equivalent emotions of anger, sympathy, and distress both for political leaders and common people. Minority vote together, which they think, would help them to get assimilated into the national mainstream.[25]

Age is a difficult factor to treat as an independent variable, but even if we could resolve such methodological difficulties, other problems of explanation remain. Older voters tend to vote for conservative parties, but this may be a simple reflection of the historical period when the electors' voting habits were being formed; age may be less important than the strength of the voters' attachment to a political party, and it is this allegiance that hardens with age.[26] The electorate is constantly being replaced, and the personality of candidates and issues may be factors in persuading the voter to change his party allegiance but it often comes with the maturity of age.[27] Though there is no final finding regarding gender as a determinant of voting behaviour but Lipset found that women are more sensitive towards ethical issues and therefore corruption, criminalization adversely affects their voting behaviour. As it is women have less interest in politics as compared to men so their voting behaviour needs to be surcharged with heart rendering issues.

Political Factors

The following are the major political determinants of voting behaviour:

1. Political orientation
2. Political issues and events
3. Political ideological allegiance
4. Political efficacy
5. Anti-incumbency factor

The comparative study of mass electoral behaviour and elitist behaviour exhibits the fact that voters are dominated by parochial considerations. They do not understand the basic issues and cast vote swayed by emotions.

V.M. Sirsikar pointed out that even in the highly politically conscious constituency of Pune, more than 33% of the voters did not know anything about the political issues involved, and nearly 25% were ignorant of the candidates and the party for which they were contesting.[28] Political variables have not generally received due attention. What motivates the electorate to become a voter is its sense of political security rather than performance efficacy. Electoral experiences in the country rely more on family socialization and the electoral maturity as an indicator of political mobilization is dangerously missing. Political awareness, political involvement, political judgement and political adjustment need special attention to stop democracy from being at the cross-roads. Matured political system demands political orientation of the electorate. Here the role of political party becomes very responsible. Political parties act as a broker of ideas, disseminate information and make voters aware of their voting power. In other words, political parties educate electorate through manifestos and agenda. Mass media of communication (both print and electronic) have wide range of roles to play in reinforcing sentiments towards political goals. The problem of democracy lies in the ignorance of citizens. So, increasing general interest in politics is highly desirable for effective functioning of political institutions.

Elections are contested primarily based on issues, where there is ideological ambiguity in the party system. India provides such a system where the national parties have mainly emerged from the umbrella character of Indian National Congress. Even in USA, it is often said that the Republican and the Democratic are the two parties with similar ideological orientations. So, elections are mainly held on the basis of events and issues, unlike Britain. Sometimes voters become polarised on an issue as emphasized by V.O. Key, Jr. as 'issue voting.' However, how far voters are influenced by issues is a subject of considerable debate. Ideally speaking, Indian political system has evolved serious issues from time-to-time, from '*Indira hatao, Desh bachao*' to 'Feel Good India', but either voter fails to understand the intensity of political issues or they are ignorant of the same.

Long-term continuities in allegiance to particular group or ideologies inspite of changes in the issues or in the role of different political parties remain stable conditions underlying mandate. For example, old people have very strong affiliation with the Indian National Congress and they are not ready to undermine its importance even with changing behavioural pattern of the party. People link themselves with the political system and political parties as they do with caste or community. Over a period of time, sometimes accumulation of grievances may deviate the voting behaviour, but that is very rare. Most of the time consistency prevails. It has also been found that ideological allegiance varies from area to area. The voting behaviour of the people of Kashmir stands in direct contrast with that of Tamil Nadu. As society is stratified, the influences of political parties also differ. There are many factors responsible for political allegiance. The family orientation, the individual interest or the ideological affiliation work together as man is a product of multiple and dynamic environmental factors.

Ideology still remains a powerful factor in electoral behaviour though critics, like Francis, Fukuyama claims that there is end of ideology.

The most analytical and critical voting behaviour is based on evaluating performance of political parties. Electorate in a democratic set-up enjoys freedom of choice. In a bi-party or a multi-party system, voters get a chance to eliminate evils and select efficacy. This however, is not a simple phenomenon, because it requires high level of awareness, critical thinking and assessment without bias or predilection. It is really difficult to sterilize the emotions and cast vote, exclusively on the basis of performance. Political participation is a human activity fundamentally and therefore, cannot be completely free from personal preferences. The analysis of the past elections provide us many examples where voters were influenced by immediate political speeches and normative agendas. It would not be out of place to say that people must take into account five years' performance and not issues cropping just before elections. As Lipset has remarked, "Since voting is a recurrent and periodic event in the life of individuals and social groups, we must consider it over longer periods of time, extending our perspective beyond static relationships between social positions, and beyond the immediate events of one election." The issue of reservation of seats for women crops up before every election, but is never settled down for reasons quite known. The Food Security Ordinance of July 2013 before ensuing 2014 parliamentary elections cannot be seen beyond doubt. The Common Minimum Programme (CMP) of BJP is also cashed by power mongers however they are aware of the fact that it cannot be implemented in secular India. They blame other political parties aligning with them for not enacting the bill. The harsh reality is that it is a mere political gimmick.

Anti-incumbency feeling is a real factor in Indian elections—ruling parties are routinely routed. To avoid anti-establishment wrath, governing coalitions usually replace incumbents with fresh candidates, untainted by corruption. As Butler, Lahiri and Roy points out, "The electorate seems to be increasingly dissatisfied with the performance of his government and is constantly looking for a change."[29]

ELECTION STRATEGY

The influencing factors in political field have less impact than the social variables. This is almost a universal phenomenon with a changing degree. The emergence of 'new politics, new social movements and the third and the fourth generation of the Human Rights' movement have successfully ensured extra electoral mobilization of a heavy chunk of population, mainly marginalized. Modern writers are of the opinion that in the cyber-space election of the future internet users or 'netizens' will come to play a crucial role. Internet use is not only popular in western world, but simultaneously engulfing countries. With the internet communication revolution cyber-polling have become common. Barack

Obama's campaign through extensive use of satellite and e-mail is known to all. In recent years, political marketing has also been used to analyse marginalized electoral politics. In India, Marketing Advisory and Research Group (MARG), India Market Research Bureau (IMRB) and Operations Research Group (ORG) have helped political parties and candidates to develop a marketing strategy.

The increasing use of opinion polls show that not only is political marketing going to stay, but it will also thrive with the help of media hype.[30] During last two decades, the use of polling in electoral analysis has gone up. Social Scientists have developed an impressive array of techniques for discovering and measuring electoral behaviour. The media is also held responsible for making fairly accurate predictions about 'hung parliament.' Psephologists, like Vinod Dua (Hindi), Prannoy Roy (English), Rajat Sharma and the likes have actually increased the craze for pre-poll and exit-poll opinions. Now there are many in the race.

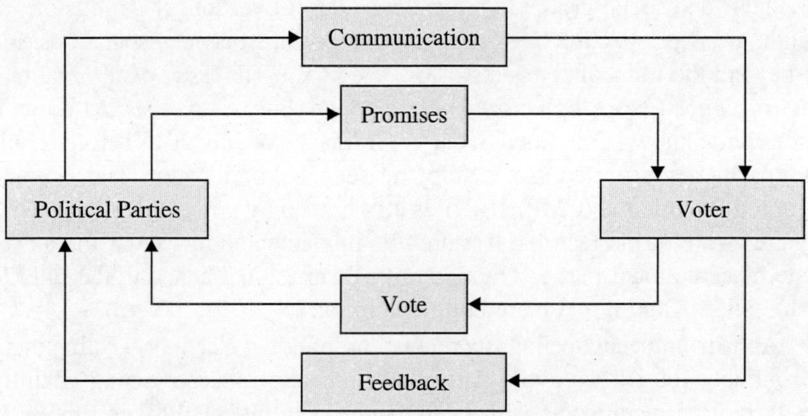

Figure 5.1 Elite vs. Mass Political Participation.

Source: Dilip M. Sarwate (1990), *Political Marketing, The Indian Experience*, Tata McGraw-Hill Publication, pp. 12–13.

Questions for Discussion

1. Political participation is a must for successful functioning of democracy. Elucidate.
2. Critically examine the nature and forms of political participation.
3. Highlight the bases of political participation in a developing country.
4. What is political participation? Discuss its various kinds and styles.
5. Define political non-participation. Discuss the various factors responsible for it.
6. What are the factors responsible for electoral behaviour?

References

1. *International Encyclopedia of Social Sciences* (Ed.) Shills David L. Articles, *Participation Political* by Herbert McClosky Vol. 12, Macmillan and Free Press, p. 253.
2. *Ibid.*
3. Nie, Norman H. and Verba, S. (1975), *Political Participation* in Greenstein, F.I. and Polsbey, N.W. (Eds.), *Handbook of Political Science*, Vol. 4, Massachusetts, Addison-Wesley Publishing Company, p. 1.
4. Huntington, Samuel P. and Nelson, Joan M. (1976), *No Easy Choice*, Cambridge, Harvard University Press, p. 4.
5. Mathews, D.R. and Protho, J.W. (1966), *Negroes and New Southern Politics*, New York, Harcourt, Brace and World, p. 37.
6. Rush, M. and Althoff, P. (1971), *An Introduction to Political Sociology*, London, Nelson.
7. Woodward, Julian L. and Roper, E., *Political Activity of American Citizens* in Eulau, et al. (Eds.), *Political Behaviour: A Reader in Theory and Research*, Delhi, American Publication Company, p. 133.
8. Huntington, Samuel P. and Nelson, Joan M. (1976), *op. cit.*
9. Das, Hari Hara and Choudhury, B.C. (1997), *Introduction to Political Sociology*, New Delhi, Vikas Publishing, p. 150.
10. Banerjee, Sunanda (2002), *An Introduction to Political Sociology*, New Delhi, Janaki Prakashan, p. 54.
11. Nie and Verba, *op. cit.*, p. 3; Huntington and Nelson, *op. cit.*, p. 5.
12. Sharma, L.N. and Ashraf, Ali (1983), *Political Sociology: A New Grammar of Politics*, New Delhi University Press, pp. 144–145.
13. Campbell, Amngus, et al. (1954), *The Voters Decide*, Evanston, Row, Peterson and Company, p. 187.
14. Das, Hari Hara and Choudhury, B.C., *op. cit.*, p. 156.
15. *Ibid.*
16. Sharma, L.N. and Ashraf, Ali, *op. cit.*, p. 146.
17. Das, Hari Hara and Choudhury, B.C., *op. cit.*, p. 157.
18. Durkheim, Emile (1951), *Suicide: A Study in Sociology*, Translated by Spandling and Simpson, Glencoe, Illinois, Free Press, pp. 246–254.
19. Riesman, David (1950), *The Lonely Crowd*, New Haven, Yale University Press, p. 287.
20. Fromm, Erich (1955), *The Sane Society*, New York, Rinehart, pp. 120–208.
21. Titus, Charles H., *Voting Behaviour in the United States*, Berkeley, University of California Press, pp. 1–2.
22. Sharma, L.N. and Ashraf, Ali (1983), *op. cit.*, p.154.

23. Butler, D. and Kavanagh, D. (1980), *The British General Election of 1979*, London, p. 350.
24. Sharma, L.N. and Ashraf, Ali (1983), *op. cit.*, p. 156.
25. See Report (1969), *Electoral Change in India; General Elections 1967*, Bombay, Academic Books.
26. Butler, D. and Stokes, D. (1974), *Political Change in Britain*, London, Oxford University Press, pp. 323–337.
27. Ball, Alan R., *op. cit.*, p. 130.
28. Sirsikar, V.M. (1965), *Political Behaviour in India: A Case Study of the 1962 General Elections*, Bombay, Manaktalas; L.N. Sharma and Ali Ashraf, *op. cit.*, p. 156.
29. Butler, D., Lahiri, A. and Roy, P. (1997), *India Decides: Elections 1993–1995*, in Partha Chatterjee (Ed.), *State and Politics in India*, Delhi; Oxford University Press, pp. 125–176.
30. Chakraborty, Satyabrata (Ed.) (2005), *Political Sociology, Electoral Politics*, Gautum Mukhopadhyay, New Delhi, Macmillan India, p. 384.

Suggested Reading

Alan R. Ball, *Modern Politics and Government*

N. Jayapalan, *Political Sociology*

L.N. Sharma and Ali Ashraf, *Political Sociology, A New Grammar of Politics*

Satyabrata, Chakraborty, *Political Sociology*

Web Link

www.ndi.org/women's-political.participation.

6
Political Development

CRUX

This heuristic concept has a fluctuating fortune, as it is not an absolute notion rather relative product of changing values and conflict of civilizations. Time, culture, leadership and motives result in political development closely linked with crises which are system specific. The variation in defining the concept makes the subject more intriguing. Lucian Pye and many other thinkers have failed to generalize the theories of political development, but all are in accord that it essentially stems from the idea of change resulting in changing contours of power structure. However the concept strives to strike a balance between normative philosophy of East and empirical analysis of the West which helps to make comparative study of political systems.

MEANING AND DEFINITION

The imaginary sketch of civilization conceived political development as a synonym of progress, mainly in economic arena with change in per capita income, standard of living which, however was subject to vehement criticisms on the ground of being parochial and partial. With the passage of time, the discourse shifted its focus from economy to overall growth, and is strengthened by good governance, which in turn, depends on cultural milieu, potential leadership and awakened citizenry. Satisfaction of basic needs of children in their family is a primary condition of growth, but yet cannot be regarded as an exclusive condition, more imperative to mention that involvement of child in family decisions develops his or her personality. Likewise in a political system involvement of citizens in decision-making process leads to political development. The end of Second World War opened gates for newly liberated states of Asia, Africa and Latin America, which colonized into third world countries, and their citizens collectively tried to emerge as a developing south block by involving their perspective in world decision-making. This shift had an adverse impact on European great powers like Great Britain, France, Germany and the optimum benefit went to USA, which established its hegemony. This opened a new era of cold War between the two giants USA and USSR. The conflict between the capitalist and communist philosophy tore the world into a bi-polar one, and each block tried to woo its allies with aim of imperialism. This situation inspired political scientists of America to carve out new theory of development where countries large or small will enjoy sovereignty and will determined their foreign policies without any imposition. The influence of America became more significant after the dismantling of Soviet Union into newly liberated democratic states. Post 1990 period witnessed a new vista of political development theory.

Lucian Pye was among the earlier batch of writers to analyze the concept in depth. He regarded political development in terms of "cultural diffusion, and adapting, fusing and adjusting old patterns of life to new demands."[1]

Samuel P. Huntington and Jorge I. Dominguez define political development as "a pattern of change which occurs in a particular type of society which is produced by a particular cause which is directed towards particular goals or which is fundamentally required by particular social and economic conditions."[2] Huntington and Dominguez have identified four major uses of the term:

1. **Geographical:** This refers, precisely, to any aspect of the politics of what has been called the developing societies. For example, the political role of the military in Pakistan would be considered a subject relating to political development, while the same problematic situation for Germany would not be viewed as such.
2. **Derivative:** Sometimes political development is used to mean 'political aspects and consequences of the broader process of modernization.'
3. **Teleological:** Political development means movement towards certain goals such as democracy, participation, institutionalization, etc.
4. **Functional:** A modern society can function if it has certain political features like, for instance, political party. Party building, therefore, is a move towards political development.

Combining all these different uses they write, 'political development has thus been variously defined as a pattern of change which occurs in a particular type of society, which is produced by a particular cause, which is directed toward particular goals, or which is functionally required by particular social and economic conditions.[3]

The second theoretical influence on political development studies came from positivism. August Comte believed that the principles of natural or positive sciences could be meaningfully applied to the study of society. And it could also facilitate changes toward progress. Also, studies on political development borrowed considerably from Talcott Parson's functionalism. Parsons had identified the basic functions any social system must perform in order to persist. Similarly, early developmentalists like Almond, Coleman, and Powell sought to measure political development by linking specialized functions with differentiated structures. Another major influence came from the writings of the noted German sociologist Max Weber, whose book '*The Protestant Ethic and the Spirit of Capitalism*' sensitized economists as well as political scientists to appreciate the role of cultural factors in development.[4]

Gabriel Almond and G.S. Powell define political development as "the increased differentiation and specialization of political structures and the increased secularization of political culture."[5]

According to Alfred Diamant, political development is not "a process which aims at a particular condition, but is one which creates an institutional framework for solving an ever widening range of social problems."[6]

The concept of political development has provided a new direction to the study of political culture. In the fifties, with the launching of the developmental activities in a large number of underdeveloped Afro-Asian countries, this concept attracted the attention of the western scholars. Scholars like Lucian W. Pye, Joseph La Palombara, Samuel P. Huntington and Leonard Binder have made remarkable contributions to this area of study. But still definition of political development remains puzzling to the researchers.

The concept of political development views the operation of a political system in terms of its increasing democratization, while that of political decay does the same for its regression and disintegration leading to the advent of some form of totalitarianism. Moreover, as the advanced liberal democracies of the West have been able to solve their gigantic problems and face challenges in an effective manner, the idea of political development also involves the capacity of a political system "to control and co-ordinate various processes of change in society generated by the socio-demographic and structural changes."[7]

APPROACHES TO THE STUDY OF POLITICAL DEVELOPMENT

System Approach

Different scholars made vast array of empirical studies in political development. Anthropologists, Political Scientists, Sociologists and Economists provided various approaches to the study of political development. The most significant is system analysis and its offshoot structural functional approach which regarded polity as a system and development as effectiveness of the performance of the system as a whole. They analyze functions at three levels first in relation to environment which is of four types: extractive, regulative, distributive and responsive. Second in relation to the functions of the input process, and third in relation to the functions of output process.

Social Process Approach

This approach tried to relate political behaviour and processes as a dependent variable on social process. Karl Marx can be regarded as its founding father which was further elaborated by Lerner and Deutsch. The four variables of the society, viz. urbanization, industrialization, secularization and politicization are co-related with each other and political development cannot afford to ignore them.

Will and Capacity Approach

Eisenstadt was the protagonist of will and capacity approach which are also known as problem-solving approach, institutionalization approach and ability to sustain new goals approach. He defined political development as an institutional framework capable of continuous absorption of change.[8]

Marxian Approach

According to Marx political development means movement from a discredited bourgeois order to fully socialist system in which the state is required during the transitional phase so as to accomplish the ideal of classless society that would eventually culminate in a stateless condition of life. Thus, it can be safely asserted that the ultimate goal of political development is something pre-determined—the coming of communist system.

Economic Approach

Kenneth Organski suggested the process of political development through four stages, which are as follows:

1. Political unification designed to achieve a centralization of power in the hands of the state
2. Industrialization with a view to bring about economic development
3. National welfare where the result of the political and economic power gained by the state are available to the masses
4. Abundance where people begin to achieve high standards of material affluence.[9]

THEORIES OF POLITICAL DEVELOPMENT

Broadly speaking, three theories are popularly interpreted in political development. The first theory is given by Samuel Huntington. He elaborated the 'componential theory'. There are five components determining the nature and scope of political development. These are as follows:

1. Structure
2. Culture
3. Group
4. Leader
5. Values

His hypothesis is based on the concept of change as inevitable law of nature. He studied political development by observing change in any or all of the components. Nature of change, pacc of change, direction of change and the impact of change in one component on the other are specifically studied. Political development does not merely depict progress towards stability or growth; it also covers chaos and disintegration which he calls as political decay. Politics must look towards war, aggression, inflation as natural phenomena of the political system.

The second theory came to be known as 'Crisis theory'. Protagonists of this theory are Gabriel Almond and W.W. Rustow. They two represented two schools of thought. Former believed that development is the natural outcome of civilization. It essentially emerges from the idea of change. Change or desire for change comes from dissatisfaction. If the nature of change is constitutional and goal justified it definitely leads to political progress, on the contrary if the methodology is not legitimized then political system may decay. Hence, all changes are not political development.

The second school claims that there are certain factors responsible for political development. Political development may be a political change, but the factors contributing to it are mainly non-political. They are called residential or domestic factors, like caste, ethnic, minorities, industrialization, urbanization, political elites and the like. Factors are termed as antecedents and political development is regarded as consequence. The relationship is quite dialectical.

'Complex theory' is given by Ronald D. Brunner and Garry D. Brewer who developed a methodologically ambitious model for relating economic change to popular political support for governments in developing areas subject to discipline of democratic elections.[10] Whole society is divided into two blocks—rural and urban. They deal with 22 variables existing in the society, its nature of change in 20 parameters in 12 equations. It is a quantitative statistical analysis of two mathematicians working in socio-political scenario.

Theories concerning "componential change, crisis change and complex change would liberate political science from the teleological concerns with modernization and development."[11]

Lucian Pye's Concept of Political Development

Lucian Pye should be regarded as the leading light of the earlier batch of writers "to analyze the concept of development in depth, and has kept on evolving his impression on the entire literature of political development." He says that the signs of political development could be traced at three different levels:[12]

1. With respect to the population as a whole;
2. With respect to the level of governmental and general systematic performance;
3. With respect to the organization of the polity.

Pye makes it clear that all three characteristic may or may not fit and balance, hence there can grow tension between the demand for equality, the requirements for capacity and the process of greater differentiation. For example, pressure for greater equality may upset the political system as it did in Soviet Russia in 1990s. Differentiation may reduce equality in order to enhance specialization. He further explains that political development is clearly not unilinear, nor is it governed by sharp and distinct stages but rather buy a range of problems that may arise separately or concurrently. Equality, capacity, political development and differentiation all are interrelated.

Lucian Pye's concept of political development is elaborately presented in his book "Aspects of Political Development." Pye in his book discusses diverse definitions and goes ahead after rejecting many, accepting one and being silent on one definition.

1. **Political development as the prerequisite of economic development:** Economists like Paul A. Baron, Benjamin Higgins have laid stress on the point that political and social conditions can play a quite decisive role in impeding or facilitating the economic growth. Pye discovers four weaknesses in this concept of political development.
   (i) It has a negative character in the sense that it is easier to be precise about the ways in which performance of a political system may impede economic growth/development then about how it can facilitate economic growth.
   (ii) It does not focus on a common set of theoretical considerations.
   (iii) The prospects of rapid economic development have become 'exceedingly dim' in most poor countries.
   (iv) Lastly, in most of the slow paced developing countries people are concerned not only with material development rather political liberation and political development irrespective of economic abundance. Therefore to link political development solely to economic events would be to ignore much that is of dramatic importance in the developing countries.[13]
2. **Political development as the politics typical of industrial societies:** W.W. Rostow tried to identify the process of political development with the pace of industrialization. Pye rejects it on the ground that it ignores the role of several other factors in the process of political development viz. welfare programmes and finally, an acceptance of some form of mass participation.[14]

3. **Political development as political modernization:** According to James S. Coleman, Karl Deutsch and S.M. Lipset, political development means study of political modernization process which characterize western countries, and is emulated by developing countries. Pye rejects it on the ground that it fails to distinguish between 'western' and the 'modern'. Former reflects merely visible traits whereas latter highlights mind set up. Moreover, developing states take pride in their cultural and traditional heritage, and rarely exposes its lifestyle or imposes outer norms.
4. **Political development as the operation of nation-state:** K.H. Silvert, Edward A. Shils and William McCord looked political development as consisting of the organization of political life and the performance of political functions in accordance with the standards expected of a modern nation-state. Pye criticized it on the ground that nationalism is a necessary but not a sufficient condition to ensure political development. Political development is concerned with nation building and not with merely a nation-state. Pye claimed that political development entails translation of diffused and unorganized sentiments of nationalism into a spirit of citizenship.[15]
5. **Political development as administrative and legal development:** According to Max Weber, Talcott Parsons, A.M. Henderson and Joseph la Palombara, political development is linked with legal and administrative order of a community because it depicts rationality in the decision-making process. Pye argues that the process of political development includes not only bureaucracy but the entire gamut of the political activities. If administration is over stressed it can create imbalances in the polity that may impede political development. Pye further claims that this view also entirely overlooks the problem of citizenship, training and popular participation that is one of the essential features of political development.[16]
6. **Political development as mobilization and participation:** Clifford Geertz, Robert Emerson, Bert F. Hoselitz and Eisenstadt and many others have presented the view that politically awakened citizenry, expanded popular participation on a massive scale signifies political development. But Pye retorts that such a view is also fraught with the dangers of either mass-manipulation or "sterile-emotionalism" or corrupting demagoguery, both of which can sap the strength of a society.[17]
7. **Political development as the building of democracy:** Joseph la Palombara and J. Ronald Pennock claims that political development is integrally connected with the building of democracy and inculcating 'values' of a democratic order in the minds of the people. According to Pye, this view mistakenly identified democracy with development,

and thus, ignores political system which are not practising democratic values. Pye says that democracy is 'value-laden', whereas political development is 'value free'. Therefore he condemns the idea as imposing American or Western values.[18]

8. **Political development as stability or orderly change:** Karl Deutsch and F.W. Riggs have laid stress on the point that stability is legitimately linked with the concept of development or orderly change. Lucian Pye rejects the idea because stability and orderly change characterize already developed societies and not developing ones. Moreover he says that protagonists of this theory fail to explain the terms stability or orderly change and further they also did not make clear as to what extent equilibrium should be established and when to bring an orderly change, what will exactly come under the perview of 'change'.
9. **Political development as mobilization and power:** James S. Coleman, G.A. Almond and Talcott Parsons have taken the view that the concept of political development can be evaluated in terms of the level or degree of absolute power which the system is able to mobilize. Pye is critical of this view on the plea that such an explanation is applicable to the case of a democratic political system, and thus, it ignores the case of development in others where the mobilization of power is deliberately kept limited.[19]
10. **Political development as one aspect of a multi-dimensional process of social change:** Socialist theorists like Daniel Lerner, Max F. Millikan, Donald L.M. Blackmer have advanced the view that all forms of development are integrated, and cannot therefore, be understood in isolation. Hence, it is not appropriate to isolate political development from the total process of modernization, polity or society as a whole. According to Pye, this view relates to all the forms of development such as economic, political and social. He appreciates this view and claims that different aspects of society—the economy, the polity and the social order—all impinge on each other.[20]
11. **Political development as a sense of national respect in international affairs:** Pye says nothing about the critical examination of this interpretation, it appears that he either accepts or ignores it altogether, and instead goes ahead to give his own explanation of political development that includes some element of all the diverse definition and interpretations that has discussed before coming to his own interpretation.[21]

Pye, after reviewing these various concepts of political development, seeks to isolate these characteristics of political development which seem to be most widely held and most fundamental in the general thinking about problems of development.[22] He then notes three characteristics—equality, capacity and differentiation.

Equality is implied in mass participation and popular involvement in political activities. Active citizenship calls for equality which also means universalism and achievement. It also means that "laws should be of universalistic nature, applicable to all and more or less impersonal in their operation."[23]

Capacity is related to the outputs of a political system and to the extent to which the political system can affect the rest of the society and economy. It means effectiveness and efficiency in the execution of public policy. Capacity is also closely associated with governmental performance and the conditions that affect such performance that seek to relate ends and means in a systematic manner.[24]

Differentiation and specialization of structures refers to the functional specificity of the various political roles within the system. Pye points out that differentiation is not 'fragmentation and the isolation of the different parts of the political system but specialization based on ultimate sense of integration.'[25]

In recognizing these three dimensions of equality, capacity and differentiation as lying at the heart of the development process we do not mean to suggest that they necessarily fit easily together. On the contrary, historically the tendency has usually been that there are acute tensions between the demands for equality, the requirements for capacity and the processes of great differentiation.[26] A study of political development in the wider perspective of comparative politics also shows that while the characteristic of equality is concerned with political culture, the problems of capacity are related to the performance of the authoritative structures of government, and the questions of differentiation touch mainly the performance of the non-authoritative structures and the general political processes in the society at large.[27]

The concept of political development was popularized by Pye, but was later refined by Leonard Binder. Leonard Binder came forward with his thesis of political development. It was appreciated by the Committee on Comparative Politics (USA) under whose auspices another important work appeared in which he attributed the following implications:[28]

1. Change of identity from religious to ethnic and from parochial to societal
2. Change of legitimacy from transcendental to immanent sources
3. Change in political participation from elite to mass and from family to group
4. Change of distribution from status and privilege to achievement
5. Change in the degree of administrative and legal penetration into social structure and to remote regions of the country

CRISIS IN POLITICAL DEVELOPMENT

According to Lucian Pye, the political development faces the following crises in the course of its progress:[29]

1. **Identity crisis:** The people should identify themselves with their political system. That is, they must recognize their national territory as their homeland and they must feel that their own personal identities are in part defined by their identification with their territorially delimited country. In the absence of such an identity with the political system, the system faces danger to it.
2. **Legitimacy crisis:** It refers to the problem of achieving agreement about the legitimate nature of authority and the proper responsibility of government. Legitimacy crisis leads to change and revolution.
3. **Penetration crisis:** It refers to the problem of the government in reaching down to the society and effecting basic policies.
4. **Participation crisis:** It occurs when there is uncertainty over the appropriate rate of expansion and when the influx of new participants creates serious strains on the existing institutions.
5. **Integration crisis:** Each political system comprises the government and the governed. In the government, there are various levels of bureaucracy, various organs of the government—administrative, legislative and judiciary. Again, among the governed there are so many groups based upon region, language, religion, race, class, sex, etc. In a sound political system all these must be fairly integrated. If this does not happen the political development faces integration crisis.
6. **Distribution crisis:** It refers to the questions about how governmental powers are to be used to influence the distribution of goods, services and values throughout the society. If these means are not available, the political system faces distribution crisis. It is due to this crisis that communist revolutions have been made in so many countries.

CRITICAL ESTIMATE

Political development has been subject to vehement criticisms. Almond and Powell have identified four challenges as follows:

1. Penetration and integration or state building
2. Loyalty and commitment or nation building
3. Pressure from various interest groups in the society for sharing in the decision-making process or participation
4. Pressure from the society to employ coercive power of the state to distribute opportunities, honour, income and wealth or the problem of distribution.[30]

This concept lacks a precise definition. Even after studying the enormous literature on this subject, one wonders as to what it really covers and what it really excludes. It becomes like the very subject of comparative politics, 'either everything or nothing.'[31]

Studies on the subject of political development 'suffer from the absence of any coherent political model of the developmental process, and that the entire analysis is left at the point where extra-political factors have set the stage for political change.'[32]

The greatest drawback of these studies, however, was that they treated political development as a dependent variable generated by something else, a world-wide wave of modernization, nationalism or democracy and not as an independent or intervening variable which, in its own turn, could shape things.[33]

The concept of political development does not offer a model that may be uniformly applicable to all countries of the world and, for this reason, be appreciated by social theorists belonging to any school, whether Liberal or Marxist.

The Marxian approach to political development may be criticized for offering a deterministic course of social evolution. The Marxists look like faced with a traditionalism that confuses them, and they find it very difficult to fit traditional societies into the rather rigid Marxian framework.[34] One may say how dictatorship of the proletariat may be treated as a sign of political development, and not that of a decay or decline in view of the fact that here people have a closed society and a singularity order under the iron hold of an elite of the Communist party. It may be commented that the dictatorship of the proletariat 'would represent the actual interest of a minority which only by some metaphysical sleight of hand could be made out to represent not only the interests of the whole, but of the future also.'[35]

In words of Nettl political development carries a number of definitional problems that include the following:[36]

1. A set of definitional priorities which constitute the meaning of development as a process and the notion of being developed or underdeveloped as a state; it leaves an impression that the concept of political development offers a hesitant and discordant division between normative and empirical categories of political system.
2. A set of values which make development desirable, if not mandatory; at the same time make it perplexing. 'Free' and 'closed', 'tradition' and 'modernity' are such terms which have at times been mismatched with the development models. The immutability of the western world as a value has been challenged in western society. For example, post modernity theory.
3. The inter-connection between the two categories of developed and underdeveloped societies may lead to rewriting of European, American and even Soviet history for developmental process.
4. The recognition of the implicit rank order of development—at least in the mind of analysts, but possibly also in the minds of

participants becomes meaningless if we consider development as a highly differential process. The subject of development originated from economics but later became catalyst for social scientists. Thus it appears wrong to have predominance of any one discipline.

After discussing the shortcomings, Nettl mentioned about four basic requirements in understanding political development theory.

1. In the inter-related world, the emphasis should be on integrating all parameters of development and not blindly follow western model based on abundance which invariably makes the concept dependent and narrow.
2. Political development does not merely mean progress, growth and stability; it also refers to instability or disintegration.
3. The social and political consequences of the demographic explosion need to be addressed in a study of development.
4. The theories of development must also accommodate racial conflicts which were ignored by Social Scientists altogether (Marxist influence).

Nettl, however, recognized the importance of this subject and appreciated the fact that such a study has contributed substantially to the infusion of a dynamic approach to the study of society.[37]

CONCLUSION

Despite these serious drawbacks, this approach has certainly broadened the scope of empirical political investigations by aligning the frontiers of comparative politics with those of other sister sciences and also by engaging the attention of a host of new social theorists towards the study of the political conditions of the new and developing societies of the Third World. As a last word, it may be said that the concept of political development cannot be identified with a rigid or fixed pattern within which the overall development of a country must take place. Just as different soils and climates produce different types of vegetation, similarly different socio-economic factors need different courses for their growth. As a matter of fact, political development 'is dependent on the evolution of society from incoherent homogeneity to coherent heterogeneity.'[38]

Political development goes on as a continuous process in response to the varied internal and external pressures of the day. It may be a shift from stone age to consumerism or tradition to modernity or even from democracy to dynasty rule to fascists' regime. More articulated deliberations in a region specific manner can, to a great extent, contribute in simplifying the process of political development.

Questions for Discussion

1. Critically examine Lucian Pye's concept of political development.
2. Discuss the various theories of political development.
3. Describe the approaches to the study of political development.
4. Write an essay on the concept of political development.
5. Define political development. Describe its difference from political modernization.

References

1. Johari, J.C. (2002), *Comparative Politics*, New Delhi, Sterling Publishers, p. 169.
2. *Ibid.*
3. Huntington, Samuel and Dominguez, J.I. (1975), *Political Development,* in Greenstein, F.I. and Polsby, N.W., (Eds.), *Handbook of Political Science*, Vol. 3, Massachusetts, Addison-Wesley, p. 5.
4. Chakraborty, Satyabrata (Ed.) (2005), *Political Sociology*, Delhi, Macmillan India, p. 306.
5. Almond, G. and Powell, G.B. (1966), *Comparative Politics, A Developmental Approach*, New York, Amerind Publishing, p. 300.
6. Illchman, W. and Uphoof, W. (1969), *The Political Economy of Change*, Berkley, University of California Press, p. 47.
7. Eisenstadt, S.N. (1966), *Modernization: Protest and Change*, Englewood Cliffs N.J. Prentice Hall, pp. 1–19.
8. Eisenstadt, S.N., *Modernization and Conditions of Sustained Growth, World Politics*, Vol. 16, Issue 4, July, 1964, pp. 576–594.
9. Organski, A.F.K. (1965), *The Stages of Political Development*, New York, Alfred Knopf, Johari, *Comparative Politics*, p. 189.
10. Brunner, Ronald and Brewer, Garry (1971), *Organized Complexity: Empirical Theories of Political Development*, New York, The Free Press.
11. Huntington, Samuel, P., *The Change to Change: Modernization, Development and Politics Comparative Politics*, Vol. 3, April, 1971, p. 299.
12. Pye, Lucian W. (1963), *Communications and Political Development*, Princeton, Princeton University press, p. 19.
13. Pye, Lucian W. (1966), *Aspects of Political Development: An Analytic Study Little*, Brown and Company, pp. 33–34.
14. *Ibid.*, pp. 34–35.
15. *Ibid.*, pp. 37–38.
16. *Ibid.*, pp. 38–39.
17. *Ibid.*, pp. 39–40.

18. *Ibid.*, pp. 40–41.
19. *Ibid.*, pp. 42–44.
20. *Ibid.*, pp. 44–45.
21. Johari (2002), *Comparative Politics*, *op. cit.*, p. 173.
22. *Ibid.*, p. 45.
23. *Ibid.*, pp. 45–46.
24. *Ibid.*, p. 46.
25. *Ibid.*, p. 47.
26. *Ibid.*, 47.
27. Johari, J.C. (2002), *Comparative Politics*, *op. cit.*, p. 174.
28. Binder, Leonard (1971), *Crises and Sequences in Political Development (Studies in Political Development)*, Princeton, Princeton University Press, p. 66.
29. *Ibid.*, pp. 62–67.
30. Das, Hari Hara and Choudhury, B.C. (1997), *Introduction to Political Sociology*, New Delhi, Vikas Publishing, p. 118.
31. Verma, S.P. (1975), *Modern Political Theory*, Delhi, Vikas Publishing, p. 274.
32. Wood, David M. and Yesilada, Birol A. (2009), *The Emerging European Union*, 9th ed., Longman p. 506.
33. Varma, *op. cit.*, pp. 279–280.
34. See Thornton, T.P. (Ed.) (1964), *The Third World in Soviet Perspective*, Princeton, Princeton University Press.
35. Krishna, Daya (1979), *Political Development: A Critical Perspective*, New Delhi, Oxford Press, p. 100.
36. Nettl, J.P. (1969), *Strategies in the Study of Political Development*, in Colin Ley's (Ed.), *Politics and Change in Developing Countries*, London, Cambridge University Press, p. 16
37. *Ibid.*, p. 32.
38. Mehta, V.R. (1980), *Political Development* in J.S. Bains and R.B. Jain (Eds.), *Contemporary Political Theory*, New Delhi, Radiant, p. 145.

Suggested Reading

Lucian W. Pye, *Aspects of Political Development*
S.P. Varma, *Modern Political Theory*
J.C. Johari, *Comparative Politics*
Tom Bottomore, *Political Sociology*

Web Link

www.chrisdonasco.blogspot.com/the theory of pol. dev. html.

7
Political Modernization

CRUX

Political Modernization is a process of change in any political system to keep it updated and contemporary. It is a long and arduous process and involves different levels of change as it is also an integrated process. Modernization comprises of elements of industrialization, secularization and urbanization. It can be categorized into three models. Capitalist, socialist and indigenous. It has a comprehensive impact on types of political system. Modern political systems face crises of modernization as human nature resist change. Thus the process of modernization is in continuous strife, conflict and change.

MEANING AND DEFINITION

The word modernization is derived from a Latin term *Mod*, meaning just now. Modernization is a process that started almost three centuries ago, and is still going on. The process was set on motion with the industrial revolution. The term modernization is used to describe the profound differences between traditional and modern societies. It is enormously used interchangeably with industrialization.[1] It essentially stems from the idea of change. Aristotle discusses the dynamics of change from one form of the political system to another; monarchy to aristocracy; aristocracy degenerates to oligarchy; oligarchy into tyranny and tyranny into democracy.[2] Robert Dahl adds 'sub-system autonomy' to Aristotelian classification. He distinguishes traditional political system from modern on grounds of structural differentiated systems in which sub-systems like political parties, pressure groups, courts and the like have autonomy, and those in which the sub-systems are subordinated and controlled.[3] Eisenstadt's classification of political system also reflects the process of change and modernization.[4] 'The ultimate objective must be to construct a scheme that incorporates these factors in a comprehensive analysis of social change.'[5]

Modernization is a complex phenomenon. It is a state of mind. Degree of modernization varies from person to person. What is modern for an individual or group may be a primitive stage for others. Some relates it with economic strata, some with consumerism, and others with social system. The same is the case with the political modernization. Different sociologists and anthropologists have attempted to define it. Like political development, it is also a term, which cannot be precisely defined. Claude E. Welch Jr. defines modernization as "the process based upon the national utilization of resources and aimed at the establishment of a modern society". This term stands for the transformation of the political culture in response to the changes in social and physical environments in view of this essential fact that political change "is intricately related to a wide spectrum of social and economic factors".[6] D.A. Rustow defines modernization as the process of "rapidly widening control over nature through closed cooperation among men." Samuel P. Huntington defines modernization as a multifaceted process involving change in all areas of human thought and activity.[7]

On the basis of these definitions we can say that political modernization refers to the process of transmutation of a pre-modernization of 'traditional' polity into post traditional 'modern polity'. Thus, modernization implies a change in the existing traditional order. It is the effect of the new on the old, not the eradication of the old and its substitution by the new. Analyzing the meaning of modernization, David Apter claims that the work of modernization is the burden of our age.[8]

CHARACTERISTICS

Modernization is a multifaceted process and for this reason political modernization is a concept having several dimensions as:[9]

1. **At the psychological level:** It involves a change in the norms, values, attitudes and orientations of the people;
2. **At the intellectual level:** It involves a tremendous expansion of man's knowledge about his environment and the diffusion of this knowledge throughout society through increased literacy and mass communications;
3. **At the demographic level:** It implies improvements in the standards of living and progress towards the mobility of people and urbanization;
4. **At the social level:** It has a tendency to replace the focus of individual's loyalty to family and other primary groups to voluntarily organized secondary associations; and
5. **At the economic level:** It involves the growth of market agriculture, improvement in commerce of the expense of agriculture, development of industrialization and widening of the economic activity.

Thus, modernization is regarded as a comprehensive phenomenon which brings about radical changes in social, economic and political systems. This is certainly not as complicated as political development.

Lucian Pye claims that as a process of change it includes the following changes:[10]

1. General attitude towards equality that allows equality of opportunity to participate in politics and compete for government office;
2. Capacity of the political system to formulate policies and to have them carried out;
3. Differentiation and specialization of political functions, though not at the expense of their overall integration; and
4. Secularization of the political process—the separation of politics from religious and other influences.

MODELS

Barrington Moore points out three models of modernization: The Capitalist Democratic; The Communist; and The Fascist. In the first situation, landed elite is either promoted to abundance production or is ruined by economic crunch. In the second, landed elite or bourgeoisie have no urge to modernize and thus peasantry takes the initiative and in the third situation, landed elite spurs the change before bourgeoisie seize the power. However, he also refers to the fourth situation, where landed upper class has no incentive to change, bourgeoisie is weak and peasantry lack cohesion for required change. This could be a situation of stagnancy where modernization is hindered and traditional orthodoxies prevail in its self-inflicted rigidity.

However, a still liberal classification can be provided, which is as follows:

1. **Capitalist model of modernization:** It exists when there are abundant resources, affluence and where there is no scarcity and dearth of possibilities and no demographic imbalance.
2. **Socialist model of modernization:** It will take place where there is an equality at primary level and where there is equally distributive wealth, goods and services. Here basic amenities of every person is fulfilled.
3. **Indigenous model of modernization:** It is a regional specific to the type of society where we live. There are some indications and symbols through which we can separate our model with that of other two models (mentioned above).

According to David Apter four stages can be earmarked in the modernization process.[11]

1. **Stage of contact and control:** It began with a few hardy and enterprising individuals with a particular strong sense of mission, or greed, or zeal, or desire for adventure.
2. **Stage of reaction and counter-action:** It was a mixture of local and foreign elements interacting and forming new developed associations.

Innovative foreign elites renovated the old structure and the native persons drew closer to them. At the same time exploitation of the dependent peoples became more severe and heinous. Thus, organized reaction took place despite desirable change.

3. **Stage of contradiction and imagination:** With the growth of new elites, more complex associations in politics arose. The base of National Movement widened. To face the challenge of growing nationalism, the colonial powers carved democratic system, which proved to be a catalyst in fermenting national zeal and organizing independence movement.
4. **Stage of search for a new generative solution:** It occurred after the advent of independence and, as such, it was marked by the inauguration of second revolution in the social, economic and technological spheres. Strikingly leaders lose their charisma with the fulfilment of goal and 'imported democratic system' is replaced by some authoritarian model.

Political modernization is the result of social mobilization and economic development. Eisenstadt discusses certain characteristics of modernization:[12]

1. **Social mobilization:** The indices of social mobilization are following:
   (a) Exposure to aspects of modern life such as machinery and mass media;
   (b) Change of residence, urbanization;
   (c) Change from agricultural occupations; and literacy and the growth of per capita income.
2. **Social differentiation:** It refers to the specialization of institutional structures and recruitment based on universal achievement.
3. **Economic change:** This change refers to technology and development of secondary and tertiary occupations, and mass consumption.
4. **Political change:** It includes
   (a) Concentration of power at centre;
   (b) Spread of potential power to wider groups;
   (c) Populistic and democratic politics and participation;
   (d) Fluidity of political support;
   (e) Interest oriented politics; and
   (f) Political institutions, such as political parties and pressure groups.

C.E. Black in his work "The Dynamics of modernization" identifies four challenges to the modernization process:

(a) A challenge to modernity;
(b) The consolidation of modernizing leadership;
(c) Economic and social transformation; and
(d) Integration of society.

Edward A. Shills has used political modernization as a variable for classifying political system on the ground as to how modernized a society is and divided societies in three broad categories. They are as follows: The impact of modernization is seen both on social and political systems. Karl Deutsch says "a process by which major clusters of old social, economic and psychological commitments are eroded or broken down and the people become available for new patterns of socialization and behaviour".[13]

1. **Primitive and backward societies:** This category includes highly backward social systems of the world where traditional responses, customs and rituals still carry the authority with them. Authority remains where it has been and no serious effort is made in the direction of political mobilization, socialization and recruitment. Nepal, Bhutan, Kenya and Sierra Leone may be put in this category. Here primitive political norms and values are dominant.[14]
2. **Developing social system:** The countries coming in this category show a dichotomy of tradition and modernity that may be visualized most clearly in those parts of the world where people lived under the colonial control. For example, Turkey, India, Sri Lanka, etc.
3. **Western or developed social system:** This category includes those countries where the people are affluent and highly educated, the country is well urbanized and institutional arrangements are such that the decision-makers are either elected by the people at large, or are legally answerable to, and act on behalf of, those who are representatives of the people. For example, Britain, America and France.

Edward A. Shills presents a classification of modern political systems into two varieties—democracy and oligarchy—and their further classification into political and tutelary democracies of the former and modernizing, totalitarian and traditional oligarchies of the latter. Their characteristics are as follows:[15]

1. **Political democracy:** It represents the best form of political system as one obtaining in a country like Britain or the United States of America. Political democracy is known by: the stability, coherence and effectiveness of the ruling elite; the practice and acceptance of opposition; adequate machinery of authority for the protection of the constitutional order; the civil order.

   Its main characteristics are following:

   (a) It has a legislature as a focal point of political system;
   (b) Political Parties constitute an integral part of the political system;
   (c) Power is held for comparatively short and well defined period;
   (d) Freedom of dissent or opposition is fully allowed;
   (e) Independence and impartiality of Judiciary is maintained;

(f) Demagogues exercise self control and discipline;
(g) There is a trained civil service;
(h) Adequate police and armed forces are maintained;
(i) People are expected to repose their trust on government;
(j) People are committed to the norms of democratic order.

2. **Tutelary democracy:** It constitutes the second best form of a political system as described by Shils. It refers to a political system that is committed to observe the norms and values of democracy and thus it tries to emulate the ways of countries known for having political democracy. It has certain distinguished features:
   (a) Executive is real centre of power;
   (b) Legislature operates under the strict control of the executive;
   (c) Channels of opposition are allowed, but within the executive control;
   (d) There is a competent and loyal democracy; and
   (e) Safeguards of rule of law and public liberties are maintained. India is the glaring example.
3. **Modernizing oligarchy:** In such a system, minority ruling group takes upon itself the task of purifying political life and establishing peace and order in the country. The ruling group is motivated by modernized ideology and process to lead the country towards modernization. For example, Sudan, Pakistan, UAR and Iraq. Its main characteristics' are:
   (a) Parliament is merely an acclamatory body;
   (b) Opposition is outlawed, free fair elections are not held and communication is censured;
   (c) Position of bureaucracy is highly strengthened; and
   (d) Rule of law is not enforced.
4. **Totalitarian oligarchy:** Like Nazi in Germany and Fascist in Italy, totalitarian oligarchy is based on a particular ideology. There is full concentration of authority in the hands of the ruling party. It has a well-knit, well-organized ruling elite bound by ideology. Rule of law and independence of the judiciary do not exist. It exhibits certain features:
   (a) Full concentration of authority in the hands of ruling class;
   (b) Highly disciplined and organized elite;
   (c) No place for rule of law;
   (d) All credentials of democracy is used for propaganda purpose; and
   (e) Attempt is made to create intelligentsia support.
5. **Traditional oligarchy:** It is based on strong dynastic constitution associated with traditional religious belief. Rulers emerge on the

basis of kinship. The state play a limited role, hence, there exist no need for a strong bureaucracy. Examples—Saudi Arabia and Nepal. It has these main characteristics:

(a) Political authority is exercised by the ruler;
(b) Efficient bureaucracy is not required;
(c) The ruler keeps a small armed force and police for his own interest;
(d) Feudalism prevails on the basis of kinship; and
(e) Public opinion is not created and legitimacy of the rule depends mainly on tradition.

CRITICAL ESTIMATE

Lucian Pye gives detailed information of the challenges of modernization, which include:[16]

1. General attitude towards equality that allows equality of opportunity to participate in politics and compete for government office;
2. Capacity of the political system to formulate policies and to have them carried out;
3. Differentiation and specialization of political functions, though not at the expense of their overall integration; and
4. Secularization of the political process—the separation of politics from religious and other influences. If these challenges are not addressed immediately, then the political system may decay, disintegrate and decline ultimately leading to the demise of the political system.

According to J.C. Johari, Edward Shils has failed to produce a 'plausible picture of modern political systems.' The five categories suggested by Shils fail to include all the existing political systems of the world. Thus, we cannot place all prevailing political systems of the world in a neat and water-tight manner in these five categories as suggested by him.

The typology of Shils has been modified in various ways by other writers who have adopted the scheme of classification of political systems on the basis of political modernization. The names of Kautsky and Apter need special mention in this connection. Kautsky suggested that we might analyze political modernization in terms of four categories:[17]

(i) Traditional aristocratic totalitarianism
(ii) Aristocratic totalitarianism
(iii) Totalitarianism of the intellectuals
(iv) Democracy

He also makes it clear about this scheme that it "should not be mistaken for an adequate description of any or all existing political systems." And he adds "There are an infinite number of variations, sub-types, and mixed and transitional forms that make it impossible to find any of the four types in pure form."

David Apter offers a complex, but intriguing theory of stages and alternate paths of political development in the larger framework of political modernization. He pays particular attention to the characteristics of traditional societies as the starting point of change, using a two-dimensional classification based on three authority types hierarchical, pyramidal and segmental and the value types were categorized as instrumental or consummatory. Depending on the character of the traditional base, and subject to the contradictory and varied influences of the western social and political systems, Apter discerns two main development consequences: a secular—libertarian model approaching democracy through mobilization systems, and a sacred collectivity model approaching totalitarianism through mobilization system.

CRISES IN POLITICAL MODERNIZATION

There are many crises that every modernizing polity encounters. These are as follows:

- Firstly, there is the problem of national identity, i.e., the transfer of ultimate loyalty and commitment from primordial groups to the large national political system.
- Secondly, there is political legitimacy, which implies legitimization of modernizing elites and the new authority structure.
- Thirdly, there is problem of penetration, which means centralization of power, bridging communication gap and effective implementation of policies throughout the society by the central institutions of the government.
- Fourthly, there is participation which refers to the development of symbolic or participatory institutions and a political infrastructure to organize and channelize the characteristically modern mass demand for a share in the process of decision-making.
- Fifthly, there is integration, which implies the organization of a coherent political process and pattern of interacting relationship for the making of public policy, and the pursuit and achievement of societal goals.
- Sixthly, the problems of distribution, refers to the effective use of governmental power to bring about economic growth, mobilize resources, and distribute goods and response in response to the mass demands and expectations.

POLITICAL MODERNIZATION AND POLITICAL DEVELOPMENT

There is a lot of confusion regarding modernization and development. Both the notions emerge from the idea of change. Both promote social change in the form of either mobilization or disintegration. They appear as interchangeable and at times synonymous. Some of the political scientists fail to differentiate the two concepts, but some others regard the two as two different world. Samuel Huntington made a sharp divide between the two. According to him, political development is mainly concerned with Institution, whereas modernization is functional part of it. The crux of political development lies in the process of 'institutionalization' that must be developed to match the increasing demand of political participation. A state may be modern and yet not politically developed. Huntington cites the reverse example of India as politically developed with modern political institutions while still backward in terms of modernization. When political institution is deficient, then political modernization process produce political decay. The outcome of modernization, is therefore, dependent on the nature of political development.

Huntington's distinction between modernization and political development helps to clarify the implications of the two processes. He regards development as an autonomous feature and determinant variable. This view is supported by Indian psephologist Rajani Kothari who believes that for a realistic theory of state building it is necessary to divorce it from modernization, as conceived so far, and to admit in its framework the primacy of politics in social development.[18]

CONCLUSION

Modernization, is thus, a process which helps a rapid change from traditional to modern concepts. It also helps the society to utilize all its resources for the development purpose and thus a society become modern from all points of view—social, economic, cultural, political, intellectual, religious, psychological and so on. Whether modernization and development are same or different, but this is quite certain that they study the performance or capabilities of political systems and also present the strategy to address the issue of political change. The changing needs and demands of the new environment should be accommodated, then only state can cope with new ideas and functions. It can be therefore not an exaggeration to say that rigidity of the political system would make it anachronistic and such system faces stagnancy and decay.

Questions for Discussion

1. Discuss the process of modernization and its crises.
2. Define modernization and distinguish it from political development.

3. Analyze political systems on the basis of political modernization.
4. What is political modernization? Discuss its salient features.

References

1. Das, Hari Hara and Choudhury, B.C. (1997), *Introduction to Political Sociology*, New Delhi, Vikas Publishing, p. 76.
2. Almond, G.A. (1965), *The Appeals of Communism.* Princeton University Press, New Jersey, p. 214.
3. Dahl, A. Robert (1963), *Modern Political Analysis,* Prentice Hall, Englewood Cliffs, New Jersey, p. 25.
4. Eisensdat, S.N. (1962), *The Political Systems of Empire*, New York, The Free Press of Glencoe, p. 18.
5. Davies, Mortan R. and Lewis, Vaughan A. (1971), *Models of Political Systems*, Delhi, Vikas Publishing, p. 194.
6. *Ibid.*, p. 98.
7. Huntington, Samuel and Dominguez, J.I. (1975), *Political Development*, in Greenstein, F.I. and Polsby, N.W. (Eds.), *Handbook of Political Science*, Vol. 3, Massachusetts: Addison-Wesley, cited in S.P. Verma's *Modern Political Theory*, pp. 302–303.
8. Apter, David . E. (1978), *Introduction to Political Analysis*, New Delhi, Prentice-Hall of India, p. 1.
9. Varma, S.P. (1975), *Modern Political Theory*, New Delhi, Vikas Publishing, pp. 302–303.
10. Pye, Lucian W. (1966), *Aspects of Political Development*, Boston, Little Brown, pp. 45–48.
11. Apter (1978), *op. cit.*, p. 461.
12. Eisenstadt, S.N. (1969), *Modernization Protest and Change*, Delhi, Prentice-Hall, p. 11.
13. Deutsch, Karl W. (1961), *Social Mobilization and Political Development*, in *American Political Science Review*, Vol. LV, September, p. 496.
14. Johari, J.C. (1982), *Comparative Politics*, New Delhi, Sterling Publishers, pp. 200–201.
15. *Ibid.*, pp. 202–203.
16. Pye, Lucian W. (1966), *Aspects of Political Development*, Boston, Little Brown, pp. 45–48.
17. Riggs, F.W. (1967), *The Theory of Political Development*, New York, Free Press, p. 333.
18. Kothari, Rajani (Ed.), (1976), *State and Nation Building: A Third World Perspective*, Delhi, Allied Publishers, p. 6.

Suggested Reading

Gabriel Almond, *Comparative Politics*

J.C. Johari, *Comparative Politics*

L.N. Sharma and Ali Ashraf, *Political Sociology: A New Grammar of Politics*

Web Links

www.sociologyguide.com, Political Modernization

cps.sagepub.com/content/3/3/297.full.pdf

8

Political Recruitment

CRUX

Placing the right person for the right post at the right time through a proper process is known as recruitment. Administrative and Political recruitment are quite different from each other. Former is based on principles of anonymity and neutrality whereas latter regards them as disqualifications. There are various methods of recruitment. Election however is regarded as the most beneficial method of recruitment. Political parties play a vital role in the recruitment process, as they educate the electorate but at times, they also cheat the masses. The success or failure of government to a great extent depends on the validity of recruitment process. Thus, it is an issue of great importance for any society.

MEANING

Recruitment is one of the major concerns of political sociology so as to examine and account for the recruitment of those who exercise political power such as Prime Minister, President, Governor and Local Counsellors, etc.[1] Political recruitment is a function performed within every political system. Just as the general body of citizens (or citizenry) must be socialized or inducted into the broader political culture, some persons must be additionally recruited and socialized to play the roles of activists and leaders. The study of political recruitment has moved some distance from the older philosophical question of "who should rule?" The focus has shifted from normative to empirical questions. Political scientists now ask who are the elites and activists, what is their personal and social background, what is the nature of their roles, and how are they recruited? Answers to these and similar questions are being sought through comparative research in a variety of political culture.[2]

In a totalitarian State, this may be extended to the personnel of the ruling party and the governmental hierarchy.[3] The distinction between the politician and the administrator is not very clear in a totalitarian state, because the decision makers are mostly the policy makers. Therefore, it becomes very difficult to draw generalization regarding the relationship between the two.

Recruitment in general context means induction of the right person to the right post at the right time. It is generally of two types:

1. **Administrative recruitment:** Induction into administrative post is 'administrative recruitment' by the standard method of selection. There are two basic features of administrative recruitment, namely:
   (a) Neutrality—To have no ideological orientation
   (b) Anonymity—Not a known figure (one's identity should not be revealed for personal benefit and self-aggrandizement)

The doctrine of political neutrality of the civil servants is completely rejected in the totalitarian political system where a 'politically neutral bureaucracy is not only an anathema, but a contradiction in terms'.[4] Anonymity and neutrality is an essential condition in democratic set-up because here Government and Political parties are expected to change after every five years or even earlier with the no confidence motion or mandate of the people. If the bureaucrats become politically committed to any one party then they will promote spoils system which was once prevalent in USA. In other words, they will continue in office till the Party is in power. Therefore, the stability of the political system will be lost. Hence, it is desired to have political neutrality of bureaucrats for the common interest of political system and citizens.

2. **Political recruitment:** Political recruitment is induction into political post. There are two styles of political recruitment:
   (a) Informal—When persons are inducted into political posts through nominations, for example, members nominated by the President
   (b) Formal—Through elections, which is a universal phenomenon

The two basic features of administrative recruitment become negative features for political recruitment. Even if one is an independent candidate he has to have an inclination towards a particular ideology. Apart from this, he has to be a known figure. There is a process of election for political recruitment which is conducted by an autonomous body, i.e. Election Commission, which performs following major functions:

(i) Demarcation of constituencies
(ii) Preparation of electoral rolls
(iii) Recognition of political parties, i.e. of symbols
(iv) Scrutiny of the nomination papers
(v) The conduct of the fair and free poll
(vi) Election expenses (The election commission has to prepare the report after scrutinizing the account of election expenses)
(vii) Besides the above functions, the election commission is there to supervise the machinery of elections throughout the country so that elections are held in a free and fair manner

Political recruitment is affected both by ascriptive and particularistic criteria, combined with performance and universalistic criteria. In western political societies/system, recruitment is guided by ascriptive and performance criteria, but with the growing pace of modernization, performance dominates ascriptive features. Similarly, particularistic and universalistic criteria is combined differently in the performance of the recruitment functions in modern and traditional systems. In liberal system, recruitment is open to all members of the society who fulfill certain requirements and in conservative it is mainly confined to community, religion, families or and friends.[5]

METHODS OF POLITICAL RECRUITMENT

1. **Lottery/Sortition/Grid:** This is the oldest method of political recruitment, which was followed, in ancient Greece. In this method of recruitment, political leaders were selected by drawing of lots—probably it was regarded as the worst method of recruitment as it was based on an element of chance rather than merit. Plato was the greatest critic of this method, and he said that all the Donkeys will get a chance to become rulers. In present times, this method is quite obsolete and redundant.
2. **Force:** In most of the political systems, political office may be seized either by the use of force or by the threat of use of force.[6] It is a non-democratic method of selection, where virtually there is no choice. The political leaders are imposed upon the people, as in case of 'Totalitarian societies.' This is considered to be antithetical to the norms of democratic principles, so this is not accepted. But even 20th and 21st century have seen few cases of political recruitment through force, like military coup in Pakistan, Taliban in Afghanistan, Maoist attack in Nepal, etc. Hence, force theory cannot be totally eliminated or denied.
3. **Patronage:** As a contrast to the system of political recruitment, which essentially is based on electoral method. Patronage offers an example of a system in which there is continued recruitment of same type of personnel.[7] In earlier times this system was very common in the United States and in Great Britain. Today, it is followed by many developing countries. Patronage thus implies that with the help of money, name and fame and also by being God Father and God Mother one may get through political recruitment process. In USA, it is also known as loot system. In other words, seeking favour against any help or loyalty forwarded. Late Pramod Mahajan, Ms. Jayalalitha, Ms. Mayawati and others are such examples whose political incumbency resulted from favour.
4. **Growth/emergence of natural leaders:** Some persons are born to be the leaders. They exhibit leadership qualities. They have coherent

integrity of thought, words and action. They are the front benchers and take initiative for the betterment of the society. But such leaders are not always reliable, and at times, may become self-centered. They have an art of opposing things and standing alone as a winner. In times of crisis, charismatic personalities emerge to handle critical situation as Otto Von Bismarck in Germany for the unification of Germany, Pervez Musharraf in Pakistan, Benito Mussolini in Italy, Napoleon Bonaparte in France and Adolf Hitler in Germany in 20th century, and Anna Hazare and Arvind Kejriwal in Indian political system in 21st century. So, the theory of emergence of natural leaders is not very reliable and is not universally accepted.

5. **Co-option:** Recruitment of particular types of leaders is made by means of co-option. Co-option stands for the election of an individual to a body of its existing members. This practice is fairly common in political institutions like the local councils in England and Wales and in the Municipality and the Panchayat bodies in some of the Indian states.[8] In India it was initiated by Rajasthan Political System at the grass roots level. However, this method is not popularly accepted.
6. **Elections:** Last but not the least, elections are one the best method of political recruitment. Through the method of elections, people get the opportunity of choosing between two or more alternatives by casting of votes. But in practice, this is not as simple as there is an infinite variety of electorate and voting behaviour. The recruitment of political candidates is a basic function of political parties: a party that cannot attract and then nominate candidates surrenders its elementary opportunity for power.[9] This process includes two stages: certification and eligibility. In most democratic countries, there is universal adult suffrage, but it is usually restricted by age, status, literacy, gender and region.

ROLE OF POLITICAL PARTIES IN POLITICAL RECRUITMENT

Induction of the right person to the right post at the right time is possible only through electoral process. It is the most accepted and most commonly used method of political recruitment. No democracy can survive without election and party is a pre-condition for election. A party is a permanent organization consisting of people who consciously aim at capturing political power through the elections. Today, party politics has become a universal phenomenon leaving aside the case of some. Every state of the world has a party system of its own whether it pertains to a single-party model, or to a bi-party model, or to a multi-party model, or to a peculiar admixture of them. A party, which claims to serve the interest of the entire country, is a pseudo party, and a nation that claims to serve the interest of the entire population with one party is a pseudo nation. Therefore, Giovanni Sartori, a political sociologist says that there should be many parties, as party is a part of the whole.

Direct democracy is difficult in modern states, and some form of representative system is found in all states with the exception of some conservative autocratic systems.[10]

Liberal democracy implies not only an extension of the franchise, but an equality of voting rights.[11] Robert Dahl rightly affirms that "Populist Democracy" is that which postulates only two goals to be maximized-political equality and popular sovereignty.[12] The complex role of elections in the political system is underlined by an examination of the voting behaviour of electorates.

In India, from 1950–1967 there was one party dominance model as prescribed by Maurice Duverger. During this period congress party was the one and the only party in power. However, things changed, and there was a mushroom growth of pressure groups and gradually most of them were transformed into political parties for the lust for power, for example, Jharkhand Mukti Morcha, Assam Gan Sangram Parishad, etc. Due to growth of regionalism, many regional party also came into existence like AIDMK, DMK, TDP, JDU, JDU (Devgoda), TMC, etc. However, multi-party system has its own merits as one has a wider choice, people can use various political parties as medium of expressing their opinions. In spite of all these, this system is not devoid of demerits as it invites political chaos in the state, multi-party state hardly gets any opportunity to have a stable government and shows all it leads to complete and utter confusion among the voters and the net result is a coalition government. At the national level, the first ever coalition government was formed under the Prime Ministership of Late Shri Morarji Desai, which existed from 24 March 1977 to 15 July 1979 heading the Janata Party. Since 1996, Indian politics has been dominated with coalition government, which is continuing till date. Though there is a prediction that there will be once again dominance of the congress party in near future, but the possibilities are quite remote.

Political recruitment in coalition party system is highly inefficient and corrupt. Even Prime Minister becomes a puppet in the hands of a coalition government, the present UPA Government is a testimony to the fact. Thus, a bi-party is the best system of political recruitment which successfully operates as in the case of Britain and United States. In a multi-party system, there are a lot of lacunae, therefore, the entire purpose of choosing the right person is defeated.

So, what political party actually should do are as follows:

1. They should be ideologically clear so that one party could be distinguished from the other. This will enable the electorate to make his/her choice easily.

2. The role of political parties should be matured enough and they should educate the masses by giving them the facts.
3. They should serve as the broker of ideas by selecting a number of issues and focusing attention on them.
4. Above all, in the newly liberated and developing nations of the world, political parties should do the job of political modernization. That is how they strive to give a particular shape to the government.
5. Decentralization and democracy within the party will surely give an opportunity to select the people who have the potential and leadership quality.

Thus, if all the above said functions are properly performed by the political parties, then only there will be proper political recruitment.

CRITICAL ESTIMATE

The effective performance of the recruitment functions by an electorate is dependent on an open and multi-directional flow of communications reporting on the performance of other functions by the incumbents of the authoritative offices to the mass of citizens.[13] Any form of hindrance may create flaw in political induction and the adverse impact is the rule of corrupt bureaucrat and ministers ultimately leading to the decay of political system. Even in largest democracy, critics retort there is an every possibility of error in selection process. Public are usually not reasonable rather they are swayed by emotions and their casting vote are mainly guided by the non-political factors like, caste, religion, region, personality and the like. The required condition of efficacy of performance, political issues, political ideology and political orientation play a secondary role. Even in democracy, elites have an edge in getting tickets and winning elections, as compared to common people. Status, popularity, Personality, fear, bullet plays vital role in determining voting behaviour. Thus the seriousness of the issue is lost.

Success in politics, both as a career and a service, very much depends upon the combination of merit, luck and tactics. Public purpose becomes handmaid in the orbit of power politics. Masses are duped and leaders continue with their seat with flattery and mesmerizing talks.

Political parties instead of educating electorate confuses them and with their false promises and manifestoes. They woo electorate through political gimmick and fabricated agendas like Women Reservation Bill which is hanging since 1996, when it was first tabled by the then Prime Minister Mr. Devegoda After winning elections, all political parties forget about their voters and tolerant voters every time forgive their leaders as they have no better choice. It is rightly said that democracy is a choice between lesser evils.

CONCLUSION

Despite the criticisms levelled against recruitment process, we can safely assert that there can be no better style of political recruitment than elections in a democratic set up. What is required is the maturity of electorate in casting vote. Much depends on the demagogue. We can never escape criticisms by just drawing attention towards systemic impediments; we have to bear the responsibility of an active citizen. Thus, we may conclude by saying that political recruitment is an important aspect of any political system. If certain norms and conditions are properly followed then that will lead to proper political recruitment, which ultimately will be conducive to political development.

Questions for Discussion

1. Define political recruitment. Discuss its various forms.
2. What is the meaning of recruitment? Examine administrative and political recruitment.
3. Discuss the role of Political party in making political recruitment.

References

1. Das, Hari Hara and Choudhury, B.C. (1997), *Introduction to Political Sociology*, New Delhi, Vikas Publishing, p. 120.
2. Jayapalan, N. (2000), *Political Sociology*, New Delhi, Atlantic Publishers, p. 100.
3. Das, Hari Hara and Choudhury, B.C. (1997), *op. cit.*, p. 120.
4. *Ibid.*, p. 121.
5. Jayapalan, N. (2000), *op. cit.*, p. 110.
6. *Ibid.*, p. 122.
7. *Ibid.*, p. 123.
8. *Ibid.*, p. 124.
9. Schattschneider, E.E. (1940), *Party Government: American Government in Action*, New Brunswick (USA) and London (UK), Transaction Publishers, First Publication by Rhinehart and Company, 1942, p. 64.
10. Ball, Allan (1983), *Modern Politics and Government*, 3rd ed., London, Macmillan Press, p. 118.
11. *Ibid.*, p. 121.
12. Dahl, Robert, (1956), *A Preface to Democratic Theory*, Chicago, Chicago Press, p. 4.
13. Jayapalan, *op. cit.*, p. 111.

Suggested Reading

N. Jayapalan, *Political Sociology*

Harihar Das and B.C. Choudhury, *Introduction to Political Sociology*

Satyabrata Chakraborty (Ed.), *Political Sociology*

Web Links

www.olemiss.edu/courses/pol/324/politrec.ppt.

www.jstor.org/stable/1976051.html

9
Elites and Society

CRUX

Democracy is a government by popular choice. It gives ample opportunity to masses to select their representatives to run the political system. This is however not to suggest that people are the makers and breakers of government. Indian polity is virtually operating in the commands of chosen privileged few. Despite acclaimed policy of popular mandate, elites rule over the people and at times become dictatorial. The making of elites in its various forms has been the political history of India. Though being one of the oldest and largest democracies of the world, it still promotes dynasty rule. Hence elitism is a guaranteed age-old practice of decision-making and will continue to do so in coming years. Democracy and elitism therefore appears compatible to each other as opposed to the conventional notion.

MEANING AND DEFINITION

In every society there exists a selected group of people who belong to the highest echelon of the social hierarchy and enjoy power, position, wealth and a superior status, which distinguishes them from the mass. Such a group is called elite. Whatever is the form of government, whether democracy or totalitarian dictatorship elite will be there at the top to control and balance power. Elite is always in minority yet it rules over majority. This is possible because the elite have the distinction of superior knowledge, intelligence and skills and by their management capacity they easily reach to the top and control the mass which is inert, apolitical and willing to submit to the decisions of the elite.

Today elite theory has become very popular in order to explain the political processes of the state. The term 'elite' has been explained by different writers in different ways. According to some thinkers, elites are the decision-makers of the society; for some, elites are the sole source of values in the society; some regard elites as a threat to the survival of democracy, while others see elite as the bulwarks of democracy. Some thinkers attempted to reconcile the value of democracy with the fact of power. Schumpeter stands out as a prominent thinker. According to him, it is not the people but the few who rule with the consent of the majority.[1] Pareto uses the word elite in its etymological sense, referring to the strongest, the most energetic and the most capable for good as well as for evils.[2]

The study of elite started in the late nineteenth century. It was initially used to denote a superior commodity, but with the passage of time, it talked about superior social groups possessing triple C's viz. Consciousness, Cohesiveness and Conspiracy. A leader or elite must essentially be aware of the fact that he or she is made to rule over the people. They must make constant effort to create a halo around them. At the same time, elite is required to be coherent in behaviour, in other words, elite must think, speak and act in one direction. Above all, elite however strong, cannot make everyone happy, so he must cleverly use his skills in appeasing all either through flattery or mesmerizing talks. A person can become elite either by birth or by possession of wealth or intellectual pursuits. Elite is an expertise in his field, utilizing the capacity to the fullest for optimum result. The term did not become widely used in social and political writings until late in the nineteenth century in Europe.[3] The political sociologist Pareto seems to be the first man who used the term 'elite.'

The concept of political elite was presented by Mosca and Pareto as a key term in a new social science. Oxford English Dictionary in 1823 applied the term to social groups.[4] Vilfredo Pareto defines elite as "people in a society who possess in a marked degree, qualities of intelligence, character, skill and capacity of whatever kind."[5] According to Gaetano Mosca "The management of public affairs is in the hands of a minority of influential persons, to whom willingly or unwillingly the majority differs.[6] Harold Laswell writes "The political elite comprise the power holders of body politics."[7] James Miesel has pointed out that "elitism thrives because of its three characteristics: group cohesion, consciousness and conspiracy."[8] The above definitions made it clear that in the conventional mode it is the aristocratic class and in contemporary world, it is the policy making class. They take all major decisions, which affect the society. They control the whole society by using power not only to fulfill the aspirations of masses but also to promote their vested interests.

THE ELITE THEORY OF VILFREDO PARETO (1848–1923)

Elite is seen by Pareto not as the product of economic forces nor as building their dominance on their organizational ability but as the outcome of human attributes. He provides psychological orientation to the understanding of elitist theory. Individuals are 'physically, morally and intellectually different. Pareto uses the term elite to refer to superiority in intelligence, character, skill, capacity, power, etc., and those who possess these qualities become elites. Pareto divides human thinking into two blocks—rational and irrational. He begins with making a distinction between the logical and non-logical actions of individuals in social life: logical actions are those directed to attainable ends and employing means which are appropriate to the attainment of the end; non-logical actions are those not directed by any end, or directed to unattainable ends, or using means which cannot attain the end. Pareto takes the view that most human actions are non-logical, and he goes on to enquire what are the forces behind non-logical action and how it comes to be represented, as frequently happens, as logical action. These forces he discovers in six 'residues' which he calls residues of combination (1) of persistence of aggregates (2) of sociability (3) of expressiveness (4) of the integrity of the individual (5) and of sex (6).[9] The ways in which the action determined by these residues assume the appearance of logical actions are discussed by Pareto under the heading of 'Derivation', which bear some resemblance ideology in Marx's sense. The rule of governing elite he argues may be of two kinds; it may be maintained either by cunningness (predominance of residues of combination) or by force (predominance of residues of the persistence of aggregates). Residues 1 and 2 are thus treated as categories within which all political attitudes can be classified. Pareto's two types of elite, animated by residues 1 and 2 respectively, types which he also refers to as the within 'speculators' and the 'rentiers': bear a close resemblance to Machiavelli's 'Foxes' and 'Lions' but they are dressed up in a most scientific garb.[10]

On the basis of above-mentioned residues he classifies society into two parts—mass, common people, ruled and majority, and elite, representatives, ruler and minority.

Former exhibits non-logical action swayed by emotions and impulse. They do not have critical thinking and cannot decide any crucial issue based on justified reasoning and understanding. Latter represents the class, which behaves in a rational manner. This class possesses highest indices in their branch of activity.[11] This class is further divided into two categories, i.e. a governing elite and a non-governing elite.[12]

1. **Governing elites:** In this class he included persons who are directly or indirectly concerned with administration, governance, decision-making and policy-making. They play pivotal role in public affairs and enjoys prestigious place in the society.
2. **Non-governing elites:** Non-governing elites are all those persons who are not directly associated with administration, but occupy a very influential position in society because of their expertise and excellence in their professional field. They influence the administration and government decisions and constantly work as a pressure group. Pareto writes about six residues which are determining factor for the rise and maintenance of the elite to power. They are the following:
    (a) *Combination:* A tendency to invent and embark on new venture
    (b) *Persistence of preservation:* A tendency to consolidate on the present move and make sure to accrue gains and move ahead with the new ideas

(c) *Expressiveness:* A tendency to make inner feeling manifest through words and actions in a convincing manner

(d) *Sociability:* A tendency to shun isolation and affiliate with others for human good

(e) *Integrity:* A tendency to maintain a good self-image by coherence of thinking words and deeds

(f) *Sex:* Tendency to see social events in erotic terms and not as an aberration and to have control over pleasure

As a matter of fact, Pareto makes use of the first two residues and on that basis lays down his doctrine of 'innovation' and 'consolidation.' An imbalance between the elements of 'innovation' and 'consolidation' causes replacement of one elite by another. Pareto writes of fox and lion like qualities necessary to maintain the elite power. The ways by which actions were determined by these residues assume the appearance of logical actions is discussed by Pareto under the heading of "derivations." Derivation gives a show of rationality to the actions of the elite.

Apart from this, he refers to certain 'derivatives' (like assertion, appeals to authority, appeals to sentiments or principles, and verbal proofs) or the ways by which actions are made to assume the logical base.[13]

In his classical work 'The Mind and Society' he discusses the rise and fall of elites, which he terms as 'circulation of elites' and claims that history is a graveyard of aristocracies. He further says "A history of man is the history of the continuous replacement of elites; as one ascends, another declines."[14] This theory has been precisely dealt by one of Pareto's pupils Marie Kolabinska in a work entitled 'La Circulation des elites en France'. Kolabinska distinguishes three types of circulations, first the circulation, which takes place between different categories of governing elite itself. Secondly, there is the circulation between the elite and the rest of the population which may take either of two forms: individuals from the lower strata may succeed in entering the existing elite; or individuals in the lower strata may form new elite groups which then engage in a struggle for power with the existing elite.[15]

There is up and down movement of members of elite and non-elite class. Elite may degenerate into non-elite and non-elite may rise to become elite, technically this process is known as "Circulation of Elites". It is in this explanation that Pareto develops his concept of 'Residues'. By 'Residues', Pareto actually means the qualities through which a person can rise up and maintain him or herself in power. He attaches the primary importance to the residues of 'combination' and the 'persistence of aggregates', with the help of which the governing elites tries to maintain itself in power.

The 'residues' of 'combination means cunningness, and the residues of 'the persistent aggregates' means force, capacity and strength. Pareto has called these two types of elites as 'speculators' and 'rentiers.'

Pareto's study of the rise and decline of elites as such is equally unsatisfactory. He does not attempt to assemble all the available instances (even for limited period) and to show that there are regularities in elite circulation, which might be connected with changes in sentiments, supposing that the leader could be independently established. He produces only historical illustrations of contemporary Italian politics to support his general articles.[16]

Pareto however fails to provide a link between the rise and fall of elites in the society. There is no substantial evidence in support of his proposition that there are marked differences between elite and non-elite. Pareto fails to investigate upon this idea, and therefore, his claim to be a democratic elitist thinker finds no support.

THE ELITE THEORY OF GAETANO MOSCA (1858–1941)

Another leading exponent of the elite theory is G. Mosca whose work 'The Ruling Class' is considered as an independent contribution less on sociology but more on politics. Mosca uses the term elite in a restricted sense. By elite he means the ruling class. He provides political orientation to the study of elite. He repudiated Aristotle's classification of states and accepted that there was only one kind of government, namely oligarchy. He writes, 'in all societies—two classes of people appear—a class that rules and a class that is ruled. The first class, always the less numerous, performs all political functions, monopolizes power and enjoys the advantages that power brings, whereas the second, the more numerous class, is directed and controlled by the first, in a manner that is now more or less legal, now more or less arbitrary and violent, and supplies the first, in appearance at least, with material means of subsistence and with the instrumentalities that are essential to the vitality of the political organism.'[17] Mosca says that in reality minorities rule majorities, rather than majorities rule minorities. Mosca is much more aware of the heterogeneity of the elite, the higher stratum of the political class, itself; of the interests or social forces which are represented in it; and, in the case of modern societies, of its intimate bonds with the rest of society, principally through the lower stratum of the political class, the 'new middle class.'[18] Thus, Mosca allows difference between modern democracies and other types of polity, and to some extent he recognizes that there is interaction between the ruling minority and the majority, instead of a simple dominance by the former over the latter.[19] The more disorganized is the majority, the more easy for minority to govern. So it is the deliberate attempt of elite to create conflict, resolve and evolve a new one for their survival. Mosca believes that the governing elites within certain time are not able to fulfill its duties, and in such a case change becomes inevitable. The ruling class has a tendency to stabilize themselves. Even in democratic elections; successful candidates show certain heredity characteristics. This interesting observation was made by Mosca when he says 'all political classes tend to become hereditary in fact if not in law.'[20] This is why, says Mosca, we frequently see in English, French and Italian parliament the sons, grandsons, brothers, nephews and son-in-laws of members and deputies, ex-members and ex-deputies. India is a glaring example of dynasty rule despite being one of the largest and oldest democracies. Congress as a party is held synonym with the yesteryears J.L. Nehru and presently the Gandhi family. This legacy is carried within the garb of democracy. Mosca has pointed out that other social forces influence the political elite itself. Elite do not rule only by force, the influential groups of the society also play a very important role in determining the decisions of elite. Mosca also introduces a concept of sub elite, consisting of 'new middle class' of civil servants, managers of industries, scientists and scholars and they form a link between the elite and the society.

Like Pareto, Mosca also believes in the circulation of elite theory, and thereby, claims to be a democratic elitist thinker. He emphatically points out that the whole history of civilized mankind comes down to a conflict between the tendency of dominant elements to monopolize political power and transmit it by inheritance, and the tendency towards dislocation of old forces and an emergence of new forces. But the change in elite comes when a new source of wealth develops or knowledge grows and old regime declines and a new one are born or a new current of ideas spreads. Mosca says "as soon as there is a shift in the balance of political forces, when a need is felt for new capacities different from the old in the management of the state, the old capacities lose their importance and the constitution of elite undergoes a change."[21]

THE ELITE THEORY OF ROBERT MICHELS (1876–1936)

Robert Michels reveals another dimension of the elite phenomenon. He proposes a law governing all social organizations and calls it 'the iron law of oligarchy.'[22] Michels' celebrated formulation was: 'who says organization, says oligarchy.'[23] According to him democracy requires organization, which leads to oligarchy. Michels insists that mass members cannot control the large-scale organizations of the modern age. Leadership is technically indispensable.[24] Most democratic modern societies, and within those societies the most advanced parties have been unable to escape oligarchy.[25] In support of the growth of oligarchy, Michels gives his concept of mass mind. The majority of human beings are apathetic, which he calls 'the Perennial incompetence of masses.' Hence, the masses are incapable of self-government. Leaders easily take advantage of these qualities of masses to perpetuate themselves in power. Once the leaders come in power, nothing can bring them down. Though sometimes revolutions occur in history and tyrants are disposed, but new tyrants arise, and the world goes on as before. At the outset, leaders arise spontaneously; their functions are accessory and gratuitous. Soon, however, they become professional leaders, and in this second stage of development they are stable and irremovable.[26]

According to Michels, majority can never rule despite the formal apparatus of universal suffrage. In any democracy the major decisions will be taken by a powerful oligarchy. Michels strongly believes that the apathy of mass enables the elite to keep themselves in power by at times duping the masses.

THE ELITE THEORY OF MARX

In every society beyond the most primitive, two categories of people may be distinguished: a ruling class and one or more subject classes. The dominant position of the ruling class is to be explained by its possession of the major instruments of economic production, but its political dominance is consolidated by the hold, which it establishes over military force and over the production of ideas. There is perpetual class conflict between the ruling classes and the subject class or classes; and the nature and the course of such conflict is influenced primarily by the development of productive forces, i.e. by changes in technology. The lines of class conflict are most sharply drawn in the modern capitalist societies. The class conflict reaches to its climax due to great concentration of wealth at one end and poverty on the other end. When the classes become most radically polarized, the class-conflict within the capitalist society ends only with the victory of the working class, followed by the emergence of a classless society.[27] Marx does not glorify elitist theory and at the end makes a prophecy of the withering of elitist rule. His assumption, however, did not happen in the advanced countries and secondly, Marx failed to assess the role of new middle classes, so a group of communist thinkers modified his theory, and disagreed with the concept of the end of elitist rule.

Burnham agrees with Marx that control of production give rise to political power, social prestige as well as wealth, and also that capitalism is in decline.[28] Burnham approached the political Elite from the economic viewpoint. He says that power comes from the control of the means of production. According to him "to discover what to see what group gets the biggest income." Burnham, however, is not a Marxist. He on the other hand, tries to modify capitalism and the capitalist system and rejects the idea that elites and capitalism will come to an end. He says that society will never ever have absolute equality; hence elites will not be removed from the society. It will only change its form. Managers will take up the responsibility, and will act as elites exercising power. The cycle will go on. Even before James Burnham, Veblen had drawn the picture of capitalists being replaced by the 'engineers' or the 'technical specialists'[29] who would emerge as elites. Djilas describes how after the Bolshevik Revolution in Russia a new class, previously unknown to history, has been formed.[30] The new class Djilas speaks of springs from the Proletariat, but emerges as the newly formed elite. Having achieved industrialization, the new class can do nothing more than to strengthen its political as well as administrative hegemony. Djilas bitterly predicts that 'when the new class leaves the historical scene—and this must happen—there will be less sorrow over its passing than there was for any other class before it.'[31] He definitely believed in the rule of political bureaucracy which possessed all characteristics of elite.

THE ELITE THEORY OF C. WRIGHT MILLS

C. Wright Mills dealt with the idea of political elites in his book 'The Power elite', which was published in the year 1959. In his view, the elite are product of the 'institutional landscape' of the society. Mills defines the power elite in terms of power as those who occupy the command posts. Mills has studied the elite phenomenon in the American Social Context. He categorized three major elites in America—the corporation heads the political leaders and the military chiefs. Mills believed that even in democracy the elites are united and form a cohesive group as they have homogeneity and they come from the same social origin.[32] Taking American Society as an example he proceeded to write that the elite takes all important decisions and the masses are kept quiet by flattery, deception and entertainment. The elite can easily indulge in corruption as the public is not organized in their protest against corruption. The elite is therefore always in an advantageous position. Indian political history is replete with examples of 'scams' boffors, fodder, adarsh, commonwealth games, coalgate, etc. but the tolerance of people never challenged their rising scale. A few incidences of protest made headlines but it gradually died its natural death due to lack of mass support.

THE ELITE THEORY OF HAROLD LASSWELL

Harold Lasswell is another distinguished writer on the subject of elite phenomenon. For him, 'the study of politics is the study of influence and the influential' and 'the influential are those who get the most of what there is to get.'[33] Most of what people want to get are termed by Lasswell as 'values' and according to him the basic values are: deference, income and safety. Those who get the most of these values are elites, the rest are masses. Lasswell discusses the method by which the elites are protected or superseded. According to him, the fate of elite is profoundly affected by the ways it manipulates the environment that is to say by the use of violence, goods, symbols of the common destiny.[34] He further talks of personality and attitude groups and discusses the meaning of social change for the relative ascendancy of such formations. elite is subject to domestic attack when it fails to bring in prosperity. The security of elites is tied up with shifts in goods and prices.[35] According to Lasswell, a revolution is a shift in the class composition of elites. The French Revolution marked the rise of the bourgeoisie; the Russian Revolution marked the rise of lesser bourgeoisie.[36] He further claimed that revolution is initiated by a few, and then gains momentum with popular support. However, consistency of followers are not guaranteed.

THE ELITE THEORY OF ROBERT A. DAHL

Robert A. Dahl has suggested the decision-making approach in his book *Who Governs*? He has tested a number of hypotheses concerning who governs in a democracy from the elitist interpretation; Dahl defines as the view that there exist inequalities in the distribution of resources of power in the community. He further noticed that power is cumulative in nature and is held by those who have wealth, status or high business position. He selected New Haven Society for the study. Dahl selected three 'Issue areas' to test the rule of elites' influence. These were decision-making on urban redevelopment, decision on public schools and decision on political nominations, particularly for the post of Mayor. Dahl also distinguished three groups of potential leaders: Politicians, social notables and economic notables. Dahl found that decision-making was done in pluralist way, which he termed as 'polyarchy'. Dahl points out that equal political participation does not exist in the elite, but there is also not single elite, a group of people who possess intellect, always put a check on the activities of rulers. The people exercise indirect influence through political voting. The political awareness of the masses ensures that the leaders will hear every minority. The vast majority of the population participates very little in politics, but Dahl does not recognize this majority as ineffective mass of the elitist theory. He does not deny that a small stratum of individuals is much more involved in political thought, discussion and action than the rest of the population.[37] Such leaders have direct influence on decisions in the sense that they can initiate proposals for policies, or successfully veto the proposals of others.[38] Robert Dahl, along with Talcott Parsons identifies a 'bargaining model' in America in which political elite perform the mediating and adjusting role among the various institutional sectors of society.[39] The basic issue for the elites is not arbitrary exercise of power, but to create a welfare state based on the aspirations of the common people. Dahl explains the phenomena of power, that every group has ability to affect political decisions.

ELITE AND DEMOCRACY

The idea of elitism is denied by those who uphold classical democratic or socialist ideas.[40] In reality, the elites in any society, wield power-political or economic, formulates policies, shape the destiny of the nation, decide the most vital issues of political life, according to their own attitudes and interests, though in the name of the welfare of common man. The existence of elites in a society influences and even shapes the entire outlooks of the masses and orientates values. But Schumpeter has tried to show the compatibility of elitism and democracy. He defines democracy as 'an institutional arrangement for arriving at political decisions in which individuals acquire the power to decide by means of a competitive struggle for the people's vote.[41] Polsby also challenges the thesis that a socio-economic elite dominates political life or that there is a single all-purposive elite.[42] They are actually the value-givers to the entire political, social, economic structure of the society of all types. The emergence of elites has exposed the very foundation of the democratic system, to which, unfortunately ruling or governing elites, pay only lip service. In modern political institutions, political power, political ideology and political behaviour of ordinary persons constitute the community. Mass participation in the government system has become a myth in the true sense of the term, particularly in the big states of modern times.

The foregoing discussion makes it explicit to the idea of the elitist democracy as against the classical concept of democracy.[43] Karl Mannheim, was a critic of the elitist theorist for their irrational justification of 'direct action' and unconditional subordination to rule by a leader. However, he modified his view and observed later that elitist theories do not stand antagonized to the norms of democracy. The conception of democracy as the elite rule was legitimized in the 20th century obviously because of the rise of Nazism and fascism regimes in contrast to the credibility of the democratic identification along with multi-party representative and parliamentary system. The reasons for the emergence, in the twentieth century, of a static conception of democracy in which elite rule is sanctioned by periodic elections have to be sought in the political circumstances of the century. Karl Mannheim claimed that a society is made democratic when individual citizens have at least the possibility of making their aspirations felt at certain intervals. Schumpeter and Raymond Aron need to be quoted who found fundamental difference between a society of the soviet type and of the western type where the former has united elite and the latter has a divided elite and set out explicitly conditions for the success of the democratic method which they classify under four headings:

(i) that the human material of politics (i.e., the elites) should be of sufficiently high quality;

(ii) that the effective range of political decision should not be extended too far;

(iii) that the government should be able to command the services of a well trained bureaucracy of good standing and tradition; and

(iv) that there should be democratic self control, i.e. the competing elites should tolerate each other's rule Aron added a few: (a) restoration of government authority capable of settling the disputes between groups and enforcing the decisions necessary in the community's joint interest; (b) an efficient economic administration which will preserve mobility and revive incentives; and (c) a limitation on the influence of those individuals and groups which want to change the whole framework of society.[44] In developing countries like India, elitism has acquired different dimensions. In the rural environment caste mobilization, class distinctions and feudal subordination is commonly practiced which empowers elite, whereas in urban sectors or for that matter in cosmopolitan culture, social mobilization are issue based thereby replacing one elite with the other. The elitist nature of modern democratic states denies mass-oriented power structure, mass-oriented political process as the major political decisions cannot afford the luxury of mass involvement. What we find in today's democratic states is only a class or a few persons of dominance, i.e. some sorts of elite, formulate, decide and execute the norms of behaviour of common people. In fact, this elites-oriented politics of modern democratic states makes the participation of common people a 'farce' a result of which ordinary citizen witnesses the entire game of politics as a silent spectator from a distant angle.

CRITICAL ESTIMATE

Different writers have subjected elite theory to vehement criticisms. It has been pointed out that the elite theory is neo Machiavellian in nature, as it relies on the cunning and manipulating capacity of the leaders. The reference of fox and lion like qualities are likely to remind the readers of Machiavellian 'Prince'. Moreover the elite theory has been taken by some as justification on the rule of minority; hence undemocratic. The protagonists of elitist theories are under attack from different quarters. Carl J. Friedrich points out that the elitist doctrines are the 'offspring of a society containing feudal remnants'. G. Lukacs suggests that the elitist problem has been raised precisely in those countries where liberal traditions are weak.[45] The elite do not exist in the classical sense of a single self-conscious, united and ruling group.[46] Andre Beteille refers to political elite, that is, the people in concrete political structures such as cabinets, parties and legislatures. According to him they are the dominating class of any society and can never merge in the common society. They extract benefits from the apathy of the people and create a class hierarchy of its own, whether it is a democracy or a despotic government. Power elite therefore is not drawn from the commoners. In fact they are the people who are most resourceful and generally well connected with the power position than the majority of people.[47] Despite all these criticisms, the theorists of elite defend, by various means, the legacy from the inegalitarian societies of the past, while making concessions to the spirit of equality.[48]

CONCLUSION

However, such criticisms cannot lessen the importance of a theory so meticulously built on real observations of the seat of power. A modern democratic state cannot ignore the role of elite, but it ought to be borne in mind that, those elite today is not merely the governing elite. The elite include the rising number of talented persons coming out of various fields who contribute much to the social welfare and progress. Thus, existence of elites in a society influence and even shape the entire outlook of the masses.

To sum up, one can say that elite is group of people either which rules the country or supports in ruling. In ancient Indian context during Kingship advisors's of King helped them to rule the states. Kautilya named them as *Amatya and Mahamatya*.

It is accepted by all the political sociologists that elite class has played a very important role in democratic as well as in socialistic state. The elite class has brought economic and political revolution in developing countries too. In India elite survive on the wealth of capitalist class and votes of demagogue. Though apparently we feel that elite theory is diametrically opposed to democratic values, but actually, both are complementary to each other. At times, it becomes too blurred to make a demarcating line between the two, though they represent two different worlds.

Questions for Discussion

1. Critically examine the elitist theories of Pareto and Mosca.
2. Evaluate the role of elite in democracy.
3. Discuss the theories of elitism.
4. Write an essay on elite and Indian democracy.

References

1. Schumpeter, Joseph A. (1950), *Capitalism, Socialism and Democracy*, 3rd ed., New York, Harper and Row Publishers.
2. Pareto, Vilfredo (1901), *The Rise and Fall of Elites*, New Jersey, The Bedminton Press, p. 1136.
3. Bottomore, T.B. (1964), *Elites and Society*, England, Penguin p. 7.
4. *Ibid.*
5. *Ibid.*
6. Mosca, Gaetano (1939), *The Ruling Class* (English edition), New York, McGraw Hill, p. 50.
7. Laswell, Harold (1951), *Politics: Who Gets What When and How*, Illinois, Free Press, p. 259.
8. Miesel, J.H. (1956), *The Myth of the Ruling Class*, Ann Arbor, University of Michigan Press, p. 4.
9. Bottomore, T.B. (1964), *op. cit.*, pp. 50–51.
10. *Ibid.*, p. 51.
11. Pareto, Vilfredo (1935), *The Mind and Society*, Vol. III, English Translation of an Italian Work (1916), Harcourt Brace, pp. 1423–1424.
12. Bottomore, T.B. (1964), *op. cit.*, p. 8.
13. *Ibid.*, p. 50.
14. Pareto (1901), *op. cit.*, p. 36.
15. *Ibid.*, pp. 48–49.
16. *Ibid.*, p. 52.
17. Mosca, G. (1939), *op. cit.*, p. 50.

18. *Ibid.*, p. 12.

19. *Ibid.*, pp. 12–13.

20. *Ibid.*, pp. 60–62.

21. *Ibid.*, p. 65.

22. Michels, R. (1949), *First Lectures in Political Sociology*, Translated by Alfred D. Grazia, New York, Harper and Row Publishers, pp. 141–142.

23. Michels, R. (1915), *Political Parties: A Sociological Study of the Oligarchical Tendencies of Modern Democracy*, Illinois, Free Press, p. 418.

24. *Ibid.*, p. 417.

25. Michels, *op. cit.*, p. 142.

26. *Ibid.*, p. 418.

27. Bottomore, *op. cit.*, pp. 24–25.

28. Burnham, J. (1942), *The Managerial Revolution*, London, Putnam, pp. 27–28 and 72–73.

29. Veblen, T. (1921), *The Engineers and the Price System*, New York, The Viking Press, p. 74.

30. Djilas, M. (1957), *The New Class*, London, Thames and Hudson, p. 38.

31. *Ibid.*, p. 69.

32. Sharma, L.N. and Ashraf, Ali (1983), *Political Sociology: A New Grammar of Politics*, New Delhi, University Press, p. 70.

33. Lasswell, H.D. (1951), *Politics: Who gets What, When, How*, Illinois, Free Press, p. 259.

34. *Ibid.*, p. 311.

35. Sharma, *op. cit.*, p. 71.

36. *Ibid.*

37. Dahl, R.A. (1961), *Who Governs*? New Haven, Yale University Press, p. 90.

38. *Ibid.*, p. 102.

39. Sharma, *op. cit.*, p. 72.

40. Parry, G. (1969), *Political Elites*, London,George Allen and Unwin, p. 30.

41. Schumpeter (1950), *op. cit.*, p. 269.

42. Polsby, Nelson. W. (1963), *Community, Power and Political Theory*, New Haven, Yale University Press, p. 128.

43. Lipset, S.M. (1962), *Political Parties*, New York, Collier, p. 33.

44. Das and Choudhury, *op. cit.*, p. 240.

45. Bottomore, *op. cit.*, p. 15.

46. Sharma, *op. cit.*, p. 74.

47. Sharma, K.L., *Power Elite in Rural India* in B.K. Nagla (Ed.) (1999) *Political Sociology*, Jaipur, Rawat Publications, pp. 163–167.

48. Bottomore, *op. cit.*, p. 148.

Suggested Reading

T.B. Bottomore, *Elites and Society*

L.N. Sharma and Ali Ashraf, *Political Sociology: A New Grammar of Politics*

Harihar Das and B.C. Choudhury, *Introduction to Political Sociology*

Web Links

www.udel.edu/htr/Amertican/Texts/power/html

Sf.oxfordjournals.org/content/50/4/462.full.pdf

10
Bureaucracy Society and Polity

CRUX

Representative democracy can promote sometimes an inefficient government because it is based on electoral politics and masses cannot always be wise and awakened. The obvious consequence can be poor governance and can give a set-back to the development process of the political system. Despite this problem, we cannot do away with democracy. Therefore, the best possible way is to form a 'class' of permanent executives to assist political executives in delivery of services and construct good governance. The committed bureaucracy or the bureaucratization of politics, sometimes adversely affects the integrity of the society. So, it becomes essential as students of political sociology to comprehend the role of bureaucracy in striking a balance between the society and politics.

MEANING AND DEFINITION

The etymological meaning of the term bureaucracy is hierarchical arrangement of authority. It is derived from the French word *bureau* which means 'desk.' Finer has rightly termed bureaucracy as the desk government. Harold Laski defines bureaucracy as a system, the control of which is so completely in the hands of officials that their power jeopardises the liberties of ordinary citizens. His definition appears to be more in nature of critique. Robert K. Merton defines bureaucracy as a secondary group structure designed to carry on certain activities, which cannot be performed on the basis of primary group criteria. Louis Coser defines bureaucracy as that type of hierarchical organization, which is designed rationally to coordinate the work of many individuals in the pursuit of large-scale administrative tasks. Max Weber claims that bureaucracy is the system of administration characterized by expertness, impartiality and absence of humanity. All these definitions characterize bureaucracy as official business dependent on documentation and technical training. Max Weber

(1864–1920), the German political sociologist is regarded as the father of the concept of bureaucracy. Public administration identifies bureaucracy with governance and claims Weberian model to be administration-centric. However, political sociology determines the scope of bureaucracy in both government and non-government performance. Weber looked at bureaucracy as a process of authority, legitimacy and development. It is imperative to understand the nature and role of bureaucracy in harmonising polity with society. Weber talked about authority and its classification into the three—traditional, charismatic and rational. Traditional authority was based on kinship and strengthened from the idea of hereditary element, which Weberian found to be erroneous as the skill of ruling cannot be transmitted from one generation to the other. It prevailed in feudal Europe and is an accepted form of authority in pre-modern societies. Obedience to such an authority is based on customs. By and large, ancient India also belonged to this category. In the pure type of traditional authority, the following features of a bureaucratic administrative staff are absent:[1]

1. A clearly defined sphere of competence subject to impersonal rules
2. A rational ordering of relations or superiority and inferiority
3. A regular system of appointment and promotion on the basis of free contract
4. Technical training as a regular requirement
5. Fixed salaries

His second type of authority, popularly known as charismatic, emerges out of a crisis situation and is transitory in nature, meaning to say, after the crisis management the charisma fades away and the authority turns into power without legitimacy. In this case, ordinary people come predominantly under spell of emotional action. The obedience stems from their reverence to the person. Adolf Hitler, Nepolean, Gandhi, Maozedong, Nelson Mandela and Anna Hazare may be considered as charismatic authorities. However, the death of the leader or erosion in his personal charm may lead to the end of such an authority. It is for this reason; Weber terms it as routinization of charisma.[2] Weber decries it and finally recommends legal or rational authority as the best possible authority of administration. It is a characteristic of modern political system. In contrast to the earlier two, it derives legitimacy from a set of rationally drawn impersonal rules. According to Weber, bureaucracy is the ideal representation of rational-legal authority where there is a clear-cut goal, and people obey the legal framework because they see their own good in the decisions of bureaucrats. Rational authority means bureaucratic process. Weber laid down the theory of 'bureaucratic rationality' that includes his five beliefs about the foundation and structure of bureaucracy:[3]

1. That legal norm can be established either by agreement or by imposition with a claim to be obedient on the part of the members of a corporate group or organization.

2. That the law is the system of abstract rules convincing all possible cases of conduct within the organization, the administration of law being the application of these rules to particular cases.
3. The fundamental source of authority in the legal type is the authority to the impersonal order of an officer holding a specifically legitimized status under the rules with powers to issue commands.
4. That the person who obeys authority does so in his capacity as a member of the corporate group and what he obeys is only the law.
5. That the members of the corporate group, in so far as they obey a person in authority, do not owe this obedience to him as an individual but to the impersonal order. In other words, there is an obligation to obedience only within the sphere of the rationally delimited authority, which, in terms of the order, has been conferred upon him.

Max Weber laid down eight fundamental features of rational legal authority:[4]

1. Organization of official functions on a continuous rule-bound basis
2. A specified sphere of competence and of distinct functions based on systematic division of labour
3. Principle of hierarchy with a lower office under the control and supervision of a higher one
4. Trained personnel for the conduct of business
5. Complete separation of members of the administrative staff from the ownership of the means of production or administration, with a clear separation likewise in principle of the property belonging to the organization and controlled within the sphere of office and the personal property of the official available for private use
6. A complete absence of appropriation of official position by the incumbent
7. The formulation and recording in writing of all acts, decisions and rules
8. The ideal type being the purest form of legal authority or 'imperative co-ordination'

Weber argues that only rational authority does not characterize bureaucracy, but it is also endowed with technical superiority, and is therefore, conducive to efficiency. As he writes, 'the decisive reason for the advance for bureaucratic organization has always been its technical superiority over any form of organization. The fully-developed bureaucratic mechanism compares with other organizations exactly as does the machine with non-mechanical modes of production.[5]

Max Weber gives a model, which makes the role of bureaucracy a leviathan without any chains. The critics vehemently criticize the excessive faith reposed on bureaucracy by Weber. Bureaucrats are social beings, and therefore, cannot sterilize their emotions while making policies of development administration. Talcott Parson affirms the idea of Weber and strongly recommends the idea of bureaucratic control, but history is repleted with cases of bureaucratization, and undue interference in policy making. There are several examples of conflict between permanent executive and political executive, which has often resulted in hindering the pace of political development. The concept of bureaucracy has almost become synonymous with the name of Max Weber as the name of class theory with Karl Marx. In modern age, complexities of life have changed the traditional meaning of bureau, but even then, no one can afford to ignore the basic features of Weberian bureaucracy in understanding administration and management.

Bureaucracy, for him is a hierarchical arrangement, which is run by professional, specialized and efficient personnel. It supervises, controls and co-ordinates complex and multi-faceted works. According to him, bureaucracy has become even more important in industrial society. Every aspect of such a society—its political institutions, armed forces, educational institutions, business organizations, or ecclesiastical institutions like the church—has transformed into the bureaucratic organization. It leads Weber to consider bureaucracy and bureaucratization as among the most important aspects of sociology.[6]

There are two views to look at bureaucracy: narrow view and broad view. Narrow view is confined to those important public servants who occupy policy making positions, whereas broad view refers to the totality of personnel occupying posts from top to the bottom.[7] Fritz Morstein Marx makes an effort to bring out the difference between bureaucracy and desk-work on following grounds:

1. The type of organization used by modern government for the conduct of its various specialized functions, embodied in the administrative system and personified more specifically by the civil service
2. A mechanistic and formal approach in carrying out such functions, literal and 'inhuman', to the point of indifference towards the effects achieved
3. The kind of government that shoulders a large burden of responsibilities in support of the economic and social order or/as well as a political condition in which the executive branch plays a role increasingly more important in relation to the legislative and judicial branches as visible in a welfare state or a social-service state
4. A government subject to control not by the electorate but rather by a group of power-hungry visionary functionaries[8]

TENETS OF BUREAUCRACY

Max Weber's characterization of bureaucracy has been summed-up in the following manner:

1. A continuous organization of official functions bound by rules;
2. A specific sphere of competence, and a sphere of obligations to perform functions which have been marked off as part of a systematic division of labour, and the provision of the incumbent with the necessary authority to carry out these functions;
3. The organization of office follows the principle of hierarchy, that is, each lower office is under the control and supervision of a higher one;
4. The rules which regulate the conduct of an office may be technical rules or norms. In such cases, if their application is to be fully rational, specialized training is necessary. It is thus normally true that only a person who has demonstrated an adequate technical training is qualified to be a member of the administrative staff;
5. It is a matter of principle that the members of the administrative staff should be completely separated from ownership of the means of production or administration. There exists further more in principle, complete separation of property belonging to the organization, which is controlled within the spheres of the office, and the personal property of an official;
6. Administrative acts, decisions and rules are formulated and recorded in writing.[9]

TYPES OF BUREAUCRACY

In the typology of Almond and Powell, one can perceive several types of bureaucracy as followed: democratic, Marxist-Leninist, patriarchal, patrimonial, medieval and monarchical, amongst others. Yet Almond and Powell argue that there is also merit in the classification of bureaucracy as set out by Merle Fainsod, namely:[10]

1. Representatives bureaucracies,
2. Party-state bureaucracies,
3. Military-dominated bureaucracies,
4. Ruler-dominated bureaucracies, and
5. Ruling bureaucracies.

According to Max Weber there are three types of bureaucracy—representative bureaucracy, mock bureaucracy and punishment-centered bureaucracy.

BUREAUCRACY IN SOCIETY

Bureaucracy though being an inevitable part of running administration vis-a-vis politics is also inseparable part of society. Its major component is power, which is essentially a sociological notion. Bureaucrats create a social class of its own because they are part and parcel of the society. In modern society, bureaucracy is emerging as a special category of society and secondly political sociology is not only concerned with political factors influencing political actors but also non-political factors determining political behaviour. Harold Lasswell, Talcott Parson and the Neo-Machiavellians: Mosca, Pareto and Michells and some of the communist thinkers like Veblen, Djilas and Burnham perceive bureaucrats or managers as the rising class of the future in all modern societies.[11] The bureaucracy represents the elite of merit which dominates the public and private administration. The upper class/caste bias in the composition of both the bureaucratic and political elites of the early post independent decades that had created a more or less one-class ensemble in administration and politics has been gradually changing over time. Yet, since bureaucratic and political recruitments have been subject to reservations and larger status reversals in the society and economy, a sharp class confrontation between the bureaucratic and political classes has been staved off.[12]

In order to make bureaucracy more representative reservation of seats was incorporated as an affirmative strategy. India is a developing country where food security still remains the basic problem to grapple with. Population explosion has its dire consequences like abject poverty, illiteracy, unemployment, malnutrition and epidemic, which adversely affects the human development index. In such a scenario, involvement of less privileged class in administrative set-up is not possible until and unless some inducements are provided. In Indian democracy bureaucrats represents the dominant sections of the society. By its very nature, Indian bureaucracy cannot be representative of Indian society.[13]

The reservation of administrative posts was initially introduced for the scheduled castes and tribes, but later seats were reserved for the backward castes to make bureaucracy more broad based and representative of the cross-sections of the Indian society. But unfortunately, once a person becomes a bureaucrat he develops the caste and class of his own irrespective of his phylum background. It is observed that even the members of lower caste or class who join the civil service get increasingly alienated from their own kinship group, and gradually form new elite with interaction limited to their own caste group in the administration and to the bureaucracy in general.[14] This has virtually defeated the very purpose of creating a representative bureaucracy. Even the practice of quota or reservations has failed to produce tangible results in developing society like India because of enormous gap in the life-style of its people. This is true of the military and the industrial bureaucracy. Officers of the army, navy and air force; engineers and managers; as well as secretaries and commissioners of the government are the top elite in terms of social prestige and power.[15]

Bureaucrats are essentially human beings, and therefore, cannot be fully neutral in their approach or action. They also cannot be value-free or value less. They are not robots but a human being with a heart and a brain. So, they cannot perfectly fit into the classification of Max Weber. Weber entrusts excessive idealism in the performance of bureaucrats. In actual practice, administrators are not only rational but also emotional in their deeds. They are not above law or flaw. Weber fails to understand this intricacy of human being. He never doubts the abilities of a civil servant in state affairs and seriously demands for a high degree of reliability in the behaviour of bureaucrats. But Robert Merton finds serious flaws in this concept. Such formalism and rigidity, according to Merton, is derived from structural sources. He accepts the quality of discipline, dexterity and adherence with rules and regulations, but does not make it obligatory for the elites. Merton points out that as 'adherence to the rules originally conceived as a means becomes transformed into an end in itself, there occurs the familiar process of displacement of goals whereby an instrumental value becomes a terminal value.'[16] If a bureaucrat fails to perform his profile duty even for some very humane and sanguine reasons, he cannot be spared by Weber, whereas Merton calls it 'dysfunction.' Merton's exposition of bureaucratic dysfunction is illuminating.[17]

Another dysfunctional aspect of bureaucracy pertains to the rise of defense mechanism of an informal order which tend to arise whenever there is a threat to the integrity of a group. The bureaucrats tend to develop a sense of a common destiny and an espirite-de-corps. Bureaucrats are the servants of the people and are expected to serve the interests of masses but in a due course of time they distance themselves from the masses and the stress and depersonalization of relationships further widens the gap between the elite and the masses. In other words, they become masters exercising, immense power and prestige of government and tend to develop an arrogant and superior attitude in sharp contrast to the descriptive norms of public servant. This type of behaviour makes bureaucrat a superior human being with a halo and public becomes hesitant in approaching them for the solution of their problems. The Hindi translation of the term bureaucrat is *naukarshahi* which is self-explanatory, where bureaucrat instead of becoming a *naukar* (servant) turns out to be a *shahi* (royal).

Max Weber claims that bureaucracy is the means of carrying community action over into rationally ordered societal action. Bureaucrats serve as an instrument of power and raises important questions regarding its relationship with democracy. Bureaucracy is increasingly becoming over dominant but Sir William Beveridge rightly says that "democracy, if it knows its business, has no reason to fear bureaucracy."

BUREAUCRACY IN POLITY

Bureaucrats are expected to maintain neutrality in their performance of functions according to the Weberian model. In practice, bureaucracy performs multiple functions and as G.A. Almond and G.B. Powell write 'bureaucracies tend to monopolise outputs'. They also intervene in the government's function of rule making and rule-adjudication. Therefore it is almost unbelievable to assess the role of bureaucracy without involvement or commitment. In the course of implementing the policies, their personal likes and dislikes influence the intent and purposes of programmes. Since it is the permanent executives, there exists a special bond between the ministers and the administrators. Ministers have uncertain period of performance and in any case a temporary tenure and most of them are not well-versed with the administrative techniques. So, they have to depend upon bureaucrats who are recruited primarily on the basis of knowledge, intelligence and merit. The long and arduous training after their recruitment makes them efficient and therefore they become indispensible in a liberal democracy. It is further observed that the individual members of the bureaucracy tend to identify themselves with the ideology of a particular political party or with interests of a particular group. Lobbies and legislators often work in concert with administrators, and together mould public policies.[18]

Fred W. Riggs has been very vocal in emphasizing the folly of assuming separatism between bureaucracy and politics. He says, this idea of separatism has in my judgement been erroneously equated with the idea that the bureaucracy should serve only administrative functions, and a constitutive system, i.e. Legislature, parties and elected politicians-should serve only political functions. This formulation obscures the fact that if bureaucrats are to give priority to managerial and rational-legal criteria in the conduct of their offices, they must have some degree of power. It obscures also the proposition that the administrative effectiveness of a bureaucracy depends in no small measure on its relations with a constitutive system.[19]

Representation is strengthened rather than weakened by being linked with the sober insights that originate in the perspective of public management.[20] The fact of the politicization of bureaucracy in developed and developing country of the world has forced us to redefine the related term of its 'neutrality' and 'commitment'. While the notion of neutrality implies acceptance of the discipline of working without reservation—indeed with devotion—for the success of every government lawfully in power.[21] Government cannot realize effectively its objective unless the civil servants are fully dedicated to them and to the political process through which they are formulated.[22] Thus, it can be safely asserted that administrative neutrality means devotion for the success of every government lawfully in power and administrators cannot allow themselves to have intimate identification with any particular policy or programme as to create for them an emotional disability when it comes to turning in the opposite direction under a different government ideology. So, there is a thin line of demarcation between neutrality and commitment, which needs to be tactfully handled for optimum results. As La Palombara writes, 'keeping the bureaucracy out of politics is a vain hope.' Therefore the conflict between the two sometimes becomes inevitable. Fred W. Riggs says, despite the conflict they must get a parallel platform because overpowering bureaucratic institution can make political organ weak and extreme political control over the bureaucracy will ruin the democratic values. We need to balance the two for political stability, economic growth, administrative effectiveness and human development. The concept of a politicised bureaucracy is one, which is involved or influences or is influenced to any degree, consciously or unconsciously, by covert or by implicit actions, in the streams of the politics of the day whether of the party in power or the party/parties in opposition. Such an involvement may mean the bureaucratic promotion of special interests of political party at the expense of national objectives. In a more extended form, it may also be regarded as a type of bureaucracy which uses political parties in furtherance of their collective or individual objectives or which is used by political parties in the achievements of party objectives.[23]

The role of bureaucracy tends to become more important in third world developing countries. Both development and democracy have remained a pious hope in many developing countries, with the bureaucracies continuing to enjoy and exercise undiminished, often enhanced, power.[24] The transfer of power from elected representatives of the people to bureaucracy is a serious threat to a democratic spirit.

In a struggle for power between public bureaucracy and political leadership (elected representatives), the former thrives if the leadership authority is weak. Closely connected with it is also the hypothesis that the bureaucracy gets immobilized if political leadership is sharply fluctuating or unstable.[25]

Role of Bureaucracy in Developing Society/Polity

The dominant position of bureaucracy in all societies, in general, and in developing societies, in particular, has created a debate regarding the role of bureaucracy, the degree of power it enjoys and its relation with social harmony and political stability. The independence of new states and many of the third world countries project economic growth and political development as their first and foremost objective. The high position of bureaucrats reinforced by popular esteem gives them additional power and dependence of politicians on them. With the emergence of bureaucracies, third world countries depicted a transitional phase of growth, be it western, modern or traditional. Bureaucracy establishes and strengthens the pace of economic growth and can also facilitate necessary initiatives for transforming inputs into outputs of political development. The problems of third world countries are so complex that sometimes government fails to tackle them, and there, the bureaucratic intervention becomes necessary. Bureaucracy has a very responsible role to play in a politically developing democracy, but the moment bureaucracy is marked with corruption, self-aggrandizement, internal bickering national development is obstructed. The phenomenon of the pre-dominance of bureaucracy in the third world has sought to be captured by many post-colonial theorists. One of the best exponents of this concept is a Sociologist from Pakistan named Hamza Alavi. He strongly believed that cohesive bureaucracy helps in the considerable growth of the political system endowed with what Marx called 'relative-autonomy', but it has been found that third world is no homogeneous entity and the relative power position of the bureaucracy and the democratic institutions varies from one state to another. In India, for e.g., political parties and elected institutions have proved more deeply entrenched. It does not however indicate that bureaucracy is not a strong force in India.[26] But it only wants to show that it is not promoting 'bureaucratic-military oligarchy' as it is in the case of Pakistan.[27]

Political parties and interests groups are chief political agencies in the mobilization of power. Parties aspire to make governments; groups seek to influence government policies. It is however, government bureaucracy that makes and implements public policies, often in concert with parties and interests groups. Amidst fluctuating fortunes of parties and the rivalries of groups, bureaucracy provides administrative expertise and stability. Also, with the expansion of the government activities, bureaucracy has come to acquire a vital role and enormous power in modern governments that rely heavily on trained civil servants to carry out complicated tasks of administration.[28]

Perhaps the most important case anywhere of a post-colonial bureaucracy is to be found in India. Ministers in India are, as in the British system, important political figures who oversee large ministerial portfolios both at central level and in liaison with the individual states. While the British ruled India, they effectively reproduced a class of administrative officers, which paralleled the British model. The result is the Indian Civil Service may be seen as modern Elite derived from both Indian and British traditions. Thus, while responsibility for policy is political, and not administrative matter, senior civil servants nevertheless are close interpreters of policies.[29]

India's administrative steel frame has been frequently attacked and many attempts of reform have been made by the government following the model of western public administration, but the combination of history and culture made it impossible to happen.[30]

CRITICAL ESTIMATE

If administration were purely mechanical then there would be no problem of corruption, but however, it is not the case. Administrators are human beings and they also exercise discretion. Discretion is a serious matter for administrators who are required to weigh up the various factors in any decision before actually making a decision. Administration is essentially a human activity, which always has a risk of becoming perverted for the greed of money and power. Corruption, in a technical sense, is probably corruption in a moral sense. This point was made clear by the Indian Prime Minister, Rajiv Gandhi in late 1985, when he linked corruption with cultural bankruptcy. Administrators may become intoxicated with power and 'power corrupts, absolute power corrupts absolutely' (Lord Acton, letters, 1904).

The term 'nepotism', a second form of corruption covers the idea that a public official rewarded his family with the fruits of office high or low. Here corruption hinges upon the love and to serve the vested interests of the family.

'Red-tapism' is another form of corruption, where files move from one table to the other under hierarchical rules and regulations, thereby making the process cumbersome for the common people. Good governance simply means a welfare state, which caters to the needs of the people and where bureaucracy performs civil responsibility.[31]

CONCLUSION

Bureaucracies' role in third world countries: very complicated. In some countries, it acts like bulwark of socio-economic and political justice, and in some others it is anti-thetical to the norms of democratic development. More so in the age of Liberalization, Privatization and Globalization (LPG), the role of bureaucracy has radically enhanced which remains the area of concern and interest for social and political scientists.

In true terms, bureaucracy should be committed to the constitution and rule of law, but things have changed and now bureaucracy tends to be more committed to their political Godfathers. Many examples are there in Indian context right from Mr. Mani Shankar Aiyar to R.K. Singh. They just favour or act to the tune of their political masters to get good birth even after retirement. Examples are numerous where retired bureaucrats were awarded with the post of Governor and offered party tickets to fight elections. How can one imagine about their neutrality. This is dangerous for any democratic country. Once Mrs. Tarkeswari Sinha, the then Deputy Minister in Nehru's Cabinet mentioned in an interview for a newspaper that, the earth is burdened with the growing weight of bureaucrats. For the implementation of any scheme, planning or law, government is completely dependent on bureaucracy; therefore they do things as per their own whims and fancies or their priorities.

Questions for Discussion

1. Examine the role of bureaucracy in a democracy.
2. Discuss the meaning and importance of bureaucracy in developing societies.
3. Bureaucracy has strong links with the society and the polity. Elucidate.
4. Critically marginalized the growing power of bureaucracy in the process of modernization.

References

1. Jayapalan, N. (2000), *Political Sociology*, New Delhi, Atlantic Publishers and Distributors, p. 171.
2. Chakraborty, Satyabrata (2005), *Political Sociology*, New Delhi, Macmillan India, p. 117.

3. Misra, B.B. (1947), *The Bureaucracy in India: A Historical Analysis of Development upto 1947*, Delhi, Oxford University Press, p. 28.

4. Weber, Max (1958), *Bureaucracy* in Geith and Mills (Eds.) *From Max Weber, Essays in Sociology*, New York, Oxford University Press, pp. 196–200.

5. *Ibid.*, p. 214.

6. Chakraborty, Satyabrata, *op. cit.*, p. 116.

7. Maheshwari, S.R. (1978), *Bureaucracy and Political Development in India, Indian Journal of Political Science*, Vol. XXXIX, No. 3, July–September, p. 332.

8. Marx, F.M. (1957), *The Administrative State: An Introduction to Bureaucracy*, Chicago, Chicago University Press, pp. 19–20.

9. Weber, Max (1958), *op. cit.*, pp. 196–204.

10. Harris, Peter (1990), *Foundations of Public Administration: A Comparative Approach*, Hong Kong, Hong Kong University Press, p. 116.

11. Sharma, L.N. and Ashraf, Ali (1983), *Political Sociology: A New Grammar of Politics*, New Delhi, University Press, p. 117.

12. Singh, M.P. and Saxena, Rekha (2011), *Indian Politics: Constitutional Foundations and Institutional Functioning*, Delhi, PHI Learning, p. 235.

13. Subramaniam, V., *Representative Bureaucracy*, *American Political Science Review*, Vol. 61, No. 4, pp. 1009–1010.

14. Sharma, L.N. and Ashraf, Ali (1983), *op. cit.*, p. 118.

15. *Ibid.*

16. Merton, R.K. (1957), *Social Theory and Social Structure*, Glencoe, Illinois, Free Press, p. 254.

17. *Ibid.*

18. Sharma, L.N. and Ashraf, Ali (1983), *op. cit.*, p. 114.

19. Riggs, F.W. (1970), *The Context of Development Administrator* in Riggs, F.W. (Ed.), *Frontiers of Development Administration*, Durham, Duke University Press, p. 80.

20. Marx, F.M. (1963), *The Higher Civil Service as an Action Group in Western Political Development* in La Palombara (Ed.) *Bureaucracy and Political Development*, New Jersey, Princeton University Press, p. 64.

21. *Ibid.*, p. 93.

22. Rai, Haridwar, Singh, S.P. and Gour, M.K. (1978), *Neutrality Versus Commitment: A Futile Debate*, *Indian Journal of Political Science*, Delhi, Vol. XXXIX, No. 2, pp. 177–178.

23. Jain, R.B. (1976), *Contemporary Issues in Indian Administration*, Delhi, Vishal Publications, p. 156.

24. Chakraborty, Satyabrata (2005), *op. cit.*, p. 126.

25. Bhambhari (1971), *A Study of the Relationship between Prime Minister and Bureaucracy in India* in *Indian Journal of Public Administration*, New Delhi, Vol. 17, No. 3, p. 367.
26. Chakraborty, Satyabrata, *op. cit.*, p. 127.
27. *Ibid.*
28. Sharma, L.N. and Ashraf, Ali (1983), *op. cit.*, p. 106.
29. Harris, Peter (1990), *Foundations of Public Administration: A Comparative Approach*, Hong Kong, Hong Kong University Press, p. 135.
30. *Ibid.*, p. 135.
31. *Ibid.*, p. 107.

Suggested Reading

J.C. Johari, *Comparative Politics*

L.N. Sharma and Ali Ashraf, *Political Sociology: A New Grammar of Politics*

Satyabrata Chakraborty, *Political Sociology*

Web Link

www.en.wikipedia.org/wiki/bureaucracy.

11
Political Communication

CRUX

The science of control is not essentially a part of human body; it also regulates a political system in producing optimum result. It is the blood stream of any organization. Two way traffic. Instruction coming from top to bottom and information moving from bottom to the top. It is required in all types of organizations. Hierarchical, Pyramidical or Segmental. Its importance is increasing day-by-day with growing democratization of political systems. Theories of political communication are dynamic in nature and provides new role of polity and governance.

POLITICAL COMMUNICATION: Meaning and Definition

As per Webster dictionary, the act or process of using words, sounds, signs, or behaviours to express or exchange information or to express your ideas, thoughts, feelings, etc., to someone else; a message that is given to someone; a letter, telephone call, etc. is called **communication**. It is a way of sending information to people by either using conventional method or modern technology.

All forms of human interactions involve communication, symbolic or formal. The mass media, such as print or electronics (newspaper, radio, internet television and now social media), make up only the most specialized and differentiated communication structures in a society.[1] Communication is so pervasive an element in all human life that it is encountered with every facet of social activity. All of political science can be reconceptualized in terms of communication, and of the factors, which generate messages and determine their impact.[2] Democratic theorists have insisted on the necessity of freedom of speech and expression in general and freedom of press in particular. Richard R. Fagen in his classic work 'Politics and Communication' suggests that the body of potentially relevant literature for the study of communication and comparative politics is almost unlimited. Communication performance can hinder or enhance the development of other kinds of social activity. The making and implementing of political decisions, for instance, is clearly dependent on accurate information and on the successful communication of messages to subordinates, military or civilian, throughout the system.[3]

Karl Deutsch regarded political communication as the main driving force of political system. He called it as 'the dynamic element of a political system'.[4] A procedure by which one mind may affects another. However, even before Deutsch, sociologist Harold Lasswell sought to define the original form of political communication in a well known article, 'The Structure and function of Communication in Society' in 1948. To him the focal issue is to make a psycho-political analysis of 'Who gets what, when and how?' He also believed that revolution is involvement of many, but it is initiated by a few and later is propagated to make it widespread. R.E. Denton and G.C. Woodward write that the content and purpose of communication is discussion based on the will and intention of political activist. To them, language of Political Communication is significant because it reflects the purpose. Language includes not only the words spoken but also the body language, gestures and posture. Here we can cite the example of Mahatma Gandhi who with his dress style, walk and soft, determined utterances influenced the masses of India. Murray Edelman or Doris Graber point out that politics essentially deals with 'language-game' which is a three level phenomenon.[5]

First, it relates to exchange of information, ideas of leaders and common people to attain certain political objectives.

Second, it relates to ideas and statements of those people who are not actively involved in politics. In other words, it is a political language of apolitical people.

Third, it also relates to different kind of language, which is sourced from the media and involves complex mix of interactions between people, politicians and media personnel.

Political communication links the input with output process in a given political system. It is relatively young and evolving concept and has drawn greater importance in recent years. The Greek term *kubernetes* is translated into English word *cybernetics* which means *steersman* or 'science of control' and also has a central receptor and a feedback process as in any machine.[6] In a human body the main receptor is the brain, which receives information from different organs of body and sends instruction accordingly, and thus, functions like the bloodstream of the human body structure. Likewise in a society or even in a polity communication is the blood stream. In the words of Althoff and Rush, 'political communication is the transmission of politically relevant information from one part of the political system to another and between the social and political system.' Norbert Weiner was the first thinker to associate communication with control and command, and claims that it controls all-animals, men and inanimate objects within the universe.[7] W. Ross Ashby who is also regarded as the protagonist of this theory claims that cybernetics is the study of all political machines.[8]

According to Almond and Powell five types of structures perform communication functions.[9]

1. Informal face to face contacts, which spring up more or less independently of other societal structures. It pervades the most developed communication channels in any political system.
2. Traditional social structures, such as family or religious-group relationship. In modern society, its' role can be overlooked, but in traditional and developing societies their influence is very marked. Tribal heads and religious leaders play a powerful role as initiators or interpreters of information for large sections of the nation.
3. Political 'output' structures, such as legislatures and bureaucracies. The formal structures in a political system constitute a particularly important channel of information. The lifeline of communication holds the entire governmental structures together and makes possible coordinated implementation of laws and the mobilization of societal resources.
4. Political 'input' structures, including trade unions and similar interest groups and political parties transmit popular and special-interest demands to the political leadership
5. The Mass Media, including newspapers television, radio, magazines, and books constitute the last class of communication. They are most specialized and differentiated structures existing primarily for the purpose of communication rather than depending on it in the course of other activities. Freedom of Press since long has been integrally linked to maintenance of free government.

In free society, autonomy of such structures are maintained free from the domination of political leaders or vested interest of the society. In a totalitarian society, these structures are under great control of elites, and thus transparency is not satisfactorily secured. O.R. Young in his work 'Systems of Political Science' said that politics and government "appear in essence as processes of steering and coordinating human efforts towards the attainment of some set of goals."[10]

Almond and Powell have associated the dynamics of Political Communication with Political Socialization. They referred to processes like, and adaptation of the political system, expansion, social mobility, policy implementation and interest articulation. It is because the socialization process—which is carried on by family, relations, friends, educational institutions, political organizations and religious institutions, and is not homogeneous in nature.

Political communication is based on ideation, coding, decoding, feedback, action and reaction (see Figure 11.1).

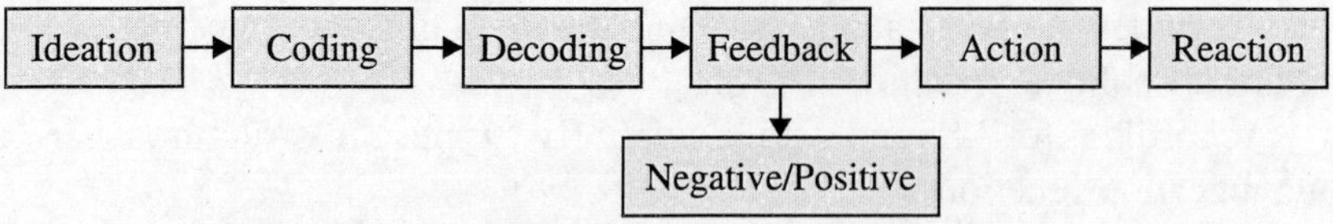

Figure 11.1 Stages of Communication.

ESSENTIAL QUALITIES OF COMMUNICATION

According to Almond, there should be four things in good communication. They are as follows:[11]

1. **Homogeneity of political information:** It should never be ambiguous or double meaning, it should not be mere jargon of words, and must not be contradictory in purport.
2. **Volume of information:** It should neither be too long nor too short. It should be adequate enough to be comprehended by receivers.
3. **Direction of the flow of information:** It should be in a single direction, if not, the purpose of the communication is defeated as the receivers may fail to act in accordance with the instruction.
4. **Mobility of information:** It cannot be rigid. It must be flexible enough to cater to changing demands of the time. It must be updated else may become anachronistic and future generation may be tempted to break it, leading to disintegration.

Information distortion can, of course, stem from many sources. But two characteristics of communications structures, which have been well-established in small-group research lend themselves to broad hypotheses. The first of these is that a given communication structure can process only a given level of information in a given period of time. When the volume and complexity of incoming information passes a certain point, either distortion or a considerable time lag will set in.

Effective activities by the elites in a large, centralized, and complex political system are hampered by the problem of the sheer volume of information, which may be processed upward through the bureaucracy.

All large organization leaders complain of the volume of relevant communications crossing their desks and of the impossibility of handling it all.

The problems of volume load and transmission error may affect elite's ability to make laws, which are effective and also responsive to social demands.

Sheer volume and complexity of information is only one of the problems, which faces elites of complex and centralized political systems. The distorting effects of bureaucratic hierarchy may also create considerable problems of information for effective decision-making.

Barrington Moore has emphasized the strenuous efforts made by totalitarian leaders to lessen their dependency on any single information source.[12] But

David Apter and others have suggested, in times of stress, the multiple channels are apt to reinforce distorted information rather than to correct it.[13] Therefore, no generalization can be drawn regarding the nature and role of communication (see Table 11.1).

Table 11.1 Styles of Communication

Open society (Liberal society)	*Close society*
Manifest	Latent
Diffuse	Specific
Universal	Particular
Neutral	Affective

Almond makes the implications of all these terms very clear by adding that a manifest political communication is a explicit message whereas latent is readable with expressive cues. A specific is the statement of a political event, whereas diffuse reflects all political events. A particular message is one, which cannot be easily transmitted beyond the limits of targeted audience. A general message is transmitted throughout the polity. A neutral information is an objective one combined with data, inference and analysis. An affective communication creates difficulties in analysis of the stream of political inputs and outputs.[14]

The open society is a democratic system where government is based on popular will and legitimacy. Such a political system is sustained by the presence of autonomous mass media, autonomous interest groups and informal personal contacts. There is no coercive government control on the channels of communication. The people freely use communication system, whereas in the totalitarian societies all channels of communications are controlled by the government. Regimentation and regulation characterize even the input part of the political system. There is no flow of communication either from the peoples' side or from the government side. Almond and Powell have observed that such a system may suffer from information distortion with serious implications.

TYPES OF COMMUNICATION SYSTEM

Communication systems vary from society to society. Lucian Pye has divided communication system in three categories.[15]

1. **Traditional/hierarchical communication system:** Such communication system is to be found mostly in traditional societies where there is dearth of professionally trained personnel to manage communication. Communication can be channelized on hierarchical pattern. Here the flow of information will be inadequate. Naturally, communication will be scrupulously manipulated by the clever hands for ulterior motive.

2. **Modern communication system:** It is characterized by the presence of trained professionals in charge of communication, like editors, writers etc. Communication is channelized through developed machines, which guarantee reliability, speed and response.
3. **Transitional communication system:** It stands between the two systems, i.e. traditional and modern communication system. On the one hand, communication revolves around modern, westernized, urban and educated people. On the other hand, the larger part of the population is under the influence of traditional communication system where the role of a priest or an 'opinion leader' or family ties becomes important.

Karl Deutsch's Communication Theory

Karl Deutsch in his classic work 'The Nerves of Government' has accorded so much importance to political communication that even the key concept like 'power' has lost much of its glamour. He called it 'the dynamic element of a political system.' Deutsch uses the method of cybernetics. He has based his analysis on cybernetics, because he found certain similarities in computer, brain and social beings. All the three are capable of receiving, transmitting, retaining and reacting on the information.

Every political system has a receptor dealing with the intake of information from internal and external environment. It also covers several other functions beyond intake like scanning, operation, data processing, load, lag, gain and lead.

Deutsch's Model

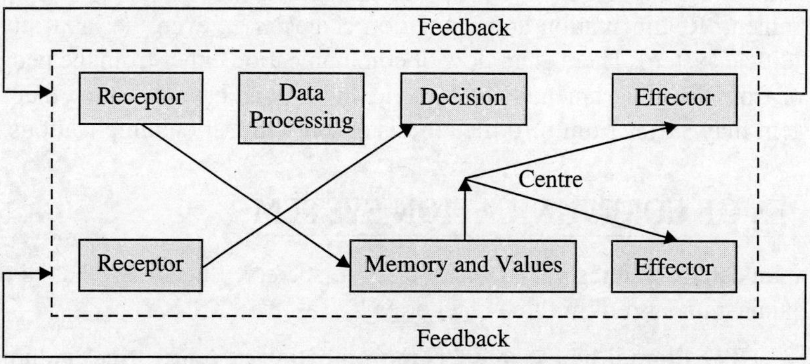

Figure 11.2 Deutsch's model of communication.
Source: J.C. Johari, *Comparative Politics*, p. 143.

The main features of Deutsch's neuropolitics may be thus summed up:

1. **Society as a machine:** According to Deutsch, the social system and political system as its part survive and develop because they contain

mechanisms which allow or encourage habit forming and other activities that go with this: the acquiring of information; the selection and development of norms relating to the use of information gained.

2. **New definition of politics:** One of the important concerns of Deutsch is to reduce the importance of the notion of *power* as a component of continuing political activity. To him, politics is concerned with the attainment of social goals; it is the sphere in which the decisions are made with respect to the whole society – decisions which are enforceable.
3. **New notion of government:** The function of government is to control the direction of information into or away from particular channels of communication. Thus, its main task is to 'steer' information rather than to exercise 'power' over the individuals.
4. **Miniature communications system:** The infrastructure of a political system is constituted by political parties and interest groups. They are interconnected and open, but they are also capable of steering themselves and with mechanism (human and institutional) that allow them to adapt and modify their structures and behaviour. Conflict between the political system and its subsystems should not be seen as 'contests of wills' but as the results of collusions caused because of the failure of steering facilities or of the signals of the system.[16]
5. **Homeostatis instead of equilibrium:** Deutsch desires to furnish a model that is not static but dynamic. That is, he is not for 'equilibrium' that indicates a stationary model of a political system. He calls the whole idea of equilibrium as being both mechanistic and excessively detached from the impact of environmental factors.
6. **Concept of feedback or servomechanism:** Feedback is, indeed, the key concept in the neuropolitics of Deutsch. It means a network of communications that produces action in response to an input of information and includes the results of its own action in the information by which it modifies its subsequent behaviour. Feedback may be negative or positive. A negative feedback system is one which transmits back to itself information that is the result of decisions and actions taken by the system, and which leads the system to change its behaviour in pursuit of the goals which it has set itself. 'Load' indicates the total amount of information which a system may possess at a particular time.

Deutsch suggests, the rapid expansion of communication may promote the consolidation of states whose people already share the same language, culture, and major social institutions; while the same process may tend to strain or destroy the unity of states whose population is already divided into several groups with different languages or basic ways of life.[17]

Various patterns of communication have great impact on conversion functions, such as rule making, as well as on socialization and on system environment. Making effective decisions requires accurate and relevant information. The decision maker must be aware of a variety of factors, such as local physical conditions, the attitudes of people involved, and the material available for action.

Karl Deutsch lays emphasis on the feedback approach, and claims that it is different from the equilibrium approach. The feedback process which is also known as servo-mechanism refers to a 'communications network that produces actions in response to an input of information, and includes the results of its own action in the information by which it modifies its subsequent behaviour in the equilibrium system.'

There are some more specific concepts that are central to an explanation of the operation of the negative feedback of the processes. They are:

Load, lag, gain and lead. Load is the function of input process of a political system. It refers to the extensiveness of the activities of a system relative to available feedback facilities and to the quantities of information involved in feedback processes relative to channel capacity. Load capacity is closely related to factors like responsiveness, fidelity, background, noise and distortion. Responsiveness refers to the facility of the apparatus in taking account of and handling incoming information. Fidelity refers to the accuracy with which the information is transmitted in the various processes of perception, selection and handling. The level of fidelity can be affected by several variables, like distortions and noise that tend to obscure relevant information. Lag is a measure of delay in reporting and acting on information about the consequences of decision and actions, whereas gain represents the extensiveness of a system's responses to this information following its receipt. On the other hand, lead is capacity to act in response to forecasts of future consequences as it is the case when one aims ahead of a moving object in order to hit it.[18]

Oran Young Suggested four characteristics of the functional aspects of political communication approach:

1. It is certainly related to an emphasis on decision-making as a process rather than on the results or consequences of decisions. As a result, the approach tends to focus on flows of information and on the forms of various structures rather than on the substance of either.[19]
2. It deals quite explicitly with various processes and dynamic movements so that it is quite well-equipped to handle questions concerning change.[20]
3. It is also attuned to the problems of evolutionary change, a fact which gives its real advantages in some areas of political analysis.[21]
4. It does consider certain externally imposed difficulties, such as overload as well as internal problems like steering pathologies and amplifying feedback.[22]

CRITICAL ESTIMATE

The communication theory emphasizes on the quantitative measurement of flows and not on the quality. Oran and Young pointed out that there could be false counting and distorting quantifications in the search for performance indicators. Man is not a machine, and thus, society cannot be regarded as a mechanistic arrangement. The entire approach depends on the extension of an analogy between a natural and a social system.

Deutsch model is highly complex, and can hardly be applied to explain the political phenomenon. Moreover, Deutsch himself admitted the fact that his neuron politics focuses more on the process than on the outcome. It tends to move away from being a working model and towards becoming a scheme. There is not only difficulty in applying models in social science; it is all the more difficult to make it useful for the purposes of social sciences.

The importance of communication theory is not universally practiced. It differs from society to society.

CONCLUSION

Despite of above criticisms, it cannot be denied that Deutsch has made outstanding contribution to the study of political science through his communication theory Deutsch's contribution is important in the sense that he has drawn the attention of political analysts to a very important direction, and has rightly claimed communication to be as nerves of government. Through his models, he has raised a number of questions regarding the performance of governments. Thus, we come to the conclusion that every social activity is possible because of communication. This is the age of communication. Whether it is good or bad, the impact of communication is very high. It is only the method and the way of communication, which either establishes the fact or distorts. We are living in a global village; any incident small or big has its impact on the whole world. Liberalization made it more receptive and sensitive.

Questions for Discussion

1. Define political communication. Discuss its importance in political system.
2. Examine the Deutsch's theory of political communication.
3. Describe the role of communication in a regimented and liberal society.
4. Write an essay on political communication.

References

1. Almond, G.A. and Powell, G.B. (1966), *Comparative Politics: A Developmental Approach*, New York, Amerind Publishing, p. 166.

2. Deutsch, Karl W., (1963), *The Nerves of Government*, New York, The Free Press of Glenco.
3. *Op. cit.*, p. 166.
4. Deutsch, Karl, (1963), *op. cit.*, pp. 1–15.
5. Chakraborty, Satyabrata (Ed.), (2005), *Political Sociology*, New Delhi, Macmillan India, p. 347.
6. North, Robert C. (1972), *The Analytical Aspects of Communications Theory*, in Charles Worth, (Ed.), *Communications Theory*, London, Longman, p. 300.
7. Weiner, Norbert, (1956), *The Human Uses of Human Beings*, Garden City, Doubleday, p. 15.
8. *Ibid.*, p. 2.
9. Almond and Powell, *op. cit.*, p. 167.
10. Young, O.R. (1968), *Systems of Political Science*, Englewood Cliffs, New Jersey, Prentice-Hall, p. 50.
11. Almond, G.A. and Powell, G.B., Jr. (1966), *op. cit.*, Indian Edition, 1972, pp. 178–183.
12. Moore, Barrington (1954), *Terror and Progress*, Cambridge, Harvard University Press, p.176.
13. Apter, David, (1965), *The Politics of Modernization*, Chicago, Chicago University Press.
14. Almond, *op. cit.*, p. 49.
15. Pye, Lucian, (1972), *Communication and Political Development*, New Delhi, Radha Krishna Prakashan, p. 6.
16. Davies and Lewis, p. 74.
17. Deutsch, Karl W. (1963), *Social Mobilization and Political Development*, in Harry Eckstein and David E. Apter (Eds.), *Comparative Politics*, New York, The Free Press of Glenco, p. 580.
18. Young, *op. cit.*, p. 53.
19. *Ibid.*, p. 56.
20. *Ibid.*, p. 58.
21. *Ibid.*
22. *Ibid.*

Suggested Reading

J.C. Johari, *Comparative Politics*
Gabriel Almond, *Comparative Politics: A Developmental Approach*
Alan R. Ball, *Modern Politics and Government*
Satyabrata Chakraborty, *Political Sociology*

Web Link

www.enwikipedia.org/wiki/pol.communication

12

Power Authority Legitimacy

CRUX

Power, authority, legitimacy and influence are of great significance in understanding politics and are crucial to political analysis. These terms are often used in political scenario but it is very difficult to define them precisely and more cumbersome to differentiate their inherent implications in the game of politics. In absence of standard terminology, Political thinkers fail to be in accord regarding the meaning and concept of power. However, if understood can enable political scientists to explain and analyze political life. Authority is essentially legitimate power and legitimacy is a harmonious blend of law and popular support. Influence is a informal impact of a personality for any length of time.

MEANING AND DEFINITION

Power is a key concept in the study of politics, for if politics is resolution of conflicts the distribution of power within a political community determines how the conflict is to be resolved, and whether the resolution is to be effectively observed by all parties; W.J.M. Mackenzie, speaks of a 'devastating confusion' in the use of terminology.[1] As there is no consensus on the meaning of influence, legitimacy and authority in corollary to power.

Political power is the capacity to affect others' behaviour by the threat of some form of sanction.[2] Political power is a relationship, if it so it is also necessary to discover exactly who or what has power in relation to whom or what. For instance, British Prime Minister is more or less like an American President which is based on statement of power relationship.

The measurement of power is a complicated process, and therefore, requires well-researched techniques. One way would be to examine the behaviour of those individuals and groups which have the reputation of being powerful, is order to see what part they played in the decision-making process.[3]

A second approach would be to begin with the decision itself and then seek to discover which individuals or groups influenced the process of decision-making.[4]

The first method may lead to the conclusion that certain powerful individuals influenced many decisions and that power was concentrated in a few hands. The second method may lead to the conclusion that political power is widely dispersed.[5]

Pluralists regard influence as analysis of distribution of power. Marxist contends wealth as source of power, which is unevenly distributed in the society, and is the source of exploitation. Max Weber's concept of power is based on domination, and he, unlike Marx is opposed to economic determinism. He believes in political autonomy and regards power as a negative variable at the polity level. According to pluralists, political power in liberal democracies is widely dispersed, that there is continual competition between organized groups, and that new groups are constantly emerging to maintain balance of influence in the political system.[6]

Further pluralists argue that the formal structure of government of liberal democratic systems is characterized by free elections based on universal suffrage, representative institutions, civil freedoms, and by a multiplicity of access points to the decision makers. Thus, although democracy is not possible in the older meaning of the term, groups do fulfil the essential democratic functions of providing control over the elites through pluralist competition.[7]

The two basic but fundamentally different uses of term 'power' says Warternberg, gives rise to essential ambiguity in the concept. Oxford English Dictionary provides two meanings. In its first meaning, it refers to do or affect something. Another meaning is possession of control or command over others domination; rule; government; survey; command; control; influence; authority.[8]

Power has so many connotations and its forms or types, mechanisms, or techniques are so diverse and variable in differential spatio-temporal contexts that it is difficult to arrive at a universal theory encapsulating all of these aspects. Everyone has power in himself. Everyone possesses the capacity to do or affect something and seeks to increase it. Nietsche's will to power in one sense implies this tendency in humans.[9]

Force, coercion, control or influence is interchangeably used with power, but all of them have distinct meaning of its own. Force is brutal manifestation of power. Influence is power sublime, and control has a wider connotation.

Some political sociologists like Dipankar Gupta believe that the discussion concerning power and authority has received a clear analytical focus in the wake of Weber's explicit distinction between two concepts. Weber looks at the distinction between power and authority with the yardstick of legitimacy in mind.[10]

J.R.P. French, Jr. and B. Raven in their book 'Bases of Social Power' identify five types of power as follows:

1. **Coercive power:** This is based on force and fear as the leader has the capacity to punish non-compliance.
2. **Legitimate power:** It is based on consent of the follower who desires to be influenced by the authority.
3. **Reward power:** This type is based on capacity to perform duties and enjoy power in fulfilling his needs and serving people.
4. **Referent power:** This is based on identification of the followers with their leaders as their role model.
5. **Expert power:** It is based on superior knowledge and skills of the leaders in modifying the behaviour of the follower.

AUTHORITY

The notion of authority is related intimately with power, influence and legitimacy. The term 'Authority' is derived from the Latin word *Auctoritas* meaning agreement or approval. Authority is defined in different ways.[11]

- Robert Michels defines Authority as a capacity, innate or acquired for exercising ascendancy over a group.
- Maclver says Authority is often defined as being the power to command obedience.
- Harold Lasswell defines authority as formal power.
- Robert Dahl regards legitimate power as Authority.
- Max Weber is the main protagonist of the development of the concept of Authority in twentieth Century. This German sociologist offered three pure types of Authority viz. (i) legal-rational, (ii) traditional (iii) charismatic.

Rational-Legal Authority

This type of authority is inherently different from traditional or charismatic authority. Here obedience is given to the impersonal order of norms and regulations, which define the status of a person issuing the command masses, follow the command with rectitude. (Obedience without doubt) Weber claims that such an authority resides with bureaucracy. Bureaucracy according to Weber, functions with immense knowledge, competent skills and neutral efficiency. Thus Weber calls this type of authority as desired and cherished one.

Traditional Authority

This type of authority is based on kinship and hereditary law. Efficiency is not considered as a criterion for selecting person for authorized office. It primarily rests on philosophy of 'Dynasty Rule' and resists innovation or change and only traditions determine the obedience to such authority. A glaring example can be cited of British Crown. This type of authority was not reliable and validated for a welfare state, in view of Weber. He believed that such an authority is losing its importance in modern age.

Charismatic Authority

This type of authority is characterized by individual's potential and management skills. It usually emerges in a moment of crisis, settles with resolution of crisis but soon, dies a natural death with normalcy of the situation. This is regarded as transitory form of authority. It is formed by impulse and fades with impulsive behaviour. Charisma creates followers and opponents simultaneously. We can here cite examples of Hitler, Mussolini or even Mahatma Gandhi. The end of such type of rule is mostly painful. Charismatic authority is based more on reverence than pragmatist assessment. Hence, such an authority facilitates integrated development, but usually is challenged by new group of elites who counter act the programmes and policies of the charismatic authority.

LEGITIMACY

Legitimacy is something lawful essentially because of popular support. The desire for legitimacy is deeply rooted in human communities, and is therefore, a universal phenomenon.[12]

The term legitimacy is derived from a Latin word *Legitimates* which means both legal and popular. Popular consent is one of the most important criteria of legitimacy despite the fact, that it is not the whole essence of legitimate governments.

The world legitimacy has different meanings. Plato claimed legitimacy in the theory of justice where each and every individual perform his stationed and assigned duties and does not meddle with functions of others. Aristotle regarded legitimacy as an essential ingredient of State till it exists for the good life of its citizens. The concept of legitimacy however changed its focus from public service delivery to power exercise. Medieval age of politics forwarded a new vista of legitimacy. Protagonists like Thomas Acquinas, St. Augustine and Marsiglio of Padua affirmed that kings are representatives of God on earth and will always be legitimate whether it gets popular support or not. City of God was the virtual nature of state. In an exceptional case, if king commits an error, God will punish him after the end of his life. People can never give them corporal punishment. This was called a dark age because legitimacy was covered with mysticism and speculation without any reason or scientific temperament. Legitimacy was challenged later by revolutionary views of John Locke an English Political thinker. He claimed that legitimacy of the government is based on agreement and consent of people. Leaders in a political system try to endow their actions with legitimacy. When the influence of the leader is clothed with legitimacy it is usually referred as authority.[13]

Weber regards rational authority as legitimate because in such, even rulers are subject to the rules of law and the authority rests on principle of lawful decision-making rather than upon the personal judgements of the ruler. Here both the ruler and the ruled are bound or constrained by law. But critics claim that legitimating process is not as simple as it is presented by Weber. The rulers claim legitimacy for their action on their own grounds and vested interest and the people's acceptance is based on their belief in the validity and reliability of the rule. Weber does not consider it necessary to explore the underlying complexity of the legitimization process. No attempt has been made to unravel the conditions for the possibility of non-compliance or of illegitimate power.[14] Weber's theory of legitimacy does not address the question why the ruled must comply with rulers' command, and if the latter's authority is believed to be legitimate what impels the former to believe in its legitimacy.

Robert Dahl rightly says that leaders in a political system try to convert their influence into authority. The greater the legitimacy of its institutions and processes, the lesser coercion will be indulged in governing and in responding to the government. Coercion is involved when a person or group of persons may be willing to submit to punishment or other forms of duress meted out by an authority deemed legitimate. Dahl affirms coercion and consent for defining legitimacy and authority consent elicit the approval of people based on moral righteousness. The authority is legitimate power when it is used in accordance with the subjects approval and the most effective method of assuring legitimacy to day is the creation of the belief that the government is being run to fulfill the aspirations of masses and to safeguard the welfare of the people. And the obedience comes from the side of subjects with firm belief of rectitude. The reposing of faith on leaders and getting the same is the reward of faith. Thus, effective performance of government and promoting values for political stability are of vital importance in creating legitimate rule or authority.

The formal structure of government of liberal democratic systems is characterized by free elections based on universal suffrage, representative institutions, and civil freedoms and by multiplicity of access points to the decision makers. Thus, although democracy is not possible in the older meanings of the term, groups do fulfil the essential democratic functions of providing control over the elites through pluralist competition.[15]

No government can be strong until and unless it holds full support. Rectitude, acceptance and affection make any government efficient and capable. The most accepted form of gaining legitimacy is to generate a mass feeling that the government strives to fulfil the aspirations of all irrespective of social divisions. This also, brings a sense of security for both the ruler and the ruled. The elements of legitimacy are found in all political systems whether democratic or dictatorial. Legitimacy creates an orderly change in environment along with maintaining equilibrium.

There is a thin line of demarcation between power and authority. This is essentially due to legitimacy.

Authority has certain distinguished features:

1. It is an institutional behaviour.
2. It is based on codification of rules regulations, laws-bye laws, precedents which are binding both on the authority and popular.
3. It is also moralization of power based on ethical norms.
4. It is pronounced in a well-defined hierarchical relationship, for example, parent child, teacher-student, ruler-ruled.
5. Authority is found at various levels from local to international.
6. Authority is essentially legitimate.

CRITICAL ESTIMATE

In a letter written in 1887, Lord Acton went well beyond these measured views in a sentence that has since become a cliché. "Power tends to corrupt and absolute power corrupts absolutely. Great men," he went on to say in words rarely quoted, "are always almost bad men, even when they exercise influence and authority..." Acton never wavered from this idea. "Among all the causes which degrade and demoralize man," he once noted, "power is the most constant and the most active."[16]

Dahl retorts that nothing is more likely to lead bad political strategies than to misunderstand "power," to misperceive "the power structure," for to be mislead about "power" is to be misleading about the prospects and means of stability, change, and revolution. The graveyards of history are strewn with the corpses of reformers who failed utterly to reform anything, of revolutionaries who failed to win power, of revolutionaries who successfully seized power and failed to make the revolution they intended, of anti-revolutionaries who failed to prevent a revolution, men and women who failed not only because of the forces arrayed against them but because the pictures in their minds about power and influence were simplistic and inaccurate.[17]

"There is no soul of man, young and irresponsible, who will be able to sustain the temptation of arbitrary power—no one who will not, under such circumstances, become filled with folly, that worst of diseases, and be hated by his nearest and dearest friends: when this happens his kingdom is undermined, and all his power vanishes from him."[18]

This however cannot be the absolute truth as one of the distinguished political philosophers has said that to the Greeks: while some men are corrupted by yielding power, others are improved by it...The full actualization of humanity would then seem to consist, not in some sort of passive membership in civil society but in the properly directed activity of the statesman, the legislator, or the founder.... The judge and ruler have larger and nobler opportunities to act justly than the ordinary man.... Politics is the field on which human excellence can show itself in its full growth.[19]

CONCLUSION

The analysis of the concept of power, authority and legitimacy is full of pitfalls rightly says Robert Dahl. He also provides remedial measures for mitigating errors in the description of decision making, influencing decisions, and being affected by the consequences of the decision, e.g. to avoid confusion of an actor's past or present power with his potential power, particularly by assuming that the greater the political resources an actor has access to, the greater his power must be.[20]

In this 21st century, power has assumed a new and a very significant role in manipulating the issues to have electoral gain. Democratic legitimacy endows leader with potential to convert influence into authority. No government can be strong unless there is wholehearted support of people. The end of 2013 Delhi assembly election results witnessed the arrival of Aam Aadmi Party (AAP) under the helm of Arvind Kejriwal, an engineer cum bureaucrat cum leader of common people. His anti-corruption drive with Anna Hazare made him representative of masses. Thus, power to continue for long requires legitimacy and acceptance in the minds of public. The best way to continue getting support of the people is to make them feel important and safeguard their interests. This will bring stability to the political system. Social change and legitimacy are interdependent. One ruler cannot serve the interest of all segments as they are highly diverse, but they can accommodate them in guise of appeasement policy. In fine, power is endangered with plurality of thoughts and culture, but it can be preserved with rational, legal and multi-pronged efforts.

Questions for Discussion

1. Critically examine the role of power in democracy.
2. Discuss the relationship between power and authority.
3. Highlight the role of legitimacy in formulating power.
4. Define authority and discuss its type as given by Max Weber.

References

1. Mackenzie, W.J.M. (1967), *Politics and Social Science*, London, Penguin Books, p. 225.
2. Dahl, R.A. (1964), *Modern Political Analysis*, Englewood Cliffs, N.J., p. 40.
3. Hunter, Floyd (1953), *Community Power Structure*, Nor Carolina University, Press.
4. Dahl, Robert (1961), *Who Governs*? USA, Yale University Press.
5. Castles, F.G., Murray, D.J., Pollitt, C.J., and Potter, D.C. (Eds.) (1976), *Decisions, Organization and Society*, 2nd ed., London, Chs. 19–23.

6. Ball, Allan R. (1983), *Modern Politics and Government*, 3rd ed., London, Macmillan Press, p. 29.
7. *Ibid.*
8. Chakraborty, Satyabrat (Ed.) (2005), *Political Sociology*, New Delhi, Macmillan India, Article by Deepak Kumar Das, p. 38.
9. *Ibid.*, p. 39.
10. *Ibid.*, p. 49.
11. Das and Choudhury, *op. cit.*, p. 160.
12. *Ibid.*, p. 169.
13. Das, Hari Hara and Choudhury, B.C. (1997), *Introduction to Political Sociology*, New Delhi, Vikas Publishing, p. 173.
14. Chakraborty (Ed.) (2005), Article by Deepak Kumar Das, *op. cit.*, p. 56.
15. Seymour Martin Lipset (1960), *Political Man: The Social Basis of Politics*, New York, Doubleday Company Inc.
16. Acton's letter can be found in his essays on Freedom and Power (Ed.) Gertrude Himmelfarb, Boston: Beacon Press, 1948, pp. 357ff. cited by Robert Dahl, *Modern Political Analysis*, p. 15.
17. *Ibid.*
18. *The Dialogues of Plato*, Trans. B. Jowett, New York, Random House Inc., 1937, Vol. II, p. 466.
19. Strauss, Leo, (1953), *Natural Right and History*, Chicago, University of Chicago press, p. 133.
20. Dahl (1964), *op. cit.*, p. 34.

Suggested Reading

Allan Ball, *Modern Politics and Government*

Satyabrata Chakraborty (Ed.), *Political Sociology*

Tom Bottomore, *Political Sociology*

Robert Dahl, *Modern Political Analysis*

Web Link

www.academia.edu/3482786/Authority_Power_and_Legitimacy

13

Political Change Conflict and Revolution

CRUX

Change is inevitable. Environment can expedite or hinder the process of change but cannot change the process of change. Change is the law of nature. It can be peaceful or violent, gradual or radical, core or peripheral, popular or illegitimate, painful or happy. Depending on the nature of change, various theories have been put forward. The fundamental truth is that change gives rise to conflict as people resist change. It therefore becomes essential to mobilize masses for making an orderly change and maintaining equilibrium as well. Amidst conflict and resistance revolution takes place, which can be either bloodless or destructive. This process of change, conflict and revolution in socio-political sphere eventually transforms society and its impact falls on the functioning of the political system.

MEANING AND DEFINITION

According to Indian mythology, there are four ages (*Yugas*)—*Satyug*, *Treta*, *Dwapar* and *Kalyug*, and as a cycle it changes as one comes after another (see Figure 13.1). Conflict of interests divides the society and gives birth to the struggle for power.

It's a continuous process.

The cycle of life itself witness innumerable changes, be it biological, psychological, intellectual, economical, social or spiritual. All these changes pass through inherent conflicts, which are settled with patience, understanding and courage. Values are undercurrent determinants of human behaviour, which is highly subjective. As a variable, it often changes with the passage of time, to cater to the new demands. The glorification of *Sati* system underwent a

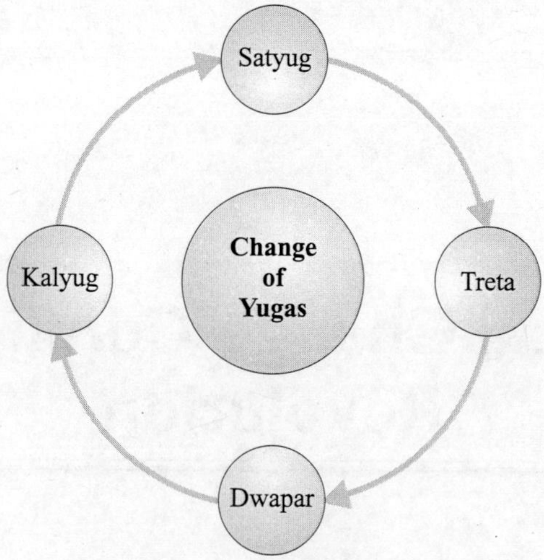

Figure 13.1 Yugas and its cycle.

change, though after a prolonged agitation by makers of modern India. History is replete with such examples, as a testimony to the fact. This is a universal phenomenon with varying degrees. Socio-political change is not always for better or desirable, as the changing norms of later Vedic society was more parochial than the early Vedic society. Earlier caste was formed on functional specialization, later it was based on kinship and hereditary law. The process of change therefore goes on from one generation to the other.

Change is a part of both the individual and the social life. No society can ever exist without bringing changes. But almost always these changes are resisted in every society, India being no exception to that. Every social change in India is vehemently opposed in the beginning because there is a psychological feeling that every change will do more harm than good to the society.

According to Jones, "Social change is a term used to describe variations or modifications of any aspect of social processes, social patterns, social interactions or social organization". According to Gillin and Gillin, "Social changes are variations from the accepted modes of life; whether due to alterations in geographical conditions, in cultural equipment, composition of the population or ideologies and whether brought about by diffusion or invention within the group".

MacIver has given a very simple definition of the term by saying that "Social change is change in social relationship".[1]

Social change cannot be studied in isolation, and as already said, each change is only a link in the series of change, which have occurred or are likely to occur.

Social change is law of society and also inevitable.[2]

In his book '*Social Change in Modern India*', M.N. Srinivas has defined "Sanskritisation as the process by which a 'Low' Hindu caste, or tribal or other group, changes its customs, rituals, ideology and way of life in the direction of a high, and frequently *twice, born caste*."[3]

THEORY OF CHANGE

Parsons interpret the aforementioned form of changes in the following ways:

One type of change is induced by endogenous forces, which is called 'structural differentiation', and the other as a result of exogenous forces, namely changes in the value system.

The first, 'structural differentiation', refers to the process by which the units of the system whose functions were fused, get differentiated.

Parsons' theory of change has always been criticised for its' failure to take conflict and change into account and persistent tension within and between systems.

No social system is as smooth as Parsons sees it. Violence, revolutions, unrest have become the order of the day.

Sorokin's Theory of Social Change

Sorokin's theory of social change pertains to the processes of cultural change in the ways, which become the life and death of a cultural system.

According to Sorokin, a cultural system grows in the following ways:

1. Quantitative increase such as the increase in human agents.
2. Qualitative increase, such as increase in the quality of such human agents.

Sorokin's theory of change has been criticised on the grounds that his theory neglects the fact that culture is a component system, i.e. an element of a particular dies out, does not imply that the whole external tradition decays.

SOCIAL WELFARE MOVEMENT

It is related to the concept of development. Therefore, directed social change is related to the planning of various policies and programmes in an attempt to bring about various welfare measures of the society.

Communist China and Cuba offer good examples of the success of planned change in peasant societies.

Although some of the gains have been a result of redistribution of societal resources. However, much we may value the democratic approach to change, it is not necessarily the most effective for all cultures, in all situations.[4]

"Political change of some kind goes on continuously in every society, in response to a variety of changing internal and external conditions, which include the relation to nature and to other societies, the interaction of groups within each society, and the unceasing circulation of personnel through the disappearance of older generations and the rise of new ones."[5]

These diverse influences have received unequal attention from social scientists, and the particular significance accorded to anyone of them has varied. Economic changes have been generally recognized as being very important, but their influence has been conceived in diverse ways. Marx's theory of the major historical transitions from one type of society to another discovers their prime cause in changes in the 'mode of production of material life', which result from the development of the forces of production and bring about a more or less rapid transformation of the 'entire immense superstructure', in a period of social revolution.[6]

With the growth of societies, war has tended to increase in scale and intensity, reaching a zenith in certain periods. One such period was the seventeenth century in Western Europe, an age characterized by the early development of capitalism and of nation states, and by religious wars; another is the twentieth century, during which wars of long duration and great destructiveness have been fought on a global scale. The warfare of the twentieth century has some distinctive features: first, it involves 'total war', in the sense that whole population and economies are mobilized for the prosecution of war; and second, it is marked by extremely rapid technological advances in the weapons employed.[7] More recently, however, there may have been a decline in the proportion of government spending allocated to the military, as a result of increased expenditure on welfare, at least in some countries.[8] However, there is no denying of the fact that defense and security of a person or institution draws more attention than anything else. Sovereignty, integrity of a state is important as it enables them to carve an independent foreign policy.

At various times in the past 'younger generation' has vigorously asserted its claims to cultural and political leadership; a notable recent example, which reawakened the interest of social scientists in the problem of generations, being the youth movements (especially the student movement) and 'youth culture' of the 1960s, which had, for a time at least, and perhaps in a more enduring way, a considerable impact upon cultural and political life in the industrial countries.[9] The total revolution movement initiated by Loknayak Jai Prakash Narain catapulted the entire political scenario and the dictatorial regime of Indira Gandhi got a setback. This movement was spearheaded by youth of India.

Mannheim's comparison between belonging to a generation and belonging to a class also provides a model for the analysis of other important 'common locations', such as those constituted by ethnicity or gender. The social movements based upon the latter affiliations, have assumed much greater political importance during the past few decades, and their development, like that of youth movements, needs to be examined in relation to wider social changes. Equally, however, they embody and express distinct cultural orientations, and like all 'common locations in the social and historical process' they have to be seen also in the context of cultural movements.[10] The Non cooperation movement of Mahatma Gandhi to the J.P. movement and the emergence of Janata party rule in 1977 can be cited as examples of youth movements.

Some kind of political change goes on at all times, produced by the succession of generations, the rise and fall of dynasties, competition among various social groups, economic and cultural developments, changing external circumstances, and more idiosyncratic factors, which can only be understood fully through detailed historical studies.[11]

Political changes of this sort may be gradual and minor but, they need not be peaceful. The replacement of a dynasty or other ruling group has frequently been accomplished by political assassinations or other forms of violence, yet without producing any fundamental change in the political system, still less in society as a whole.[12]

One of the principal forms in which this question has been discussed is the long-standing debate in the socialist movement about 'reformist' and 'revolutionary' political strategies.[13]

It is an important question how far political change, which almost always involves some kind of conflict, also tends to be accomplished by violent means. Even minor political changes may depend upon the use of force, in *coups d'etat* or sporadic revolts. Equally, however, some changes of a major character may be achieved more or less peacefully.[14]

The study of contemporary social changes in the Indian society cannot be dissociated from the initial social conditions of the society. Its historical roots provide a base for its evaluation. The social and economic distortions created by colonialism, emergence of the ideology of freedom movement, its crystallization in the form of the Indian Constitution, and the planning process for social transformation, are some of the historical factors which have set the direction and patterns of social changes in contemporary India.

Gandhiji was the pioneer in this thinking. Jawaharlal Nehru completed this process by evolving a model for Indian path to social transformation based on the parameters of modernization and integration.

Democracy, equality and freedom are revolutionary ideas. These are indeed difficult to realize through a single leap forward. To realize these ideals human resources need to be generated, which take time being essentially evolutionary in nature. It shows how revolution and evolution as social processes have an intimate relationship. One cannot be realized in totality without the other.

Revolution comprises a series of institutional innovations. At the national level, the electoral rights based on adult suffrage were introduced as an activity. It meant a great qualitative change in the social psychology of people and their social, cultural and political self-awareness. Social scientists have rightly called the elections in India as a measure of 'silent revolution'. It activated new social solidarities, satisfaction of people's aspirations. It also gave a new shape and hope to people's social and political consciousness.

CONFLICT: Meaning and Definition

Conflict is a struggle over values, status, power, or scarces, in which the aims of the conflicting parties are not only to gain an advantage but also to subjugate their rivals.[15]

Social conflict is a process of interaction between persons or groups with incompatible goals. Conflicts may also be classified in various other ways: for example, as large-scale or small-scale, as involving organized or unorganized groups, or as having various degrees of intensity. For analytical purpose, one of the most useful classifications is the following episodic conflicts are recurrent conflicts regulated by rules that participants and witnesses accepted as legitimate. Continuous conflicts are unplanned conflicts within a stable social system, terminal conflicts in which one participant attempts to disable another permanently.[16]

According to Duncan there exists inner conflict between 'natural' impulses and 'social' or 'culture' needs. A conflict is highly probable when the pursuit of an objective by one group interferes with that of another.

As conceived by Peter Harris, conflict is a negative interaction between persons and groups in pursuit of objectives, which are positively oriented toward one another and engage in social interaction to obtain the objective.

TYPES OF CONFLICT

There are different types of conflict. Here we are discussing major three types of conflict, although they are related and sometimes blend into each other have very different consequences for the social systems in which they take place.[17]

Social conflict as seen by Boskoff may be defined as those processes of interaction between persons representatives of roles, or other subsystems which serve by design or accident to (a) overcome or obviate resistance to the acquisition of desired facilities, resources or values and/or (b) interfere with the pursuit of some desired objective or value, Conflict, then, may be direct or indirect, personal or impersonal, bitter or effectively neutral. Conflict implies the existence of some differences between the parties in position, resources, values and goals. The actors are so committed to some values or goals that they try to manipulate (decrease or increase) the differences for their respective ends.

Time is a great healer of conflicts. As usual, overwhelming percentage of people have faith in resolving conflicts. In fact, it is only too evident that major political changes have very often resulted from violence, not only in revolutions and counter-revolutions, but also in wars of conquest or of national independence.[18]

But some important political changes have also been achieved by peaceful means. The welfare state, although its development has been influenced by the wars between nations, and accompanied by sporadic violence, is not essentially the product of either war or violent revolution.[19]

Any account of political conflict, however, which confined itself to these limiting cases of rational persuasion on one side, and the use of physical force on the other, would be seriously incomplete. Between these extremes there is a whole range of means which are employed to promote or resist political change: the reproduction of a dominant ideology, and the elaboration and diffusion of counter-ideologies; economic coercion of various kinds, exercised on both a national and international scale, by governments, large corporations and international agencies (for example, through economic sanctions against particular countries, through the lending policies of such agencies as the International Monetary Fund, and through the investment policies of banks and multi-national corporations); protest movements, more or less peaceful demonstrations, and political strikes.[20]

In the international context it becomes necessary to assess as to who have played the role of catalyst in bringing about political change. Harold Lasswell, an American political sociologist rightly claims that change is the initiative of a few, but it is translated into revolution with the strategy of propaganda; which is mooted by Elite and followed by masses. It requires critical analysis as Almond suggested that it is crucial to consider how conflicts between social groups develop within the limits of given structural conditions, how such conflicts bring about political change, and what kinds of social group playa major role in this process.[21]

Social changes may be simply defined as the process by which alteration occurs in the structure and function of a social system. Social change, strictly speaking, includes only those alterations that occur in the social system of groups. It is only part of a broader category called cultural change.[22]

Social change occurs both at the individual and social system levels. All social changes, changes in individuals and change through crisis and revolution should be understood as change in the social system as a whole. The process of social change includes the creation of new ideas, the way in which they are communicated and their consequences. The changes that ensure better life for the people are being characterized as progress or development.

Some other features of the process of social change may also be identified such as imitation, assimilation and acculturation. It is easier for the people of a developing country to emulate western culture, but however it cannot be termed as modernization, it is essentially westernization which erodes traditional values, as it also not easy for them to develop their own social and political ethos along with the changing values. It touches only the periphery and does not touch the soul of the society. This is exactly what is termed by Samuel Huntington as a 'Clash of Civilization'.

The first and foremost characteristic of change is that it involves two kinds of changes: quantitative and qualitative. The former type refers to many small shifts in the thinking and behavioural pattern, also shifting attitudes of diversified groups in a particular society. Quantitative change can be easily ascertained with some degree of exactitude. Data on quantitative changes like change in population (demographic change) in numbers and composition, population distribution and per-capita income are easily available. Qualitative change, on the other hand, is a kind of change that occurs sooner or later when the structure of the society as a whole is radically altered. The dismantling of USSR in 1991 and the formation of newly liberated democratic states like Ukraine and Tazakistan can be cited as some of the classic examples of qualitative change. The changing of ice into water (solid state to liquid) is the form of Marxian change. The making of democracy from authoritative polity, and adherence to qualitative norms of good governance from the closed society rule.

The process of social change can be viewed in the following sequential steps:

(a) invention,
(b) diffusion, and
(c) consequences.

Invention is the process by which new ideas are created and developed. *Diffusion* is the process by which these new ideas are communicated to the members of social system and the process by which a trait spreads from one culture to another. Those societies in close contact with others are most likely to change. Consequences is a process of assessing the impact of changes on the structure and functioning of the political system.

THEORIES OF SOCIAL CHANGE

There are different theories of social change and many writers have tried to explain all its ramifications. Each theory is different from the other. The social thinkers of nineteenth century Europe were fascinated by the problem of social change. The political revolution in England, America, and France due to industrial revolution started a new era and eminent thinkers gave their own perspectives.[23]

Evolutionary Theory

Auguste Compte (1798–1857), a French thinker was perhaps the most prominent protagonist of this theory. He explained social change as the outcome of intellectual development. He formulated his famous law of the three stages of intellectual development. It marked a progress from the theological mode of thought through metaphysical mode of thought to the positive mode of thought as represented by modern science.

The British thinker Herbert Spencer (1820–1903) was more comprehensive in his theory of social evolution and supported his analysis with empirical data.

He was to a great extent influenced by the theory of evolution propounded by Darwin. Spencer perceived that every society goes through a series of fixed and immutable stages, not because of deliberate effort on the part of the man himself, but because of the consequences of a cosmic design over which man has no control. He used the terms like *survival of the fittest* and *struggle for existence* to explain the superiority of western cultures over non-western ones. His elimination theory cannot be justified as it discriminate against the weaker section of the society. This cleavage eventually diminishes the quality of the art of governance.

Ferdinant Tonnies (1855–1935) protagonised the theory which was consistent with that of Durkheim. He felt that the individual's struggle for power as characteristic of urban societies would result in cultural disintegration. For both Durkheim and Tonnies, change did not inevitably bring progress, but it had both positive and negative consequences.

The British thinker Leonard Hobhouse (1864–1929) was strongly influenced by both Compte and Spencer. His theory of social change was worked out in a more rigorous way using historical and anthropological data.

Conflict Theory

The 'Conflict Theory' provides another perspective on social change. It was originally formulated by Karl Marx (1818–1883), the German thinker. His concern for change fundamentally differed from that of many other social theorists. Marx was interested in the most fundamental sort of-change, best characterized as qualitative rather than quantitative change. In Das Capital, first published in 1867, Marx argued that social class conflict is the most basic, fundamental, and influential source of all social changes. The classes are in conflict because of the unequal allocation of goods and services.

Conflict theory accounts for some of the major sources of social change within a society: the changing means of production and class conflict.

Sociological Theory

Max Weber, German sociologist, showed how religous ideology was influential in stimulating the growth of capitalist enterprise. He also placed great emphasis on the role of knowledge and ideology in stimulating change toward rationalisation. To Weber, change represents the development of rationality in the west, and is manifested in all major institutional spheres. Rationality represents a novel form of belief, thought, expression and action, which should be essentially above bias and prejudice.

Pareto, another leading sociologist advanced a thesis that changes within a society make for the rise of Elite position of men whose personal characteristics are appropriate to leadership under the circumstances of the time who in turn strongly affect those times.

Equilibrium Theory

The notion of equilibrium (balance) was borrowed originally from mechanics and biological sciences. The basic assumption of the equilibrium theory is that when change takes place in anyone component in a system, it tends to spur further change in the other elements, which accommodate the new element and integrate it within the structure. The best known equilibrium theory is the structural-functional view point analyzed by Talcott Parsons.

There are three types of change to which Parsons have directed his attention. The first, he describes as a circular process, which refers to the way in which the polity fulfils the function of goal-attainment under usual conditions of uncertain and scarce resources. The second type of change is the growth, which implies the amount of power increased or diminished in the polity. The third type or change is identified as the fundamental structural change.

FACTORS DETERMINING NATURE OF SOCIAL CHANGE

Factors determining the nature of social change are as follows:

Technological

The technology of a society is conceptually distinguishable from all else in that it consists of the devices, knowledge and skills by which men control and utilize physical and biological phenomena, and posses control over the antecedents and consequences of a given socio-political system.

Ideological

The term ideology is used in many ways. But generally speaking it refers to a set of interrelated religious or secular beliefs, values and norms that justify the pursuit of a given set of goals through a given set of means. Throughout history, ideologists, leaders or in other words translators are main agents in shaping the direction of social change, which can be either of a positive or a negative nature.

SOCIAL CONFLICT

Interests always clash, and hence, it becomes imperative for Elite to follow appeasement policy in order to accommodate diverse interests and bring harmony in the society. A sense of dissatisfaction creates cleavage, which is widened by power mongers, and thus clash becomes inevitable. Social conflict promotes social change as society attempts to accommodate itself to a wide variety of demands for social, economic, political and cultural reforms.

Social conflict has been widely defined. George Simmel claims that 'in every state of peace the condition of future conflict and in every conflict the conditions of peace are formed'. Social conflict may be defined as a struggle over values or claim to status, power and scarce resources. It may also be defined as struggle among groups over ideology or ways of life, or over power or scarce values, which can be explained in terms of social structure. Terms like conflict, cooperation and competition are interchangeably interrelated.

The term cooperation refers to the social process involving two or more persons or groups working jointly in a common enterprise for a shared goal. Cooperation is considered to be the most basic of social processes, because without it life would be difficult if not impossible.

The concept of *competition* is a basic process of social life. The living elements compete with one another, to have control over limited resources for survival. Society fixes the areas in which to compete and areas in which not to compete.

The concept of *conflict* is diametrically opposed to the concept of 'cooperation'. Conflict is a hostile struggle between two or more persons or groups for an object or value that each prizes. Conflict is also a process in which opposing parties attempt to injure, harm or destroy one another to achieve a certain goal. In society or polity cooperation, competition and conflict intermingles according to the interest and convenience of the conflicting parties.

Theories of Social Conflict

The analysis of the various conflict theories and their basic premises is of crucial importance to study social conflict into its proper perspective. All conflict theories can be classified into two broad categories—micro theories of conflict and macro theories of conflict. The micro theories of conflict lay emphasis on primacy of individual motivations. The macro theories on the other hand place emphasis on collective and social institutions and structures.

Marxian Approach

One of the schools of thought that have contributed immensely to the understanding of conflict is Marxism. According to Marx, there are two basic factors that lead to inter-social conflict-alienation, and class struggle. Alienation is the state of fix, which leads to compulsive aloofness, which Marx refers many a times. According to Marx, alienation arises when the working class in the capitalist society finds itself transformed into a commodity. The worker produces goods, which are owned by the proprietor of the capitalist enterprise. The other factor that gives rise to alienation is the division of labour in the capitalist society. The interests of the two classes of the society i.e., haves and have-nots are antagonized with each other which creates fight sometimes hidden, and sometimes open essentially leading to the ruin of contending class by a greater revolution.

Psychological

Ted Robert Gurr made an attempt to examine psychological factors to study social conflict. He developed his theory of 'Relative Deprivation' popularly known as 'R.D. theory' in order to study conflict behaviour of individuals. He defines relative deprivation as actions and perceptions of discrepancy between their value expectations and their value capabilities.

Socio-Political

There are many socio-political theories of conflict. One type of conflict, which is observed in multi-ethnic or multi-religious societies is internal war. The term 'internal war', here means a domestic violent process within a political order to change its constitution, rules, or policies. Some theorists have argued that conflict occurs not in conditions of abject poverty, but in times of relative economic prosperity. Others have postulated that conflict is most likely to occur when a period of economic prosperity is immediately followed by a brief period of economic austerity.

There are many causes of social conflict. In the first place, competition among individuals divides their interest. Secondly, the domination of capital in the capitalistic structures has created conflict. Thirdly, the struggle between two classes with opposing interests results in social conflict. Fourthly, social conflict may also be due to ideological differences. In a nutshell conflict is inherent and natural.

REVOLUTION: Meaning and Definition

The concept of revolution is multi-dimensional and covers not only the political but also the socio-economic and cultural aspects of human life. In broader terms, it may be identified with drastic changes in the political system whether peaceful or violent. But in specific terms, it has come to be identified as a sudden, fundamental and major transformation of a political system.

The term revolution is used interchangeable with outburst, upheaval, unrest, agitation, rebellion, revolt. In the words of Robert, a revolt is a collective and ordinarily violent action by which a group rejects the existing authority as well as the established social standards, and prepares to attack and destroy them.

According to Carl J. Fredrick, "Revolution constitutes a challenge to the established political order and eventual establishment of a new order radically different from the preceding one."

According to Laski, "Revolution may be defined as an attempt by the use of force against the government legally in power to compel a change in what are held to be, by those using such force, the actual purposes of the state."

According to Macpherson, "I take revolution to mean a transfer of state power by means of involving the use of threat of unauthorized force, and the subsequent consolidation of that transferred power, with a view a burning about a fundamental change in social, economic and political institutions."[24]

Evolution

In Plato's political philosophy, a revolution may be interpreted as the establishment of the ideal state. Aristotle was the first political thinker who made a detailed study of revolution, suggested its causes as a change in the constitution of the state. The replacement of one form of government by another or a change in the type of the rulers may amount to a revolution. Cicero, in his *De Republica*, defined the term revolution as "a disagreement among the citizens in terms of breaking up, because the citizens divide themselves into several factions". St. Augustine said that an unjust ruler should be killed to prevent things from drifting towards a revolution. Machiavelli wanted a revolution in Italy for the establishment of a strong Republican government. The credit however, goes to John Locke, who propounded a theory of revolution in his 'Second Treatise on Civil Government'. According to Locke, the government is bound by the terms of contract to guarantee the natural rights of the people to life, liberty, and pursuit of happiness, and the people have the right to Change the government by revolution, if it fails to protect or guarantee their rights.[25] Karl Marx has made a significant contribution to the theory of revolution, Fredrick Engels celebrated friend of Marx, aptly described Marx as a revolutionist, and continued to state that Marx has explained the major political revolutions of the modern age, as the result of long-term social and economic developments, in which new forms of economic exploitation and property ownership steadily develop. Thus, a political revolution also becomes a social revolution, when it involves the conflict of social classes.[26]

Although a revolution is primarily a political event; it is bound to have socio-economic and cultural dimensions. The political dimension of revolution signifies a change in the existing authority. The purpose of revolution is to change the 'unjust' authority by a just one, as perceived by those who spearhead the revolution. When there is the triumph of democracy over the forces of imperialism, it is called a liberal revolution. The American War of Independence of 1776, which overthrew colonial rule of Britain was the example of a liberal revolution. The establishment of the 'Dictatorship of the Proletariat' and the seizure of the power by the leaders of Communist Party is known as the Communist Revolution. Revolutions may be classified as 'limited' and 'unlimited' on the basis whether its implications are restricted to some aspects or they have wider manifestations. The 'negative' and positive' aspects of revolution also form the basis of classification of revolutions. In the negative revolution, political decay is taken as a sign of 'political development'. The establishment of Fascist authority in Italy in 1922, and Nazist in Germany in 1933.[27]

But no revolution can take place all of a sudden. For this, leadership is required to psychologically prepare the masses. It is difficult to bring a revolution in developing societies, which are opposed to violent changes. Without psychological preparedness of the masses revolution cannot even take place. In this connection it may be pointed out that revolution is not one time process but an ongoing and continuous process because the people are never satisfied with what the leaders of revolution promise to the people. In fact one revolution is the basis of another revolution or violent change.

There are several causes responsible for revolution. Political causes very much count in so far as revolution is concerned. Political leadership may be corrupt. The system in operation might have degenerated itself to the lowest. Political institutions might have become den of corruption and political leadership might have lost legitimacy. In the economic field there may be wide gap between the rich and the poor, and the former may be enjoying at the cost of the poor. The rich may be denying all chances of economic development of the poor. There may be uneven distribution of wealth. As the gap widens with that the chances of revolution also increases. Revolution comes in society when one race claims extreme superiority and begins to persecute and execute the members of other communities.

The leaders in a society exploit the discontent of the people against the established government which is called anti-incumbent principle and convert this into a revolutionary strategy to overthrow the existing order and establish a new order in its place. With the seizure of power by the revolutionary leaders, begins the second stage of the revolution. The third stage is identified with making desperate efforts by the revolutionary leaders to achieve the revolutionary goals and ideals. In the final stage, the revolutionary symbols gradually lose their popularity and hold on the people and dictatorship becomes more organized and strong and uses naked force for suppressing the people. At this stage, reconciliation between the overthrown authority and the new established order leads towards restoration.[28]

Theories of Revolution

Theories of Revolution are as follows:

Marxian Theory

He believed that capitalist societies always degenerate to the extent that even a little violent blow can serve the purpose and bring a revolution in society. He has said that in the first stage of revolution the proletariats will throw the capitalists out of power. They will form dictatorship of proletariat also known as socialist state but that will be a transitory phase. Next stage will come when a society will be established which will not be based on force and classes, the making of classless society in which state will also wither away. Revolution therefore according to Marx is the only feasible way to achieve communism.

Liberal Theory

Against violence based theory of Marx about revolution, the liberals are opposed to use of violence in bringing basic changes in society. Glorious Revolution of 1688 and French Revolution of 1789 was unjustified, and that those who brought about these revolutions were reactionaries.[29] They viewed and supported revolution only when existing rulers deprived the people of their rights or when the ruler was unjust. According to them, a revolution should be supposed to come when there is change in the constitution or in the form of government.

Idealist Theory

Propounder of this theory directed revolution towards a higher ethical goal of life. Hegel justified and glorified revolution and identified it with the process of unfolding of history and the development of civilization. Immanuel Kant, the father of modern idealism, described revolution as a fact of nature. A revolution is neither morally nor legally acceptable to Kant, if it enacted not with a view to· promoting national, but personal, class or regional interests. The people then lose faith in democracy.[30]

Idealist Liberal Theory

The supporters of this theory believe that a revolution is not merely a political process, but every event of historical significance directed towards a higher moral end in revolution. This theory of revolution is different from both the liberal and the Marxian theories. The idealistic liberal theory puts emphasis on an ethical, spiritual or cultural upheaval through which a group of persons seek to establish a new basis for existence. The advocates of this theory argue that, a revolution is not merely a political process, but a part of the unfolding of human personality. The idealistic liberal interpretation of revolution can also be noticed in M.N. Roy's philosophy of 'radical humanism, subjected to criticism that these theories are too abstract to be understood by the common man'.[31]

CONCLUSION

In the final analysis it may be said that a revolution is either a boon or a bane. A revolution is a means of change in the socio-economic and political life of the people. It liberates them from the shackles of bondage. Revolution, which ends only in violence and bloodshed or caters to the ulterior motive of an individual or a group should be rejected as it is harmful to the process of constructive change. Revolution with a purpose is fruitful, and is also desired when society is thoroughly degenerated and corruption, bribery, exploitation and oppression become the order of the day, no amount of reform can remove the deep-rooted wrongs from the society. At such a critical juncture, there is a need for a revolution to implement radical changes for establishing just and moral society. However, such situation demands the role of leaders who would emotionally surcharge public to a point of outburst against the forces of *stagnancy*.[32] Thus, the role of leadership in bringing about revolution cannot be underestimated. History is replete with such examples where leaders have played a vital role in augmenting revolution.

Any change is not a welcome step. It faces resistance, which gives birth to conflict between the two. One who wants status quo and the other who believes in change. Political change most of the time is the outcome of social calculations and economic unrest. A conflict gives birth to the political change, but always does not lead to a revolution.

Questions for Discussion

1. Discuss the relationship between social conflicts and revolution in a democracy.
2. Define revolution and discuss its various theories.
3. Social change is inevitable. Elucidate.
4. Critically examine the evolution and causes of conflicts in a developing society.

References

1. Ahmed, Shehzad (2007), *Social Justice*, New Delhi, Anmol Publications, p. 11.
2. *Ibid.*, p. 12.
3. *Ibid.*, p. 69.
4. *Ibid.*, pp. 3–7.
5. Bottomore, Tom (1979), *Political Sociology*, New Delhi, B.I. Publications, p. 79.
6. Marx, Karl (1859), *A Contribution to the Critique of Political Economy*, English Editions, Preface.
7. *Ibid.*, p. 82.
8. Janowitz, Morris (1978), *The Last Half-Century: Societal Change and Politics in America*, Chicago, Chicago University Press, pp. 185–189.
9. Bottomore (1979), *op. cit.*, p. 83.
10. *Ibid.*, p. 84.
11. *Ibid.*, p. 85.
12. *Ibid.*
13. *Ibid.*, p. 86.
14. *Ibid.*, p. 90.

15. Johri, P.K. (2007), *Social Conflicts*, New Delhi, Anmol Publications, p. 43.

16. *Ibid.*, p. 44.

17. *Ibid.*, pp. 44–64.

18. Bottomore (1979), *op. cit.*, p. 91.

19. *Ibid.*, p. 92.

20. *Ibid.*, p. 94.

21. *Ibid.*, p. 96.

22. Das, Hari Hara and Choudhury, B.C. (1997), *Introduction to Political Sociology*, New Delhi, Vikas Publishing, p. 196.

23. *Ibid.*, pp. 199–204.

24. Singhal, S.C. (2012), *Political Theory*, Agra, Lakshmi Narain Agarwal, p. 415.

25. Das and Choudhury (1997), *op. cit.*, p. 303.

26. *Ibid.*, p. 304.

27. *Ibid.*, p. 302.

28. *Ibid.*

29. Singhal (2012), *op. cit.*, p. 417.

30. *Ibid.*

31. Das and Choudhury (1997), *op. cit.*, p. 306.

32. Singhal (2012), *op. cit.*, p. 418.

Suggested Reading

Shashi Motilal and Bijayalaxmi Nanda (Ed.), *Understanding Social Inequality*

Hari Hara Das and B.C. Choudhury, *Introduction to Political Sociology*

S.C. Singhal, *Political Theory*

Web Links

www.marxists.org/subject/anarchism/bauer/political-revolution.htm

www.revolutionpoliticalmedia.com/

www.politicalconflict.com

www.phs.prs.k12.nj.us/ewood/AP_COMPA/CHANGE.HTM

14

Political Efficacy Mobility and Leadership

CRUX

The rectitude of followers on their leaders can be gained and sustained only when leaders take people in confidence and properly educate the electorate. The citizens' faith and trust in government have a positive impact upon the performance of political leaders. Political efficacy has a correlation with mass participation and elitist decision-making. Hence it is ideally expected that citizens would identify themselves with their national leaders, get mobilized and act as an awakened citizenry to promote and control political leadership for social welfare.

MEANING AND DEFINITION

Political efficacy means the feeling of the influence of the political events and actions upon the citizens. Political efficacy was first discussed in social psychology, a branch of knowledge falling in between sociology and psychology. Efficacy depends on the strength of the self, subjective ability, self-confidence and individual effectiveness. It has a crucial role to play in a democratic set up.

> Sense of political efficacy is the feeling that political and social change is possible and that the individual citizen can play a part in bringing about this change.[1] High levels of efficacy among citizens are usually viewed as desirable for the stability of democracy, because "in the modern democratic society, citizens should feel that they have some power to influence the actions of their government."[2]

The stability of political efficacy has often been questioned in regard to internal and external efficacy, which is moderately correlated. Some scholars also argue that more democratic forms of school of governance are able to contribute to higher levels of political efficacy.[3]

Easton & Dennis defines Political efficacy as, "a sense of the direct political potency of the individual, a belief in the responsiveness of the government to the desires of individuals, the ideas of the comprehensibility of government, the availability of adequate means of influence and a general resistance."

Types of Political Efficacy

1. **Opinion efficacy:** This means that the beliefs and the personal political opinions of the individuals are very important in determining the nature of politics.
2. **National efficacy:** In this type of efficacy, a citizen believes that he/she can influence the national government programmes and policies. National efficacy has been further subdivided into the following two types:
   (i) *Direct national efficacy:* This involves the feeling that the individual can directly influence the national government. This is the characteristic of the modern stable government.
   (ii) *Indirect national efficacy:* In this the individual feels that he/she is a part of an organization, which may influence the local and national political system and therefore, affect the functioning of government indirectly.

Efficacy is a quantified concept, which can be measured. Campbell measured the political efficacy of the American citizens for the first time in USA in the elections of the President. For this purpose, he used the following parameters of measurement:

- I do not think that the government officers particularly care about the ideas of the persons like me.
- People vote which decides how the government works in a country.
- Voting is the only means by which persons like me may determine how the government runs the things.
- Persons like me can do nothing to control what the government does.
- Sometimes politics and the term government are so complex that a person like me cannot properly understand as to what is happening.

The political efficacy may be measured by giving answers to the above questions (Hypotheses).

Another modified standard of measurement was given by Easton & Dennis. They measured political efficacy of the American citizens by modified types of the above-mentioned five questions. These modified forms were as follows:

- Voting is the only means by which my parents determine how the government carries on various things.

- Sometimes I fail to understand as to what is happening in the government.
- Whatever is happening in the government will always go on happening whatever the people do.
- There are some powerful persons in the government who are running the whole mechanism and they do not care about the ordinary persons like us.
- My family has no right to say anything about whatever the government chooses to do.
- I do not think that the men in the government care about what the family like that of us thinks.
- The extent to which these persons help in legislation is very much/ very little/nothing.

Determinants of Political Efficacy

The following variables are considered as determinants of political efficacy:

1. **Educational status of family:** Education provides the means by which a person may effectively interact with his environment. Most of the sociologists consider education and political efficacy as interdependent. But they differ on the opinion as to the political efficacy found on different levels of education. In a study in Western U.P. contradictory result were found about the political efficacy of a particular group of educated persons. This shows that there is no direct relationship between the level of education and political efficacy.
2. **Political interest:** Almond, Verba and Powell have found in their studies that a higher level of political efficacy is found among the citizens who have deep political inclination and hold voluntary membership of political or quasi-political organizations. Reading newspapers, discussion, demonstration promote public participation. Females tend to have lower level of internal efficacy. Effects of gender on external efficacy are quite low. Trust on political leadership has a strong effect on external efficacy.
3. **Socio-economic status:** From the studies by Almond and Verba it has also been found that more educated persons or persons from higher socio-economic status show more political efficacy, but some thinkers have pointed out that there is no relationship between social class and political efficacy. As in case of India less educated, low income group people give more vigilant responses unlike Aristotle's remarks, so generalization cannot be drawn.
4. **Age:** Different studies of the correlation of age and political efficacy have given different results. Aristotle claimed that middle class

community enables the government to perform effectively. Studies in Japan have shown higher efficacy among middle aged persons. S.M. Lipset talks about elderly persons who have greater level of political efficacy. He also affirms that politics is a masculine affair. Age, therefore, is not only responsible factor. Gender too has decisive role to play in political participation and this assumption is approved worldwide with varying degrees.

5. **Family and peer groups:** Experiences of the citizens in their families influence their political efficacy. For example, Psephologists' studies have shown that more political efficacy is found in the members of the family in which parents take more interest in political discussion, political participation and political activities. On the other hand, if the parents lack interest in politics, less feeling of political efficacy is found among the young members of the family.
6. **Religion and race:** Studies in USA, France and Belgium have shown the influence of religion and race upon political efficacy. India is no exception to it. Though being a secular state, Government of India keeps track of religious fervour and uses it keenly and deliberately as an appeasement policy for electoral gain.
7. **Rural and urban residence:** The residents of rural area are more influenced by versions of their role model as they fail to critically analyze the issues. Urbanization as an index of modernization has a definite impact upon the critical thinking. The electorates are aware and have an attitude to participate in politics for their own interest.
8. **Permanent residence:** Studies in USA, Great Britain, and India have shown that prolonged residing at a particular place increases intimacy and affiliation with the region, and therefore, it influences the political efficacy, attitude and voting behaviour. It is also known as regional proximity. The voting behaviour of tribe is significantly different from non-tribes. This shows the possible impact of regional culture.
9. **Psychological factors:** Studies by Robert Lane, and Harold Lasswell have shown the influence of psychological factors upon political efficacy. Intelligence has particularly favourable influence upon political efficacy. They are the champions of Psycho-pathology of Politics. Political efficacy is a complex phenomenon, which is influenced by many factors. It plays a significant role in making government accountable and responsible.

While understanding political efficacy perspective, it becomes clear that electoral participation is associated with political awareness, attitude and interest. Media plays a vital role in political communication and creates media hype on certain issues, like Anna movement in Delhi for the Jan Lokpal bill which not only gave birth to a new political party Aam Admi Party (AAP), but also got the Lokpal bill passed by the Indian parliament, same is the case with December 2013 Delhi bus rape case, which ultimately led to the formation of Justice Verma Committee and subsequent amendments in the IPC (Criminal Amendment Act 2013). Very closely related with the term Political efficacy is political mobility and political leadership.

Political Mobility

According to Karl W. Deutch, Social Mobilization is a process in which old social, economic and psychological commitments are eroded or broken and people become available for new patterns of socialization and behaviour. The term mobilize means organization for the purpose of war. Armies are mobilized during the wartime. The people are also mobilized to face foreign aggression. The political sociologist, however, is concerned with the social aspect of political mobility. Sociologically speaking, mobility is the result of urbanization, industrialization, globalization and commercialization. An important index of political mobility is the increase in the number of political and pseudo political organization and their membership.

The following problems have been pointed out in the concept of political mobility:

1. It fails to explain the process by which the people achieve new patterns of behaviour.
2. It has a tendency of accepting mobilization as an important symptom of the wide process of modernization.
3. It is vitiated by social determinism or the idea that social mobility is the result of some particular social changes.
4. According to this concept, the political development changes with the economic situations. It may be remembered that political consciousness is not correlated to economic progress. Some developing countries show more political mobility as compared to developed nations.

According to David R. Cameron the concept of political mobilization suffers from the following defects:

1. The politically mobile persons decide success of political activities. This is possible only so far as their ideology and organization modifies according to local needs and requirements.
2. Mobilization does not represent the forces opposing it, some groups do not participate in it as they consider the general policy of the government against their interest.
3. Mutually independent factors work in the process of political mobilization. It includes activities of political factions.

Traditionally, mobilizations involved regimentation. The organizational aspect of mobilization must be understood in order to comprehend it. The political parties compel their members to adopt new patterns of behaviour and conditioning. According to Karl Deutch, the political and the social changes are the index of modernization. Lerner has claimed that the extension of urbanization, literacy, growth, means of communication and the social changes consequent of it encourage more people to participate in elections.[4]

Political mobilization also includes political integration. Mobilization builds up the strength of a party. It increases the number of active members. It determines interaction of leaders and followers. It is the process of change and modernization. It is a result of some social changes. Social changes encourage political mobilization. Social factors however, are not the indices of political mobility. It is very much depends upon the policy of the government. Its' success depends on political organization and the factors and individuals influencing it. It is also influenced by ideologies. It results in the evolution of party system. It is a step in the process of nation building.[5]

POLITICAL LEADERSHIP: Meaning and Definition

The study of politics is based on the hypothesis that only few privileged people have the potential to rule over the masses. Monarchy talks of one man rule, Aristocracy of few persons rule and democracy though talks of the rule of (many) but encourages representative government which more or less is elitist rule in the shell of popular rule. Since time immemorial, it is an established fact that the capacity to rule is rare and masses have apathy and are unorganized which creates favourable situation for political leaders to flourish. Leaders have skills to mobilize population in any direction, sometimes for national welfare and at other times, for self-aggrandizement. They act like translators and they know how to sabotage an agenda and on the contrary, to blow any issue out of proportion for vested interest. Public is duped by the mesmerizing promises of leaders even in developed countries, like USA where participant political culture predominates.

Luther Gullick gives POSDCORB view of political leadership. This perception is keenly practiced in the discipline of public administration. This view is highly recommended for Prime Ministers of India, Britain, and so on.

POSDCORB stands for:

- *Planning:* Determining what is to be done to accomplish a specific purpose, objective, or the mission of the department, section, or unit.
- *Organizing:* The formal arranging and balancing of activities, the determination of who will do what, the assigning of authority and responsibility so that which is being planned will be accomplished.
- *Staffing:* All major appointments are made either by the leader himself or in accordance with the advice of subordinates.
- *Directing:* Assigning tasks, ordering, instructing, telling subordinates what to do in order to accomplish the objectives.

- *Coordinating:* Integrating a schedule of activities so that the plans will be carried out on time and also coordinates with the state head, subordinates and colleagues for optimum result.
- *Reporting:* All management staff is expected to give their report to the political leader which moves in hierarchy and the instruction is given by the leaders to the workers.
- *Budgeting:* Leaders have control over financial transaction as finance is the backbone of any institution. It is a good tool of control over the administration as it is rightly said he who controls the purse controls the power. In addition to it, there are different other methods of controlling. By checking the progress of work against plans or standards to determine if activities are under way and progressing satisfactorily; making corrections and adjustments or even new plans in the light of new developments or unforeseen circumstances. Implementing strategies for accomplishing or fulfilling the purposes or ends of the work plan also puts a control on the operation of the institutions.

Leadership is generally defined as influence—the art of influencing people to work freely toward the achievement of collective goals. Harold Lasswell regards leaders as most influential person possessing maximum of cherished values of the society. Models of excellent leadership, on the other hand, can be especially powerful in informing the study and implementation of public administration, offering salient models that can gain and maintain the attention of busy policy implementers. If better leadership 'prescriptions' are to be constructed, they will have to rely on lessons of successful leadership as viewed through new lenses.[6]

The literature of leadership focuses on partnerships as a means to attain the stated goals of a particular public policy. Programmes in public administration and public affairs, as well as in business and management, are expending much effort in undoing the assumptions that students bring to the classroom; as a consequence, they are ignoring the problems and constraints of such deep-seated, albeit simplistic, views. Those simplistic assumptions essentially follow an authoritarian, or Theory X, model.[7]

Leaders must be strong and decisive; under continuous pressure, they must act on the spot, reaching decisions without taking much time to consider the subtleties and implications of their choices.[8]

Leadership Theories

Leadership is a social phenomenon and therefore social scientists tried to define it in their own perspectives. However all were in accord that it is an essential feature of a democratic edifice.

Trait Theory

Trait theory embraces the idea that leaders are born; therefore, they must possess certain innate characteristics that make them well-suited for leadership. Height—justifiably or not—is thought to be a leadership trait; that is, there is the perception that taller individuals are better leaders. Height is often associated with dominance and power. Other leadership traits include intelligence, self-confidence, sociability, integrity, and diligence. Good reasoning skills and the ability to use language persuasively are positive leadership traits, but there is such a thing as being too smart for one's own good. Off-the-charts intelligence can sometimes be misinterpreted and can actually hinder a leader's ability to connect with his or her subordinates. The essence of leadership is getting people to follow. People are more inclined to follow someone who exudes confidence.[9]

Skills Theory

While trait theory emphasizes personal characteristics, the skills approach to leadership is centered on human capital. In other words, an individual's skills and abilities determine the extent to which he or she is fit for leadership. There are three distinct types of skills: technical, human and conceptual. Technical skill refers to the abilities and knowledge necessary to complete a particular task. Human skill is analogous to having interpersonal skill or simply being good with people. A leader with interpersonal skills is aware of individuals' needs and tries to motivate subordinates by fulfilling those needs. Conceptual skill refers to the ability to think critically and work with ideas. Long-term visioning, strategic planning, and analyzing hypothetical scenarios are conceptual skill sets. Conceptual skills are thought to be most important among top management, while human and technical skills are most important among middle and line managers.[10]

Style Theory

The style theory of leadership is framed in terms of task-oriented behaviour and relationship-oriented behaviour. Task behaviours deal exclusively with organizational goal attainment, while relationship behaviours deal with the socio-psychological aspects of managing employees—creating a harmonious and cooperative work environment and making sure that employees get along with each other and their supervisors. Style theorists examine how well leaders balance the need to achieve results (task behaviour) versus the needs of the people within the organization (relationship behaviour). Leaders who place a high priority on relationships as opposed to tasks are often described as 'country club' managers; they do a good job of creating a pleasant work environment and satisfying the needs of their subordinates. Leaders who place a high priority on tasks as opposed to relationships are said to be 'authority-compliance' managers; they are good at achieving organizational goals in an efficient manner. The needs of the employees are often disregarded, as workers are thought to be cogs within a machine-like operation. This type of leader is overly controlling. Leaders who place a high priority on both tasks and relationships are described as 'team' managers; they emphasize results and employee needs by incorporating participatory management.[11]

Situational Leadership

The idea behind situational leadership is that the leader must alter his or her leadership approaches based upon the circumstances (or the situation, hence the name). Observation of leaders' behaviours in a wide range of situations has revealed that leaders often exhibit one or a combination of these behaviours. Relationship or consideration behaviour deals with the extent to which a leader is likely to maintain personal relationships with supervises through communication, delegation, and offering opportunities for growth and potential. This is characterized by trust and respect, in addition to concern for their feelings. The leader spends time directing group activities; identifying tasks and how they should be accomplished, as well as defining patterns of organization, communication channels and schedules.[12]

Contingency Theory

Some leaders are better suited for certain situations. The idea behind contingency theory is fitting leadership style to a particular situation. The first step is to determine one's leadership style. Fiedler constructed a survey known as the Least Preferred Coworker (LPC) scale, the purpose of which is to determine whether a leader is more relationship oriented or task oriented. After assessing a leader's orientation type, the next step is to examine the leadership situation from three different vantage points: (1) leader member relations, (2) task structure, and (3) position power *Leader-member relations* centers on whether the work environment is positive or negative. Do the subordinates trust and exhibit loyalty to their leader, or is the opposite true? *Task structure* deals with whether employee tasks and responsibilities are clearly defined.[13]

Path-Goal Theory

Employee motivation is central to the path-goal theory of leadership. Leaders must embrace behaviours that deal with the motivational needs of their employees. In the context of path-goal theory, four types of leadership behaviours have been identified:

1. Directive leadership deals with clearly informing subordinates what needs to be accomplished, how it should be accomplished, and what the expected results should be.
2. Supportive leadership deals with 'human' needs (e.g., being friendly and approachable).

3. Achievement-oriented leadership deals with challenging subordinates to do their very best.
4. Participative leadership deals with including subordinates in decision-making.[14]

Transformational Leadership

Like path-goal theory, transformational leadership deals with subordinate motivation. Transformational leadership, however, goes a step further by focusing on the subordinate's values, ethics, long-term aspirations, and general workplace needs. Transformational leaders are charismatic, and serve as role model for their subordinates. They inspire by conveying high expectations. The transformational leader inspires intellectually by being creative and innovative and also by encouraging their subordinates to be the same way. This type of leader further emphasizes the importance of communication and listening, which aids in cultivating a workplace environment that addresses one's job-related and personal needs. There is a true sense of employee nurturing among transformational leaders.[15]

Life Cycle Leadership Theory

This theory deals with the levels of direction (task behaviour) and emotional support (relationship behaviour) a leader provides, while taking into consideration the subordinate's maturity level.

In the context of life cycle theory, maturity encompasses the following:

1. Motivation to achieve
2. Degree to which a subordinate desires and has ability to handle responsibility
3. Education or formal training related to tasks
4. Experience

While age may affect maturity level, it is not directly related to this type of maturity. As a subordinate's maturity increases, a leader's task behaviours should decrease and their relationship behaviours should increase to the point where the individual is sufficiently mature that the leader can decrease relationship behaviour (emotional support) as well. Style adaptability is the degree to which leader behaviour is appropriate to the demands of their situations and followers. A person with a narrow style range can be effective over a long period of time if the leader remains in situations in which his or her style has a high probability of success.[16]

Types of Leadership Power

Many leaders believe that their effectiveness as a leader is determined by how much and what kind of power they have. The five types of power are discussed below.[17]

1. **Reward power:** It is the ability to meet the needs of another, or control him or her, by giving rewards for desired behaviour. Pay, promotions, or bonuses may be ways that organizations exert reward power over their employees.
2. **Punishment power:** This is a coercive power, or the ability to deliver a painful or punishing outcome to another, and hence control him by his desire to escape the punishment. Firing, ridiculing, or disciplining an individual are common techniques of coercive power.
3. **Expert power:** This power is based on the ability to understand, use, and deliver information that others need.
4. **Legitimate power:** It is the control or influence that is exerted by virtue of the person's holding a particular position in the organizational structure. The power is vested in the rights and responsibilities of the position, not the person. Compliance with that power occurs because other individuals in the organization respect the organizational structure and the rights and responsibilities that accompany particular positions.
5. **Referent power:** Having the desire to comply with a leader's wishes because of your attraction to him/her describes referent power. Control based on referent power will be dependent on the leader's ability to persuade others to follow based on attraction or charisma.

The 'great man' or 'trait' theory popularised the conception of leadership in a way that the leader depicts him as one who has the most superior influence in directing group behaviour.[18] This school has not contributed to the knowledge as Plato in ancient political science talked of Philosopher guardian at the helm of city state affairs. Even the elitist theorists, primarily Pareto and Mosca have already established that those who have superior qualities shall guide and direct the mass of inferior qualities. No doubt the personal qualities and situation make individuals as leaders, but by this approach the student of leadership cannot articulate the types of role taking and characters of leadership building. Chambers has observed, in context of American party leaders that leaders develop unusual skills in intergroup adjustments and combination, in compromise, in aggregating as well as mobilizing interests; and practical rationalization of political methods and process.[19] This unusual skill elates a person to the position of a leader with many followers who repose their faith on his/her leadership.

Near to human relationist approach, group dynamists are intensively concerned with personal and group interactions as the most dynamic force for change in society. Emphasis is placed on process of interaction between leaders and group.[20]

The small group research approach attempts to analyze and measure interactions in small groups on the theory that findings are applicable to more complicated situations. Many of the specific studies are concerned with the emergence of leaders within the group.[21]

Early leadership research, focused on the leader himself, which is the virtual exclusion of other variables. It was assumed that leadership effectiveness would be explained by isolating psychological and physical characteristics, or traits, which were presumed to differentiate the leader from other members of his group. Studies, generally, guided by this assumption proved none too fruitful. Leaders do not emerge or function in isolation. They must be guided by certain emerging factors, like election rules, eligibility for leadership and other fundamentals of elections. Connected with this they must deal with followers within a cultural, social and physical context.

After examining various theories of leadership aimed at isolating the traits of effective leaders, we can agree to the generalization. "The qualities, characteristics and skills required in a leader are determined to a large extent, by the demands of the situation in which he is to function as leader".[22]

More recently, followers have been systematically considered as a major variable in research on leadership. However, the followers or the mass have not been taken as determinants of leadership. The existing approach examines the leader in the context of public, in which a leader is accepted by people, followed by people and is recognized by people. Leadership is a group mechanism. Though situation includes group also, it requires special emphasis and also a separate dealing. The most fundamental concept of sociology is that we live as members of groups.

The typology of leadership can be described threefold-autocratic, democratic and Laissez, faire. Autocratic type endeavours to control behaviour through unlimited and independent authority. The democratic type also endeavours to control group behaviour, but the control is not independent rather makes use of motivational forces within the group. The Laissez faire type rests on the autonomous characteristics of the group to the extent that the leader does not intervene. But more of these three kinds, in practice at least, exist in absolute form in a situation. Rather we may think of them as a matter of degree. All of them are blended in each situation.

Paul Pigors advocates that leader liberates the energy in opportunity to express them and in the service of which their powers can develop. The dominator dominates his subjects because by exploiting their momentary desires or weaknesses, he forces them into relationship which tends to keep them permanently subservient and in which he can count on them to remain under his control.[23]

"Leadership signifies the role of providing guidance, direction and coordination to a group, organization (political or otherwise), community, nation, etc. Leadership also refers to the capacity to inspire confidence in the rightness of one's purpose, courage in their collective execution and sense of obedience in the threat of resistance."[24] But the question is what makes a leader a political leader? The answer is power and authority. Here it must be made clear that simply holding an office does not make anybody a political leader as Blondel advocates "a head of the state is not a political leader if his or her activities are limited to being wholly symbolic. The English Monarch was a political leader in past, but the gradual abandonment of powers has restricted his or her power in public affairs to such an extent that there is no scope for political leadership."[25] As regards the role of a political leader, particularly in context of Indian society and that too of Bihar social milieu, the leader exercises over a wide range of subject matters comprising number of elements. These subject matters have been dogmatically decomposed into three areas[26]—diagnosis, prescription of course of action and mobilization of those who are made to ensure that action does take place. It can be safely argued in context of India that political leaders have come to be concerned, principally, with improvement of social and economic condition.

CONCLUSION

The concept of leadership is one of the basic and perennial issues of politics. But the study of leadership is not the sole concern of the political scientists. It is a social phenomenon and recently many social scientists have contributed to its literature. The meaning of the term leader varies from person to person. Political leadership can be best understood in terms of how it grows and functions. It can function both in democracy and dictatorship. There are many characteristics of leadership and is influenced by the social and political structure of that society.[27] In a way of conclusion it can be safely asserted that political efficacy, mobility and political leadership are co-related terms, which work together for democratic models and its success also depends on the mass support. Individual makes the difference in politics due to their personality. Personality may be the outcome of his social, cultural, educational, political, spiritual or economic background or environment but their political efficacy is too high. There are numerous examples like Subhash Chandra Bose, Sardar Patel, Jai Prakash Narain, Anna Hazare, etc. who gave a new direction to the Indian Polity due to their political efficacy.

Questions for Discussion

1. Define political efficacy and how it affects political leadership.
2. Discuss the various theories of political leadership.
3. Mass mobilization can be used by political leaders for institutional support. Comment.
4. Highlight the theories of leadership and how it affects political mobility.

References

1. Campbell, Gurin and Miller (1954), *The Voter Decides*, Evanston IL, Row Peterson and Company, p. 187.

2. Wright (1981), p. 69.

3. Mosher (1994), p. 83.

4. Cameron, David R., 'Toward a Theory of Political Mobilization', *The Journal of Politics*, Vol. 36, No. 1 (Feb., 1974), pp. 138–171, Published by: Cambridge University Press.

Article Stable URL: http://www.jstor.org/stable/2129113

5. *Ibid.*, p. 171.

6. Holzer, Marc and Schwester, Richard W. (2011), *Public Administration: An Introduction*, Delhi, PHI Learning, p. 321.

7. *Ibid.*, p. 322.

8. *Ibid.*, p. 323.

9. *Ibid.*, p. 325.

10. *Ibid.*, p. 328.

11. *Ibid.*, pp. 328–329.

12. *Ibid.*, p. 330.

13. *Ibid.*, p. 331.

14. *Ibid.*, p. 335.

15. *Ibid.*, pp. 335–337.

16. *Ibid.*, p. 340.

17. *Ibid.*, pp. 340–341.

18. Borgatta, E.F., Bales R.F., and Couch, A. (1954), 'Some findings Relevant to the Greatman Theory of Leadership', *American Sociological Review*, Vol. XIX, pp. 755–759.

19. Chambers, William N. (1972), *Parties and Nation Building in America*, J. La Palombara and M. Weiner, (Ed.), *Political Parties and Political Development*, New Jersey, Princeton University Press, Second Printing, pp. 79–106.

20. Lewin, Kurt (1952), *Group Decision and Social Change*, Swanson, New Comb, and Hartley (Ed.) *Readings, Social Psychology*, New York, H.M. and Co.

21. Gordon, Thomas (1954), 'Leadership: Shall It Reside in the Leader or in Group', *American Journal of Nursing*, Vol. LLV., pp. 1067–1088.

22. Stogdill, Ralph M. (1948), Personal Factors Associated with Leadership: A Survey of the Literature, Handbook of Leadership, 1774, Ohio State University, p. 63.

23. Pigors, Paul J.W. (1935), *Leadership or Domination*, USA, Houghton Mifflin Company, p. 74.

24. Verma, Ravindra Kumar (1996), 'Political Leadership: Issues in Concept and Approaches', *Journal of Social and Economic Studies*, Vol. 13 (combined), 1996.

25. Blondel, Jean (1987), *Political Leadership: Towards General Analysis*, New Delhi, Sage Publications.

26. Tucker, R.C. (1981), *Politics as Leadership*, 2nd revised edition, 1995, Brick Lecture Series, USA.

27. Das, Hari Hara and Choudhury, B.C. (1997), *Introduction to Political Sociology*, New Delhi, Vikas Publishing, p. 145.

Suggested Reading

Peter G. Northouse, *Leadership: Theory and Practice*, 3rd ed.

Marc Holzer and Richard W. Schwester, *Public Administration: An Introduction*

Hari Hara Das and B.C. Choudhury, *Introduction to Political Sociology*

Web Links

www.wisegeek.org/what-is-political-efficacy.htm

www.jstor.org/stable/2111730

www.huffingtonpost.com/tag/political-leadership

15
New Social Movements

CRUX

The desired change in the governance and community involves mass mobilization and participation. This can be either constitutional protest or sporadic outburst. The net result is transformation in parts or in whole, providing alternative ideologies. Therefore social movements are the forces, which seek to bring coveted change. This sometimes gets widely diffused. Such movements at times create conflicts as people resist change, and at a certain point, it takes the shape of popular movements. New social movements emerged in 1960s in India as a collective effort to give voice to the demands of a segment of society for socio-political action e.g. Students' movement, women's movement, ecology movement human rights movement and the like.

MEANING AND DEFINITION

Eighteenth century is known as the age of enlightenment, which opened a new vista of thinking in Europe and America. Thinkers of enlightenment age, such as John Locke, Thomas Jefferson, Thomas Paine and Voltaire fought against irrationality, superstition, rigidity and tried to incorporate ideologies supported by reason, logic, science and rationality. They believed that systematic thinking should be applied to all spheres of human activity. These ideas gradually caught the attention of Indian social scientists around the latter half of the 19th century. The constitution of India, adopted in 1950, can be regarded as the product of enlightenment convention. Other social movements that have come up in India claiming to represent the downtrodden have a very different ideology. It is trying to cover the common issues, which are otherwise overlooked. The work on environment disaster, inequality and human rights deprivation are some of the movements that can be pronounced as postmodern movement or precisely new social movement. Mahatma Jyotirao Phule, Periyar E.V. Ramaswamy

Naicker, Dr. Babasaheb Ambedkar, Mahatma Gandhi can be regarded as forerunners of enlightened humanist social movements.

Since 1960s, post industrial economy a number of new social movements flourished—among them the students' movement, various national and ethnic movements, the women's movement and the environment movement became immensely popular. It became extremely active in political life, and more attention has been given by sociologists to such forms of political action, which may be seen not only as constituting a basis or context for the development of more highly organized political activities but also as political forces in their own right, existing alongside and sometimes in conflict with, established parties and pressure groups. There was a paradigm shift from the conventional social movement in objectives, methodology and strategies. There are two claims of New Social Movement. First, that the rise of post-industrial economy is responsible for a new wave of social movement, and second, it is primarily different from previous movements. This new movement emphasizes social changes in identity, life style and culture instead of changing public policy. The protagonists of this movement belonged to the new middle class and comprised informal loosely organized social network.

We may define a social movement, in broader terms, as a collective endeavour to promote or resist change in the society of which it forms part.[1] One way of doing this is to point out the less organized character of a movement, in which there may be no regular or easily identifiable membership (no party card or dues), and little in the way of a central office or staff. Belonging to a movement is more a matter of sympathizing with a particular social outlook or doctrine, expressing it in everyday political debate and being ready to participate in occasional activities, such as demonstrations or riotous assemblies.

The distinction between a movement and a party, or other organized group, is shown also by the fact that large-scale movements tend to produce within themselves a variety of more or less directly political groups, as did the nineteenth-century labour movement; and the subsequent course of political action has then to be understood partly in terms of the relation between the broader movement and the various organized groups.[2] Indian National Congress was a movement for the liberation of the country, but with the independence of India it turned into a political party and ideological differences within the party emerged. So it can be assessed that there is blurred distinction between a movement and a party.

Having established a distinction between social movements and organized political formations, and indicated in a preliminary way the characteristics of social movements, it would not be too difficult to construct a typology of such movements, as a number of writers have attempted,[3] in terms of their size (number of participants), range (local, national, international), duration, objectives (specific or general, directed toward transforming individuals or supra-individual systems and so on.[4]

Lorenz von Stein, in his work '*History of the Social Movement in France from 1789 to the Present Day*,'[5] portrays social movement as a struggle for greater social independence culminating in the class struggle of the proletariat. Stein's book may have influenced the initial formulation of Marx's conception of the proletariat in capitalist society.[6]

To such an extent, which the social movement came to be largely identified, especially in Germany, with the labour movement. Of course, the identification was not complete, for as we have seen, Tocqueville attached greater importance to the democratic movement, animated and sustained by the middle class rather than the working class, but the impact of the labour movement grew steadily, and to a large extent it was represented as a prolongation of the democratic movement, as the term 'social democracy' indicates.[7]

Beyond any such differences of interpretation, in any case, there was a common recognition that in one form or another large numbers of people in the post-revolutionary societies of Europe and North America had begun to take part actively and consciously, in the construction and reconstruction of their societies.

It is on the basis of this historical experience of modern social movements, and with the aid of concepts which were introduced in order to understand them, that social scientists and historians have gone on to study movements of a similar though more restricted kind in other societies; for example, millenarian movements,[8] peasant rebellions,[9] the actions of 'crowds' and 'mobs'.[10] The value of such studies is that they show plainly the ubiquity of popular political action, which may be diffuse, lacking any clearly formulated doctrine, or expressing itself mainly in religious or cultural terms, but always which provides a matrix from which political organizations can emerge in favourable circumstances.

Nevertheless, the gap between movements of this kind (which have sometimes been called 'pre-political') and modern social movements remains large, for the latter exist on a vastly greater scale, are more directly involved in political conflict, are influenced by more rigorous and elaborate ideologies, and have as a rule a more enduring, less ephemeral, character.

Political apathy which was noted in many countries, and especially in Britain, in the mid-1970s, was itself an indication of the instability of existing political regimes, for it expressed a disenchantment with established political organizations and their policies.

The long-term success of social movements depends also on several general conditions. In the first place, it is essential that such movements should formulate a doctrine, which is capable of arousing enthusiasm and commitment to sustained political activity. The doctrine, which may be concerned with national liberation, the emancipation of a class, the emancipation of women, or some other general aim which is felt to be important by large numbers of people, has to include or be founded upon a social theory which can elucidate the principal issues, clarify the objectives and ways of attaining them, and outline alternative forms of society.[11]

There is a second important requirement for the success of a social movement. At some point in its development it must create more organized political groups, or convert or capture existing political organizations, which are able to engage directly in a struggle for power, and have the capacity to use power when they have gained it in order to reconstruct society.[12]

What is perhaps most striking in the past two decades is the way in which social movements of very diverse kinds have become an accepted part of political life in the democracies of the world and to some extent have provided models for movements in countries where the expression of criticism, dissent and opposition through formal political institutions is virtually impossible. There are three phases of new social movement.

The first is that in which movements such as the democratic movement and the labour movement in Europe, the women's suffrage movement and independence movements in colonial territories at a later time, or present-day, movements in autocratic states, provide only effective means for expressing grievances and seeking to bring about political changes. A second stage emerges when the achievement of representative government, universal and equal suffrage, and free elections seems to diminish the importance of political action outside the formal institutional sphere, although in periods of crisis social movements, such as the unemployed workers' movements or the fascist movements in some European countries, may develop. The third, present stage in the democracies seems to be one in which there is a considerable revival and proliferation of social movements as a more or less permanent feature of political life, reflecting a broader movement to extend democracy. Representative government, parties and elections are now seen increasingly as providing an essential framework, but as inadequate by themselves to establish a democratic society in the more radical sense of government by the people.[13]

Examples of new social movements include women's movement, gay rights movement, ecology movement and various social welfare movements. Paul Byrne, F. Parkin, Beuchler, Kendall, Alain Touraine, Ernesto laclau, Chantal Mouffe, Claus offe, Sundar Singh Bahuguna, Indira Jai Singh, Medha Patkar, are some of the main propounders in this field. It also promotes the role of civil society and NGOs for collective action rather than focusing on the instrumental role of the state.

HUMAN RIGHTS MOVEMENT

The realization that all human beings are born free and equal in dignity and rights, still violation of human rights continue to occur in various parts of the world gave rise to this movement. It is an effort to define human dignity and worth. According to United Nations human rights can generally be defined as those rights, which are inherent in our nature and without which, we cannot live as human beings. They are inalienable in the sense that it cannot be denied or taken away by any one, not even the government. No culture tolerates human oppression but unfortunately, it is in practice since time immemorial. In the garb of religion, custom, tradition and feudal mentality, human exploitation in its varied forms were legitimized. The social taboos in form of untouchability, gender discriminations, child labour, sexual abuse of queer sex, and so on and so forth created in egalitarian society.

Human rights movements in India, today, can be said to encompass a variety of groups and institutions that struggle for the rights of the marginalized.[14]

Human rights groups provide a way of mobilizing people on issues that are not mainstream. They are voices of the oppressed and the minorities. Very often, the agenda that they spearhead through long periods of struggle, gets adopted by the state as legislation, especially when new parties, alliances or groups come to power, or when those in power have to concede to determined struggles.[15]

The human rights movement represents the historical journey travelled by man ever since the beginning of the institutionalized political and social order. The first such effort was the Magna Carta of 1215 A.D., followed by Bill of Rights 1689 of England, American Declaration of Independence 1776, French declaration of three cardinal principles of democracy, i.e., liberty, equality and fraternity. More recently the first world war of 1914 led to massive destruction of life and property, and as a result in 1920 League of Nations was formed to combat war and restore universal peace and non-violence. This body failed to mobilize mass towards global peace, and as a consequence was made the declaration of the Second World War in 1939. It led to annihilation. The fear to face the dire consequences of third world war based on nuclear arms, where there will be no victor or vanquished left to taste the fruits gave rise to the formation of UNO in 1945, soon after the termination of Second World War.

For a long time several philosophers, social activists, political scientists, were continuously demanding for peace of human race. Their clarion call went unheeded. But the United Nations Declaration of Human Rights on 10 December 1948 turned out to be the first organized move for entire humanity under the Chairmanship of Eleanor Roosevelt. The preamble and the 30 articles contain principles of worth and dignity of human beings all over the world. Many countries came forward to promote respect for these rights.

The different phases of Human Rights movement created three different categories of human rights as follows:

1. **First generation rights:** These rights talk of civil and political freedom of an individual. Right to Life, Liberty, Political Participation, etc. are its various types. Such rights are guaranteed to citizens for their development and are safeguarded by the state as its primary obligation.
2. **Second generation rights:** These rights provide social and economic rights, which are fundamental for social security. It is

rightly said that he who suffers from panic of hunger finds no sense of liberty. So adequate means of livelihood is essential for the human growth.

3. **Third generation rights:** These rights evolved recently on the basis of international consensus. It includes cultural and environmental rights. This has given rise to group movement and attitude movement like gay rights, gender rights, students' rights, environment rights, child rights and the like. This type strictly comes under the category of new social movement. Despite its global impact, this movement has failed to produce desired results. Constitutions of the sovereign countries have incorporated them in their good governance plan of action, but even then, social ostracism prevails. Abject poverty and illiteracy, poses serious threat to the goal of attaining human rights for all.

A large number of human rights groups operate in various parts of the country. But they come forward to form a national alliance on a number of issues.

The groups also face many challenges in their working. Linking up with other mass movements and political parties, and responding to new issues that threaten life and livelihoods are some of the crucial challenges/tasks before the movement.

One of the most common state responses is the use of physical repression on human rights activists. Dr. Binayak Sen, a PUCL activist, was arrested by Chattishgarh government for helping naxalites to set up network against state. This arrest created doubts in the minds the believers of justice.

Critical reviews of human rights movements in India by Kothari and Sethi, note that not all limitations of the movement are on account of state repression. Nor are the challenges limited to majority parties in power. Rather many of the challenges relate to the internal structure of the groups and the differences between them. A further set of challenges arises in responding to new issues of development, environment, survival rights, and gender and community rights.

There are limits to voluntarism, which is the basis on which activists of the groups are mobilized. The volunteers often lose interest or drop out over a period of time, tired of the intense efforts in mobilizing against rights violation in isolated locations, working in remote habitation, or simply with the disappointment and inability to get adequate state cover.[16]

Human rights movements as an international basis for mobilization and resistance to oppression emerged after the Second World War with the International Bill of Rights.[17] Though the second half of the twentieth century has been characterized as 'the age of human rights' with the point being made that 'no preceding century in human history has been privileged to witness such a profusion of human rights enunciations on a global scale',[18] there have also been extraordinary silences. One such silence has been the entire discourse on the rights of queer people which finds no express mention in either the International Bill of Rights or the regional human rights conventions.[19] The silence is all the more extraordinary when one takes into account the fact that it was the supposed horror of the holocaust which triggered the development of international human rights law.[20]

In 1991, Amnesty International reinterpreted its mandate to consider as prisoners of conscience 'persons arrested for their homosexual identity or for engaging in consensual homosexual activity in private', despite considerable internal opposition.[21]

Human rights are useful when it comes to contesting abuses which occur in the public sphere, but when the discrimination is more subtle and depends on the existing social framework of homophobia, it becomes much more difficult to contest. Societal attitudes and prejudices which, cause discriminatory behaviour are difficult to target using human rights language. In such a case, the pain, isolation and rejection faced by those who come out is difficult to capture in human rights language. Further, human rights doctrines might also be unable to tackle structural factors and patriarchal structures.[22]

WOMEN'S MOVEMENT

The most far-reaching social development of the twentieth century has been the movement to end discrimination on the basis of gender. In this development, women themselves have been largely involved as activists, thinkers, researchers, organizers, and policy-makers. By the last decades of the twentieth century, women of all backgrounds, regions, religions, colours, races, and classes had moved themselves and their communities, though sometimes just a little, towards equality and empowerment. This popularly came to be known as feminism. The Oxford English Dictionary describes feminism as 'a movement supporting equal rights for women'. Feminism involves two facets—a social movement and an intellectual commitment. Both seek justice for women and the end of sexism in all forms. (Sexism means discrimination on the basis of gender). As a social movement, it aims in challenging and changing the relationship between gender and power that results in women's subordination, exploitation, and oppression in the family, place of work, society and in the state. The intellectual commitment has led to feminist writing and theorizing that question of male dominance, argue for improving the condition of women, and demand a public voice for women speaking on behalf of their sex.

In the 1960s and 1970s, feminists in the West used the term 'patriarchy' as shorthand to indicate the social system based on the domination of men over women. The term was taken from anthropology where it referred to a kinship system in which the eldest male, literally the father or patriarch was invested with authority over other men and over women. It saw the woman's role as bearer of children and caregiver and traits such as passivity and submissiveness were attributed to women. The sharp reaction of women folk all over the world put feminism under attacks from different quarters. The label 'feminism' acquired unpleasant connotations in all regions of the world. The year 1920s has been retrospectively identified as 'the first wave of feminism'. During this period, in the West, feminists fought for a legally and politically equal position in society. The period of feminist activity between the late 1960s and 1980s is seen as the second wave feminism. During this period, feminists saw cultural and political inequalities as inextricably linked.

Towards the end of the 1980s, feminists began to understand that the category of woman is far too universal and undifferentiated. In the context of caste, community and class among many other differences, it was no longer possible to talk in terms of women.[23]

The closing years of the 1980s and the 1990s have seen a new kind of political contest gaining in importance.[24]

This encouraged women to understand aspects of their own personal lives as deeply politicized and reflective of a sexist structure of power in a patriarchal society. The early 1990s saw the beginning of the third wave feminism. It arose in response to the perceived failures of the second wave and also as a response to the backlash against the initiatives and movements created by the second wave feminism. Feminists, during this period, were also influenced by post-structuralism and under its influence, they abandoned the concept of a single collective identity and accepted plurality and difference in different feminist positions and strategies. The second wave and third wave of the feminist movement are not seen as chronological. These may properly be understood as generational. The third wave feminism coexists with the second wave feminism.

In India lakhs of women participated in the struggle for liberation as followers as well as leaders in their own right. Women's organizations had begun to appear as early as the 1880s. In 1882, Sakhi Samaj was established in Calcutta and Arya Mahila Samaj in Puna. In 1917, Anne Besant established the Women's India Association in Chennai, and in 1927, the All India Women's Conference was established. These were organizations mostly of middle class women who had been beneficiaries of 'welfare' measures of Indian 'reformers'. Yet their establishment marked the emergence of a social ideology of gender roles. From its inception in 1885, the Indian National Congress exhorted women to join as equals. This can be cited as a glaring example of new social movement. In the new India that emerged after independence, the expectations of women which, grew out of their participation in the national movement remained unfulfilled. Men came to control the political process and women were ignored. In some respects, the framers of the Constitution, showed a high degree of sensitivity towards gender issues. In the Preamble to the Constitution, it is stated unequivocally that there would be 'Justice social, economic and political', and that there would be 'Equality of status and opportunity'. Article 14 of the Constitution ensures equality before law to all persons. Article 15 lays down that, 'The state shall not discriminate against any citizen on grounds only of religion, race, caste, sex, place of birth or any of them.' Article 16 provides for the equality of opportunity in matters relating to public appointment. But, in spite of these pious declarations, many sections of the constitution erode these provisions and deny equal status to women.

The United Nations initiatives in the early 1970s also played a vital role in strengthening women's movement. Yet, the character of the women's movement in India was different from west. It grew out of developments indigenous to India. Several features highlight this. In the case of India, the movement, even initially, was not confined just to the middle class urban educated women. In fact, in many areas, women at the grass-roots level took the initiative. Secondly, many of the issues that emerged were specific to India, arising out of the social norms and traditions in India. Finally, the movement was not necessarily confrontational. Men often joined these movements and the state often reacted positively.

The issues that caught public attention the most during the late 1970s were those of dowry and dowry-related violence. In the late 1970s and early 1980s many cases of rape of women caught the public eye. Women activists first tried to redress through institutions like the police, and the judiciary. But, the evidence began to highlight the indifference of the state, and as a result, civil society came forward to address the issue. In 90's empowerment cropped up as an agenda, in the women's movement. Women's invisibility in decision-making also became an issue for the women's movement in India. An analysis of women's participation in movements on many issues shows that in India the urban movements and rural movements have enriched each other. Organized political structures like political parties, trade unions, and other organizations played a role in mobilizing women in many of these movements. These grass-roots movements did not overtly attack patriarchal norms. But the very participation of women in activities like *dharna*, *gherao*, picketing, processions, and other such activities and the assumption of responsibility for social action in itself represented an assertion of that right to equal treatment. Activists themselves reported that the day-do-day participatory process made them experience freedom often far larger than their previous experiences at work. The process of struggle promoted their self-confidence, sense of power, and solidarity. India had seen an ongoing debate around the issue of meaningful participation in the political process. During 1992–1993, two constitutional amendments—73rd and 74th—were passed. These provided for reservation of one-third of seats for women in the urban and rural systems of local governance. By April 1993, these amendments were ratified by all the states. In 1996, a bill was introduced in the Indian Parliament to reserve one-third of seats in the Indian Parliament and State Legislatures for women. But, political paralysis gripped political parties and the bill was deferred. Affirmative action such as reservation of seats is not new in India, where preferential treatment to safeguard the interests of 'disadvantaged sections' of population has been an integral part of public policy as a result of new social movement. Many political parties like Congress, Leftist, BJP, etc. have assured women's reservation in parliament and assembly in their party manifesto. However, Bihar is the first state to give 50% reservation in Panchayati Raj Institutions for women, which is exemplary, and is followed by other states as well. Though we have not yet tasted the fruits of toil, however new social movement has paved the path for women empowerment.

ENVIRONMENTAL RIGHTS MOVEMENT

Until two decades ago, the world looked at economic status alone as a measure of human development. Thus, countries that were economically well-developed and where people were relatively richer were called 'advanced' nations, while the rest where poverty was widespread, and were economically backward were called 'developing' countries. Most countries of North America and Europe, which had become industrialized at an early stage, are economically more advanced. They not only exploited their own natural resources rapidly, but also used the natural resources of developing countries to grow into even larger economies. So as development progressed, the rich countries got richer while the poor nations got poorer. However, even the developed world has begun to realize that their lives were being seriously affected by environmental consequences of development based on economic growth alone. This form of development did not add to the quality of life as the environmental conditions had begun to deteriorate.

By the 1970s, most development specialists began to appreciate the fact that economic growth alone could not bring about a better way of life for people unless environmental conditions were improved. Development strategies, in which only economic considerations were used, had begun to suffer from serious environmental problems due to air and water pollution, waste management, deforestation and a variety of other ill-effects that adversely affected peoples' well-being, health and hygiene. There were also critical equity issues between the 'haves' and 'the have not's' in society, at the national and global levels. The disparity in the lifestyles between the rich and the poor were made worse by these unsustainable development strategies.[25]

This is creating vital environmental problems for our future generations. In order to propagate the notion of 'sustainable development' environmentalism emerged as a broad philosophy and ideology and a new social movement regarding concerns for environmental conservation and improvement of the health of the environment. Many terms evolved like biodiversity, eco-friendly, eco-ethics, etc. changes were made in individual behaviour and public policy. The first environmental movement could be seen in the works of romantic poet William Wordsworth in 19th century. In 1962, an American biologist Rachel Carson published a book *Silent Spring* discussing the impacts of indiscriminate spaying of DDT in US, and its serious impact on ecology or human health. In the 1970s, environmental movement gained rapid speed around the world.

Protection of environment became important in developing world. Thus, slogans like 'ecology is permanent economy' were used. In 1972, Stockholm Conference was held under the aegis of UNO on international environmental issues. There was an alarming realization that world is getting closer to natural catastrophe. We had several issues like global warming, depletion of ozone layer, green house effect which involved youth more than in any other social movement. Thus, in the 20th century, environmental movement gained both recognition and popularity. Many socio-religious organizations have come forward to support environmental issues.[26]

SOME ENVIRONMENTAL MOVEMENTS IN INDIA

There is no single environment movement in India. A large number of political initiatives, either single-issue-based or attempting to link a number of different issues-together with varying, and at times, competing ideologies-make up its mainstream.[27]

Silent Valley Movement

The Silent Valley Movement in Kerala in the 1970s was one of the earliest and fiercest ecological controversies in post-independence India. The protests were against construction of hydel power project on the Kunthi river in the ecologically rich region called Silent Valley.[28]

This movement resulted in cancellation of the project and creation of the park in 1980.

Chipko Movement

The Chipko Movement in Garhwal and Kumaon, in what is now Uttaranchal, also took place in the early 1970s, with people rising against the felling of trees for commercial reasons.[29]

It originated from Bishnoi community and picked up momentum in the hands of Sunderlal Bahuguna, whose appeal to Mrs. Gandhi resulted in the green-felling ban and whose 5,000 kilometre trans-Himalayan foot march in 1981–1983 was crucial in spreading the Chipko message.

Narmada Bachao Andolan (NBA)

One of the longest running battles against the construction of a dam has been that of the well-known Narmada Bachao Andolan, posited against the system of dams called the Sardar Sarovar Project, to be constructed on the river Narmada.[30]

It is a social movement consisting of *adivasis*, farmers, environmentalists, and human rights activists against a number of large dams being built across the Narmada river. Narmada Bachao Andolan, with its leading spokes persons Medha Patkar and Baba Amte, received the Right Livelihood Award in 1991.

Jharkhandi Organization Against Radiation (JOAR)

The Uranium Corporation of India Limited (UCIL) has three operating mines in Jadugoda, Bhatin and Narwahpur villages of Jharkhand. In 1960s, land was acquired in Jadugoda for constructing ponds, tailing ponds for dumping nuclear waste, and constructing residential colonies for the miners.[31]

ANALYSIS

Environmental movements can be understood to be a part of what are known as 'new social movements' of the 1960s and the 1970s across the world. These movements came up for reasons specific to the politics of that time. During the Cold War, the two competing ideologies of Liberalism and Marxism had so completely dominated political discussion by their fixed categories of analysis, that some issues could not be included in them.[32]

In India, persons like Medha Patkar, Maneka Gandhi, Sundarlal Bahuguna, Salim Ali, Bindeshwari Pathak, M.C. Mehta, etc. are major protagonists who championed the cause of nature protection through different styles. Their contributions are commendable.

For most of the last 30 years, these movements chose to remain outside of the institutionalized structures of politics. Disgusted by the corruption and cynicism of mainstream political actors, they did not participate in the political party/election process. They chose, instead, to challenge it from the outside, giving voice to concerns of people and making political accountability a reality, creating a base of legitimacy as the real representatives of the people.

While most of these movements by themselves were strong, it was hard for them to sustain struggles over a long period of time with limited funds and people.[33]

The principal achievements of the environmental movements in India are broadly of two kinds. The first is of introducing new rules and regulations that protected the environment and the interests of marginalized workers/tribals/peasants. The second was that of introducing new ideas in the public space that did not exist earlier, making it possible to influence public policy and other interventions in the public space.[34]

CONCLUSION

The various types of social movements very explicitly reveal the fact that it grows out of frustration, dissatisfaction and mass awareness. The recent anti-corruption movement of Anna Hazare is also a glaring example of such a movement. It essentially requires a leader to mobilize masses and translate the issue into political conflict and change. The initiative is always taken by a few (elite) and then they conspire and propagate to involve masses for social cause or goal. In fine, it is the result of awareness drive of media, zeal of a torch bearer and popular support for a longer period.

Questions for Discussion

1. Define new social movements. Critically examine its role in contemporary society.
2. Write an essay on women's rights movement.
3. Discuss the implications of human rights movement.
4. Environment issues are major concern for all. Elucidate.

References

1. Turner, Ralph H. and Killian, Lewis M. (1972), *Collective Behaviour*, 2nd ed., Prentice Hall, Englewood Cliffs, New Jersey, p. 246.
2. Bottomore, Tom (1979), *Political Sociology*, Bombay, B.I. Publications, p. 42.
3. Aberle, David F. (1966), *The Peyote Religion Among the Navaho*, Chicago, Aldine Publishing, pp. 315–333.
4. Gurvitch, Georges (1950), *La vocation actuelle de la sociologie*, Paris, Presses Universitaires de France, Vol. 1, ch. 5, *Typologie des groupements sociaux*.
5. Totowa, N.J. (1850), *Socialism and Communism in Present Day France*, Bedminster Press, Reprint 1964.
6. Avineri, S. (1972), *The Social and Political Thought of Karl Marx*, Cambridge, Cambridge University Press, pp. 53–55.
7. Bottomore (1979), *op. cit.*, p. 43.
8. Knopf, Alfred A. (1963), *The Religions of the Oppressed*, Oxford University Press, 1970.
9. Hobsbawn, E.J. (1971), *Primitive Rebels*, 3rd ed. (Manchester University Press, 1971), and Eric R. Wolf, *Peasant Wars of the 20th Century* (Harper & Row, New York, 1970).
10. Rude, George, *The Crowd in History* (New York, John Wiley, 1964).

    [The author notes how recent is the serious study of popular movements, and how widely diffused until lately was the ruling class view that riots and rebellions are simply the result of 'conspiracy.']
11. Bottomore (1979), *op. cit.*, p. 47.

12. *Ibid.*, p. 48.

13. *Ibid.*, p. 57.

14. Priyam, Manisha, Krishna Menon, Madhulika Banerjee (2009), *Human Rights, Gender and the Environment*, Noida, Dorling Kindersley (India), p. 84.

15. *Ibid.*, p. 85.

16. *Ibid.*, pp. 92–94.

17. *The Universal Declaration of Human Rights, The International Covenant on Civil and Political Rights and The International Covenant on Social and Economic Rights make up the International Bill of Rights.*

18. Baxi, Upendra (2002), *The Future of Human Rights*, New Delhi, Oxford University Press, p. 1.

19. *The European Convention of Human Rights, The African Charter on Human and People's Rights and The American Convention on Human Rights do not mention sexual orientation explicitly anywhere.*

20. Narrain, Arvind (2004), *Queer Despised Sexuality, Law and Social Change*, Bangalore, Books for Change, p. 15.

21. *Ibid.*

22. *Ibid.*, p. 28.

23. Priyam (2009), *op. cit.*, p. 178.

24. *Ibid.*

25. Chapter *Social Issues and The Environment, General and Environmental Studies* (2008), compiled by Patna Women's College, Patna University, pp. 397–402.

26. Baeyens, G. and Martinez, M.L. (2007), *Coastal Dunes: Ecology and Conservation*, Springer, p. 282.

27. Priyam (2009), *op. cit.*, p. 267.

28. *Ibid.*, p. 269.

29. *Ibid.*

30. *Ibid.*, p. 270.

31. *Ibid.*

32. *Ibid.*, p. 273.

33. *Ibid.*, p. 275.

34. *Ibid.*, pp. 276–277.

Suggested Reading

Tom Bottomore, *Political Sociology*

Robert Dahl, *Modern Political Analysis*

S.P. Verma, *Modern Political Theory*

Web Links

www.boundless.com,...,Social Movements

www.hrweb.org/history.html

www.britannica.com/EBchecked/topic/647122/womens-movement

www.cnn.com/...environmental.movement/index.html?...

http://sidshome1.blogspot.in/2007/09/new-social-movements-postmodernism.html

16
Politics and Society

CRUX

The credentials of any polity is formed by the norms of its society. Society is at times politicized by political leaders, political parties and interest and pressure groups. At the same time, political behaviour is guided by social variables like caste, community, region, language and the like. The relationship is dialectical sometimes in conflict and at other times in consonance and therefore, no one can claim to understand the nature and functions of polity or society in absence of either. Polity is the super structure and society provides the infrastructure but however, no political scientist or sociologist can affirm the autonomy of state or society.

AN INTRODUCTION

The terms state, government, and political system are not autonomous. They have partly overlapping meanings, but they have different nuances. Much of the continental European literature has taken the opposite course, thus considering government as one of the partitions of the state. Like the state, political system is also conceptualized as an entity embedded in its society and endowed with authoritative powers of allocation and distribution of resources and power. But political system is a more society-centred concept than the state. The state is supposed to be the most concrete institutional embodiment of sovereignty within a territory and political community.[1]

The monumental work of Kautilya on statecraft is known to us as '*Arthashastra*' which necessarily establishes the inter mingling of society with polity as depicted by Karl Marx and Max Weber and S.N. Eisenstadlt also comments that the major centre of Indian civilization was not political, but the religious-ritual one. Even in pre-modern India or in medieval period sovereignty and political authority allowed autonomy of the groups as an ally of the state. The British colonial states made a federal union which was unique as it comprised the mixed ideologies of medieval and ancient period significantly influenced by the colonial traditions. Thus, the modern nation state in India is the result of multicultural secularism and democratic developmentalism.[2]

The Indian political system like any other political systems of the world cannot grow in isolation. They require a foundation for proper sustenance and enhancement of administrative values. Indian political system can be best understood in connecting linkages with the social stratification and process. Social stratification is basically a sociological concept. It refers to the fact that both individuals and groups are indispensible part of the political system. Social stratification is a universal phenomenon in all societies. The social philosophers have tried to establish a dialectical relationship between the polity and the society. Karl Marx as a sociologist claimed that society precedes polity and Marxist sociology explained notion of power in relation to class. Max Weber, another renowned sociologist, propounded social stratification theory and introduced systematic, explicit and necessary differentiation into it. While Marx emphasized on economic factors, Weber propagated the concept of values. Both Weber and Marx analyzed polity in conformity with the society. Talcott Parson, Robert Merton and Emile Durkheim showed great interest in the dimension of social stratification as embodied in the political system. Contemporary students of political system strongly believe that polity functions in agreement or disagreement to social stratification of class, caste, gender, region, language or social status. As modernization proceeds stratification articulate the political behaviour along with the social mobility. The social tension, inconsistencies, deprivation, resentment and movement leads to conflict and conflict resolution which essentially remains the ultimate goal of any political system.[3]

Bernard Barber defines social stratification in its most general sense, as a sociological concept that refers to the fact that both individuals and groups of individuals are conceived of as constituting higher and lower differentiated strata or classes, in terms of some specific or generalized characteristics or set of characteristics.[4]

Melvin Tumin define social stratification as the arrangement of any social group or society into a hierarchy of positions that are unequal with regard to power, property, social evaluation and/or physical gratification.

In contrast to the above definition, which emphasise on inequality, Dipankar Gupta argues that social stratification is not only about inequality or hierarchy but also about difference or the facing of social orders as horizontal or equal blocks.[5] Social stratification has vital impact on the life of an individual. It is an ordering process in society, which carries within its fold—values and norms—and blends it with differences to produce a new era of multi-culturalism.

THEORIES OF SOCIAL STRATIFICATION

Theories of social stratification are as follows:

Marxian Theory

There are different theories of social stratification, which has made the phenomenon more intricate and analytical. Karl Marx propagated the first theory. He along with his celebrated friend Friedrich Engels in their monumental work entitled Communist Manifesto (1848) illustrates the concept of social stratification in its economic dimension—'free man and slaves, patrician and plebeian, lord and serf, guild master and journey man, in a word, oppressor and oppressed, stood in constant opposition to one another, carried out an uninterrupted, now hidden, now open fight.' This class-consciousness and antagonism is the result of production, profit and division of labour. For Marx, social stratification is nothing but a class struggle essentially ending with either transformation of the society (communism) or ruin of the contending classes (socialism). This theory was highly influenced by the works of Adam Smith who made a significant contribution towards the study of social stratification by his classical work 'Wealth of Nations'. But critics regard Marxian theory as a parochial one, because it fails to take into account the important role played by cultural networks like religious ideas, rituals, values and goals.

Weberian Theory

Max Weber was the next great thinker who propounded the theory after Marx. To begin with, he agreed with Marxian philosophy that group conflict is the basic ingredient of a society. While elaborating his theory, he gave a new dimension of status and power along with class. Weber considered Marxian theory as a pre-assumption not the real and scientific analysis. He was convinced that class consciousness is not only manifested in terms of matter, rather he believed that social stratification is also influenced by the role of status and power structure. Conflict of any form gets charged with translators (leaders). Weber argued that status reflects family origin, education, and influence in addition to wealth. The status groups are identified by their style of living, which gives them edge in the society and they command respect. Weber further defined power which according to him is not to be associated with industries or production ownership, but with vast bureaucracies that tend to become interconnected and interdependent.[6] Power signifies an imposition of will by the superordinate. When such exercises are carried out with the consent of subordinates, power becomes legitimate authority. Weber's work has been criticised, because he fails to measure and quantify both power and status.

Contemporary Theory

This theory was elucidated by Talcott Parson, Robert K. Merton, Wilbert E. Moore and Emile Durkheim. These thinkers laid emphasis on prestige as a dimension of social stratification. Prestige according to them is based on system of values and functionalism of structures. Contemporary students of the theory of stratification are divided into two groups—those urging for single dimension underlying social stratification and those who believe that social stratification may best be conceptualized as multi-dimensional.[7] In either case, the contemporary thinkers fulfill certain basic needs of complex social system as they focus on means-end relationship. This theory is however criticised on the ground that it regards inequality as a negative feature for an ordered society. Critics however, claim that social stratification is both inevitable and a necessity for bringing equilibrium in the social structure.

Despite criticisms, all the three above-mentioned theories have added a new vista in ushering modern functional and welfare state.

CLASS vs. CLEAVAGE

The oldest form of stratification of society is class. Plato conceived three classes based on the instinct of wisdom, spirit and appetite. The varna division of Indian society was based on functional division of four-fold classes which eventually evolved into the caste system. Aristotle analyzed the state in terms of three classes which were distinguished from one another by the amount of wealth each possessed, and the virtues or vices that each acquired as a result of its economic condition. He said that political community is best governed by the citizens of the middle class.[8]

In modern times, Marx, Engels and Adam Smith elaborately discussed the class concept. The class system is characterized by the consciousness of identity and solidarity within each class, and mutual hostility between them. The separate individuals form a class only in so far as they have to carry on a common battle against another class; otherwise they are on hostile terms with each other as competitors. On the other hand, the class in its turn achieves an independent existence over and against the individuals, so that the latter find their conditions of existence predestined, and hence, have their position in life and their personal development assigned to them by their class, become subsumed under it. This is the same phenomenon as the subjection of the separate individuals to the division of labour and can only be removed by the abolition of private property and of labour itself.[9]

Bendix and Lipset rightly emphasize that the important aspect of the Marxian concept of class is the individual's position in relation to the control over the organization of production. For example, if two men are carpenters, they belong to same occupation, but one may run a small shop of his own, while another works in a plant manufacturing pre-fabricating housing. The two men belong to the same occupation, but to different social classes.[10]

Classes represent the hold on economy on the basis of human action. The neo-machiavellian thinkers Vilfredo Pareto, Gaetano Mosca and Robert Mitchells creates an elitist class in the society who are wise enough to guide the masses and logically rule over the people. This view was further supported by Robert Dahl, Harold Lasswell, C. Wright Mill and some of the communist thinkers like Veblen, Burham, Djilas and Organski. Be it money or power or intellectual pursuits or birth with a silver spoon, all the forms of classes are superordinate and create cleavage in the society. But at the same time, all the thinkers believe that class is not to be blamed for social differences. Be it traditional or a modern society, differences creates competition and consciousness which subsequently lead to liberal representative politics. Ralf Dahrendorf proceeds with the inevitability of conflict in society, but rejects revolution as the means to achieve classless society as predicted by Karl Marx. They all are in accord that regulation of class activities is an ordinary, but necessary operation of the government. V.O. Key rightly says that the problem of social class in politics becomes a bit slippery when one attempts to define social classes. If a group has a sense of class consciousness, a sense of belonging to one group rather than to another, class takes on political significance.[11]

Max Weber modifies the concept of class as a comprehensive social category, by employing the concept of status based on social honour or prestige, to make a distinction between class and community, denying that class is a community; they merely represent possible and frequent bases for communal action.[12] Weber defines class as follows:

> We may speak of 'class' when (1) a number of people have in common a specific casual component of their life chances, in so far as (2) this component is represented exclusively by economic interests in the possession of goods and opportunities for income, and (3) is represented under the conditions of the community or labour market.[13]

For Weber, class is represented by the holding of property and economic resources which affect one's life chances under market conditions. Moreover, class is a situation to which individuals confirm according to their economic means and patterns of consumption.[14]

Criteria of Class Distinctions

There are various criteria on the basis of which class distinctions are being made such as status, occupation, birth, wealth, education, personality traits, etc. Status may be based upon the differences of birth, wealth, occupation, political power, race and intellectual attainment. In most cases, status is determined by a combination of two or more of these factors. Status is the social position that determines for its possessor, apart from his personal attributes, a degree of respect, prestige and influence. Occupation is an index of class in modern society. The rank of an occupation is usually rationalized in terms of its relative importance to the welfare of the community. When status is fixed by birth, then the class structure tends to be compact or 'integrated' and there is a rigid stratification. A class system came into being allowing persons to rise and fall on the basis of individual's achievement. Under modern capitalism wealth became a key factor in determining classes.[15] Knowledge skills and rectitude also create a superior class in the society as those traits are recognized as values highly cherished by people in the society.

CASTE vs. CASTEISM: Origin and Evolution

Caste is derived from a Portuguese term 'Casta' which means race or family. Caste is primarily a Hindu phenomenon which was commonly practiced in almost all religions of India. MacIver rightly believed that feudal system promotes caste and India is the glaring example of it. There are two schools of thought regarding the nature of caste. One school strongly believes that caste is based on functional specialization as was practised in early Vedic period. The second school contends that caste is determined by birth based on kinship and hereditary law. The *varna* system elaborated four orders: *Brahman* exhibiting wisdom, *kshatriya* having spirit and energy, *vaishya* predominantly business-oriented and *shudras* performing lower limb jobs. The untouchables, however, were not included in the order, and were called *atishudras*. These *varna* ranks were based on karma. But with the passage of time, Brahmans established their hegemony and gradually started exploiting the weaker castes and converted the karma principle into kinship. The British administration transformed the caste system into class order by introducing capitalist form of production in India. In colonial India two types of caste conflict were identified:

1. Backward caste peasants and upper caste zamindars; and
2. Conflict between *dalits* and upper caste Hindus. The caste–class symmetry followed a similar pattern even in post independent India.

CASTE: Definition and Meaning

Andrian. C Meyers rightly said that caste means different things to different people. Caste has assumed new role and function under the impact of modern forces and demands.[16]

Norman D. Palmer truly assessed that caste is losing its importance as a social factor and gaining importance as a political factor.

A.L. Kroeber defines caste as "an endogamous and hereditary sub-division of an ethnic unit occupying a position of superior or inferior rank or social esteem in comparison with other such sub-division."

A caste system can be said to exist when a society is composed of birth-ascribed, hierarchically ordered and culturally distinct groups.

It has been observed that, "caste is a system of stratification in which mobility, movement up and down the status ladder, at least ideally may not occur."

M.N. Srinivas as defines caste "as a hereditary endogamous, usually localized group, having a traditional association with an occupation and particular position in the hierarchy of castes. Relations between castes are governed, by concepts of pollution and purity and generally maximum commensality occurs within the caste."

"Every Hindu necessarily belongs to the caste of his parents, and in the caste he inevitably remains. No accumulation of wealth and no exercise of talents can alter his caste status, and marriage outside his caste is prohibited and severely discouraged."[17]

CASTE IN INDIAN POLITY

In India, caste is the central fact of social structure. It originally referred to the distinction between *Arya* and *Dasa* (slave). It is an endogamous kinship group known as '*Jati*', linked by marriage and lineage, and for the most part locally identifiable. It has experienced many changes because of the changing socio-economic forces in India.

Caste is a social custom, which all our great preachers and reformers have tried to abolish. The Brahmo Samaj, the Arya Samaj, the Ramakrishna Mission movement and the Theosophical movement, significantly contributed towards the end of caste division. Mahatma Gandhi was not only against the removal of untouchability but also against the caste system itself. The British Administration in India brought about a radical change by instituting a new principle of justice, which emphasized that all men are equal before the eyes of law. In the post-Independence period there have been many attempts to break the hold of the caste system. There have been legislative measures to outlaw untouchability and grant franchise to all regardless of caste considerations. Baba B.R. Ambedkar took up the cause of weaker sections of the society. Around 17.5% seats were reserved for dalits in Parliament and assemblies. The constitution of India incorporates protection and safeguards for SCs, STs and other backward castes. The forces of urbanization and industrialization have also contributed substantially to undermine the caste system by facilitating closer contact and collaboration between different castes. 'Sanskritization', which denotes that a status group aspiring to upward mobility in the system of social stratification, tends to emulate the lifestyle of higher castes, and seeks its acceptance within the great tradition of Sanskritic norms and the *varna* system.[18] This tendency among the backward castes, says Srinivas, is responsible for the continuity of the traditional structure of caste. Another concept that Srinivas uses is that of 'dominant caste'. He calls a caste dominant if it preponderates numerically over other castes, and also when it wields preponderant economic and political power.[19] But Srinivas makes an important point when he says that even a large and powerful caste group can be 'dominant' only if its position in the local caste hierarchy is not too low. The 'intermediate castes' such as the Jats in Uttar Pradesh, Punjab and Haryana, and the *Kurmies*, *Koeries* and *Yadavas* in Bihar (who once formed a Triveni Sangh), aspire for a dominant position not only in the villages, but also in recruitment to various elective and bureaucratic posts. These intermediate castes, in the process of their upward mobility, have emerged as rivals of the upper castes.

The scheduled castes, untouchables or *Harijan* (term not in practice today) still find it difficult to become a 'dominant caste'. Some outcastes in Bihar, such as *Dusadhs* and *Domes*, endowed with physical strength and traditionally in the service of landlords as musclemen, often clash with members of intermediate and upper castes. It is true that the caste system has been strengthened rather than weakened by the introduction of adult franchise and representative politics in India. According to a Report by Human Rights Watch—Dalits and indigenous peoples, known as scheduled tribes or *adivasis* continue to face discrimination, exclusion and acts of communal violence. Laws and policies adopted by Indian government provide a strong basis for protection, but are not being faithfully implemented by the local authorities.

There is another point of view, which holds that social stratification is undergoing a change as other elements of status, such as power and class are coming to the fore. Under the influence of modernization, secularization and democratization, caste is being replaced by social circles, social networks, political factions or factional alignments, pressure groups and even socio-economic classes. Andre Beteille argues that with the changes in the criteria of status in Indian society, there has occurred 'transformation from closed status groups based on caste to more open ones which accommodate other components as well.'[20]

According to a third perspective, caste has assumed new functions, such as the provision of educational, welfare and employment facilities, and other economic benefits for its members. But it is to be emphasized that caste functions today more as a political group than as a social or economic group. Hence, the phenomenon of 'politicization of castes' must assume a special significance in any discussion of caste-politics interaction. Rudolph and Rudolph, for instance, point out that caste is a medium of political mobilization, and an instrument of political education.[21] The non-Brahmin movement led by Mahatma Jyotirao Phule in Maharashtra, and by Ramaswamy Periyar in Tamil Nadu are glaring examples of caste consciousness and its liberating impact. Caste played a significant role in 'no-rent campaigns' in Bihar and Uttar Pradesh. These campaigns aimed at remitting the rent in years of scarcity or drought as well as reducing the cesses imposed upon the cultivators by the landlords or zamindars. Caste mobility movements mainly aimed for self-respect which formed an integral part of the campaign against social and economic exploitation.[22]

The Marxian interpretation is very different from other anthropologists. He talks of two castes—haves and have-nots. He blends caste and class into one frame. If we consider from Marxian angle then we find that caste carnage in Pipri, Kansara, Narainpura Belchi, Gonda and Lakshmanpur bathe can be termed as class violence as it depicts the clash between landless and land owners. Deeper study proves that it is a battle of deprivation and unfair distribution of resources.

Caste orientation of local politics has been the aspect most often emphasized. Panchayats and cooperatives are said to have come under the increasing control of dominant caste groups and their leaders. Caste is also said to fractionalize national politics. The preponderance of a certain caste (of Brahmins) in the central cabinet has been cited as an instance to prove the impact of caste.[23] A good number of voting studies, on the other hand, emphasize the role of non-caste factors in determining voting behaviour. Rajni Kothari and Tarun Sheth in their studies of Baroda East in the 1962 general elections, found that elite groups were driven by leadership and factional conflicts, and that few communities voted as a block.[24] Rajani Kothari a renowned Indian psephologist rightly says that caste and community are two easily identified social clusters, which are keenly and deliberately exploited by politicians for their electoral gain. Common people believe that politics is caste ridden, but in actual practice there is politicization of caste.

Swami Vivekananda said that in historic age caste had some value and importance, but in modern age it is totally perverted leading only to social division and suppression. The British colonial rule reaped its optimum benefit. All the states of India are caste ridden with varying degrees. Bihar and Eastern parts of U.P. is beset with caste tensions, However, ideology oriented states are also not untouched by the caste system. Kerala or West Bengal is also not free from caste politics. Comparative study reveals the fact that caste plays most dominating role in local politics. Its impact slightly diminishes at state level and minimizes at central level. Nowhere caste symmetry is overlooked. Right from distribution of tickets to voting behaviour, caste system predominates. The success and defeat of Political parties are to a great extent influenced by caste leanings. The defeat of the Congress in all the three by-elections in 1963 is also attributed to the state of Congress organization in those areas and the consolidation of the opposition forces.[25]

Now the political situation is very grim in India. In last 2009 general elections or in ensuing 2014 elections the agenda revolved and will continue to revolve round community, caste and personality politics even at the cost of national development. D.L. Sheth, therefore summarised that by drawing castes into its competitive structure politics finds its bases in society and by subjecting itself to the rules of competitive politics, caste acquires political characteristics. The controversy whether caste serves functions of politics or politics serves functions of caste is, therefore, misplaced. Indeed, the interaction between caste and politics should be conceived as a two-day process of politicization of castes and institutionalization of politics.[26]

Contemporary India is known as the country of youngsters. Young generations are more development oriented rather being caste oriented. So the wind of change is also blowing. Many political analysts believe that in 2012 assembly election victory of Samajwadi Party with two-third majority in Uttar Pradesh made a political history under the leadership of Akhilesh Yadav, which reflects the same. Delhi is another example. So, there is hope that India may come out of the caste-ridden politics.

COMMUNITY vs. COMMUNALISM

According to Cicero, religion is a word, which is derived from the verb *religare*, i.e., to inflict pains on oneself by means of repeated effort. Lactantius, a teacher of Latin rhetoric in the first half of the fourth century said it is derived from the word 'religare' which means to bind together. He interpreted religion as essentially a '*bond of piety*'. These two interpretations suggest the two-fold aspect of religion. On the objective side religion involves the recurring performance of certain human activities. On the subjective side it is the part of the hidden experience of the psychic life. Most of the definitions of religion centre on the concept of superhuman: belief and practice, rituals and rites. Vague fear of unknown powers, not the child of terror, but rather a relation of all members of a community at heart, and protects its laws and moral order." Religion, in any society, is the foundation on which the social values rest. Like marriage and the family, religion is present in every known human society. This implies that religion has a long evolutionary history.[27]

Max Weber, a German sociologist in his classic book, 'The Protestant Ethics and the Spirit of Capitalism', observed that religion responds to the basic human need to understand the purpose of life. Spirits may inhabit the bodies' of people and animals as well as inanimate phenomena such as rivers, mountains and winds. Those who practice theism believe in divine beings. They believe that God and Goddesses shape and influence human affairs. Gods are powerful beings worthy of being worshipped. This type of religion emphasises not on a belief in supernatural forces, spirits or supernatural beings, but on the abstract ideals of correct ways of thinking and behaving. Religion has been and remains a powerful source of social cohesion. Through religion, norms and values have always been internalized. It provides the main foundation on which the society rests. Emile Durkheim, one of the earliest functional theorists, noted the ability of religion to bring about group unity and cohesion. This positive notion of religion has been distorted with the passage of time and growing complexities. Religion is no longer related to ethics and morality. It has a perverted version glorified by the fanatics and power mongers. Electoral politics have further diminished the essence of religion. It is now more a community feeling than spiritualism. The gross downfall of religious divinity is a worldwide problem. Religion gradually emerged as a problem of communalism by which the entire universe is beset with. The dogmatic element of religion created 'ism' which lead to communal violence and frenzy. Secularization implies separation of matters ecclesiastical from matters temporal. Religious matters are to be separated from the other affairs—political, social and economic in actual practice, secularization has come through different stages in its historical perspective in India and elsewhere. It remains merely documented fact, but in reality, it is a redundant ideology for decision makers and populace. From the analysis of the major religions of the world we notice the existence of certain common elements in all of them. These include organizations, heads of organizations, festivals, rituals (prayer, emotion, belief) and followers. All religions have formalized social rituals. Many also have private rituals, such as prayer. Rituals are religious practices, which include viewing and handling objects. One of the functions of ritual and prayer is to produce an appropriate emotional state. In some religions, the participants performing rituals deliberately attempt to alter their state of consciousness. All religions endorse a belief system. It usually involves a supernatural order and also often includes a set of values to be applied to daily life. There is, however, variation in the belief system of different religions. Most of the religions have an organizational structure. Specialists are recruited and trained by these organizations. This facilitates interaction between the society and the members of the religion. If we address the elements we come to the generalization that they act like divisive forces and segregates humanity into conflicting groups. Too far fanatics and some anti-social elements of the society stretch it. Some Politicians flare up the conflict for their electoral gain.

Karl Marx argued that 'the ruling ideas of each age have always been the ideas of the ruling class. The dominant religion of a society is that of the dominant class'. Marxist scholars emphasized that the role of religion was to justify the political status quo. It was done by cloaking political authority with sacred legitimacy and thereby making opposition to it seem immoral. Religion, while encouraging the acceptance of supernatural causes of conditions and events, tends to create the natural and human causes of social problems in the world.[28]

Communalism is perversion of religion from a moral order to an arrangement of contemporary political convenience, from a sublime faith into a mean tactic of politics, from a spiritual end to a wicked immoral means. Communalism exploits both religion and politics, and is born out of a real or an imaginary fear of the other communities, either due to ignorance or due to misrepresentation. Communalism is opposed to secular change. It seeks to convert religiosity into political bellicosity.[29]

COMMUNALISM IN INDIAN POLITICS

Bipin Chandra in his famous work *Communalism in Modern India* observes: "the concept of communalism is based on the belief that religious distinction is the most important and fundamental distinction, and this distinction overrides all other distinctions. Since Hindus, Muslims and Sikhs are different religious entities; their social, economic, cultural and political interests are also dissimilar and divergent. As such, the loss of one religious group is the gain of another group and *vice-versa*. If a particular community seeks to better its social and economic situation, it is doing at the expense of other."[30]

It is an established fact that communal seeds in India were sown, nurtured and promoted by the British imperialism as a deliberate design to foster divide and rule policy. The type of politics approved, tolerated and encouraged by the British imperialism was only 'communal politics' as opposed to secular and national politics. Sir Syed Ahmad Khan wanted and also demanded to have a parallel socio religious reforms movement for Muslims along with Hindus, which was spear headed by Raja Ram Mohan Roy. This can be viewed as the initial mode of communal politics. The year 1857 witnessed the first war of independence which organized communal frenzy when rumour spread like a wild fire that the cartridges are greased with the fat of cows and pigs. Mangal Pandey's revolt added fuel to the fire. Lord Curzon played a nasty role in aggravating dissension by mooting the idea of partition of Bengal on communal basis in 1905. He got a setback by the Hindu-Muslim unity, but at least succeeded in creating cleavage. In 1906, Muslim league was formed as a challenge to Indian national congress, which was dubbed as a Hindu body. Though Jinnah was not in favour of its formation, but later played pivotal role in it. Morley-Minto Reforms Act of 1909 created separate communal franchise, which widened the gap between the two. Situation grew from bad to worse till Mahatma Gandhi arrived in India. He tried to rejuvenate the relationship, but it proved to be transitory. The intermittent events strengthened separatist tendency, and finally in 1940, Two Nation theory emerged. The appeasement policy of political leaders created a sharp divide. Mountbatten plan finally created Pakistan on 14 August 1947, thereby piercing a sword of communalism into the soul of secularism of Akhand Bharat (One India-United India). It was followed by a civil war and annihilation. It was considered to be the end of communal conflicts, but later proved to be wrong. The hypothesis was tested and was disapproved. In post-independent India, makers of the Indian Constitution were quite apprehensive of religious tensions. Hence, they incorporated religious freedom in the third chapter of Indian Constitution dealing with fundamental rights, running from Articles 25–28. India was declared a secular state where religion was made an individual affair and the state had no official religion of its own. This seemed not fairly good enough to bring communal harmony. Rising trend was witnessed in riots between the two, taking the form of a clash between Majority (Hindus) and Macro minority (Muslims). Mrs. Indira Gandhi, the then Prime Minister made a controversial 42nd constitutional amendment in the year 1976, by adding the term 'Secular' in the Preamble of the Indian Constitution. The pertinent question is whether such formulations can change the mindset of people or it is just a political gimmick? Unfortunately, the alien rule taught our leaders to exploit caste and community for their own vested interests.

Communalism in post-partition India struck stronger roots in medium-sized towns like Jabalpur, Jamshedpur, Aligarh, Moradabad, Ahmedabad, Godhra, Bhivandi, Bhagalpur, Kota, Muzaffarnagar and similar other places. Factors playing vital role are the following:

Muslim Marginalization

During the British rule in India, Muslims were economically and educationally more backward as compared with the Hindus. It was hoped that after independence when equal opportunities had been provided to all, the Muslims in India will also take fullest advantage of that. But even now the percentage of Muslims going to educational, technical, medical and other professional institutions is much less than their population. The result is that they are educationally as well as economically backward. This economic disparity between the two communities is creating wide gap and many misunderstanding; one community feeling that it is being constantly exploited by the other or that the richness of one is only at the cost of other.[31] Today Muslims constitute second largest religious community in India and second largest Muslim minority in the world. Thus they are called as 'macro minority' Still a sense of insecurity prevails which aggravates the antagonism between the two communities. A feeling of economic backwardness and a discontent that the benefits of modernization in terms of government's jobs, business and education opportunities, etc., have not been enjoyed by the Muslims promote separatist tendencies among them.[32]

Fanatic Organizations

The Hindu Mahasabha, Muslim League and the Akali Dal are some well-known communal parties in India. The Jammat-e-Islami, Jamaiyt-ul-Ulema, the Dini Talimi, Majlis-e-Mushawarat, the Iteahad-al-Musalmeen, the Ajnuman-e-Taraqoee-Urdu are other Muslim organizations which are informed of moreover the same communal ideology. They not only represent particular communities but also thrive on communal politics. Their leaders often use them to create communal tensions so that they may fish in troubled waters. Besides the communal parties, there are non-political organizations like Bajrang Dal, VHP, RSS, Jamaat-e-Islam, Islamic Sevak Sangh (ISS), the All India Conference of Indian Christians and Panthic Committee SIMI also responsible for sedition. These organizations declare that they have nothing to do with politics, but they have the backing of the BJP, the Muslim League and the Akali Dal. They encourage the half-educated and communally sensitive elements to indulge in communal fight in the name of religion.[33]

The emergence of communalism and the consequent threat to communal harmony in Kerala owe much to the increased activities of two fundamentalist organizations, the RSS and Islamic Sevak Sangh (lSS) of the Hindus and Muslims, respectively. The ISS is widely perceived as a Muslim Counterpart to the RSS. The rapid rise of the Islamic Sevak Sangh in Kerala is vitiating the atmosphere of communal amity in the State.[34]

Appeasement Policy

The caste-based politics in democratic India also helps perpetuating the communal cleavage. Lust for vote-catching on the part of nearly all the political parties adds fuel to the fire. The '*en bloc*' voting of the Muslims to the Congress is attributed generally to the pro-Muslim policies of the Congress government in power, and to the tendency of the Congress leadership to appease the Muslim in all possible ways. All political parties, be it in government or opposition, try to woo electorate by their mesmerizing talks and false promises. They dupe the masses by flattery and it often proves dangerous for democracy. Neither stern action is taken against the well-known anti-Hindu, anti-Muslim and anti-National leadership, nor do the governments take initiative in the matter of reforming the personal laws. Even politicians play dirty game on convicted terrorists at the cost on Nation's security. Uniform Civil Code remains a distant dream in the light of appeasement policy.

Electoral Politics

Today our politics is purely ballot-box oriented and elections have become end in themselves. Selection of candidate for a particular constituency is generally made after considering the relative strength of different castes and communities residing in that constituency. Communal loyalties of the voters are covertly and sometimes even overtly, appealed at the time of propaganda campaign. 'Mandal' and 'Kamandal' have become the punch words for contesting elections. All the political parties are interpreting secularism according to their own convenience.

Media Hype

The circulation of such openly communal newspapers as 'Akali Patrika', 'Sobat', 'Organizer', 'Marmik' and others are no less responsible, for the growth of communal forces. They often pass on news, which cause communal tensions. The textbooks on history written by different scholars have also helped perpetuating the communal cleavage. In fact, the Indian civilization and culture owe very much to both the people. "The Hindu and Muslim Communities came to imbibe each-other's thoughts and customs; and beneath the ruffled surface of storm and stress, there followed a genial current of mutual harmony and toleration in different spheres of line.[35]

After the partition of the country many among the Hindus forcefully argued that since the Muslims had got their homeland, India, which was now left behind, should be the land of the Hindus. The RSS always blames Muslims for any communal riot in the country and refuses to see the other side of the picture. Muslims always feel threatened by the Hindu majority in spite of government's affirmative policies. All these 'communal forces' among the Hindus have resented the concept of 'secular India' and demanded of the government to take steps to ban cow slaughter all over India, to introduce Hindu religious, ethical and spiritual teachings in educational institutions and to propagate the tenets of Hinduism through such mass media as the press and radio.[36]

Political Apathy

Governments fail to assess the dire consequences of communal war. They either overlook it or resolve it for a short period. They have never tried to put an end to it forever. For securing advantageous position in the struggle for power, political parties do not even hesitate to use the communal factor. The government first gave in to Muslim fundamentalists on the Shah Bano case, and later it equally blatantly gave it to Hindu fundamentalists. Both these acts were used for election propaganda. It was pure political opportunism. No conviction was involved in either case. The partition of the Punjab brought about the most radical change in the life of this region, since the fall of the Sikh Empire.

Issue of Conversion

Constitutional law does not permit the mass conversion in India. Before independence, Christian Missionaries while taking the benefit of Hindu orthodoxies promoted conversion at a large scale, which posed a positive threat to the unity and integrity of India. There was a lot of resentment, which was suppressed by the ruthless attitude of Britishers. This followed even in post independent phase in the closet. Sometimes, coercive conversion made the headlines in the news. Dr. Graham Stuart Staines was an Australian Christian missionary, who along with his two sons Philip and Timothy was burnt to death by Hindu fanatics who alleged that Staines had forcibly converted or lured many Hindus into Christianity. Such incidents also provoked riots and ruined the unity of Indian nation.

The following remedies have been suggested for eradicating communalism:

1. Banning communal organizations without fear or bias whatsoever. Conviction of government should be visible.
2. Communities should learn to either separate religion from politics or include morality in religious fervour.
3. The law and order machinery should be depoliticized. The District Magistrate and SP be made directly responsible for communal riots, and such other occurrences in the areas under their jurisdiction.
4. Positive measures include educative efforts to inculcate among the people mutual respect and tolerance towards all the religion, to mitigate value erosion and facilitate moral education and civic education.
5. Removal of communal/controversial contents in textbooks and reading material prepared for students.
6. T.V., radio and media must behave in a more responsible manner in dealing with such sensitive issues. They should avoid coverage of news and views, which are likely to flourish communal prejudice and hatred.

Nationalism can infuse spirit of belongingness which can definitely prevent communal oppression. Government must be competent enough to set limits to undue dominance of social variables in determining political functioning.

REGIONAL AFFINITY vs. SEPARATISM

Man is a social animal. A statement heard and said in all generations. Regional proximity is the natural outcome of human beings. It is not only desired, rather promoted by sociologists for development of the nation. Feeling of oneness and belongingness are such ingredients, which are essentially required for national integration. Identity seeks certainty; it seeks clear-cut boundaries. One is either a citizen or an alien, either an Indian or a foreigner.[37] The moment this feeling is subjugated to parochial regional interest, it fosters separatist tendency and converts nationalism into regionalism. It simply means giving priority to sectional interests over national good. This poses a positive threat to the security and integrity of a country. Hence, there is a thin line of demarcation between regional proximity and national identity.

After independence, efforts were made to make Indians realize the worth of being an Indian. Though India is a federal state, yet we practice single citizenship. We have adopted single Judiciary broadest at the base and tapering towards the top. At the apex is Supreme Court, which remains the highest court of appeal. India has a cultural, pluralism having diversity of caste, community, creed, language and culture, which is both an opportunity and threat for India. At times, it had created apprehension in the minds of its citizens. Soon after independence nationalist fervour were subdued under ulterior motive of selfish few. Indian National Congress was termed as north Indian political party trying to override interests of people of South India. Centralizing tendency in Indian federation led to stiff opposition. The emergence and growth of demands of separate independent states, regional advocacy and regional autonomy flared up the issue out of proportion and eventually regionalism characterized Indian Political system. However during the Nehru era Centre has resorted to coercive measures to suppress political dissent proving the fact that balance of power in Indian federal system has shifted to the centre.[38]

Tamil Nadu was the first state, which demanded to secede from the Indian federation, however it was not successful because stringent action was taken by the Central government. Sixteenth Constitutional amendment was made which declared India as a union of states and no state will be excused for making a separatist demand. Territorial integrity of India will not be tolerated to be violated. Tamil Nadu requested the other three states of south to join hands in this secession movement, but they all expressed their unwillingness, and hence, the movement died its natural death. This event however sowed the seeds of regional politics. The period of 60's and 70's witnessed regional agitation of an extreme form. Shri Jarnail Singh Bhinderwale preached the idea of separate state for Sikhs called khalistan. This promoted loot, killing and arson and misuse of Akal Takht which intensified terrorist activities. Government of India decided to have Blue Star operation in golden temple, Amritsar which led to the assassination of former Prime Minister Mrs. Indira Gandhi. Another secessionist demand was made in eastern India by Mizos. The insurgency came to an end when the protagonist Laldenga signed an accord with the centre and Mizoram was declared a full fledged state. The problem of Kashmir has also given birth to militancy. The making of Punjab and Haryana or Bombay and Gujarat are glaring examples of regional rift. The operation of Rhino in Assam to contain UlFA movement, the Cauvery water dispute between Karnataka and Tamil Nadu, the Belgaun boundary dispute between Karnataka and Maharashtra, the making of Jharkhand state on tribal identity and Uttrakhand on hilly culture, the agitation and the making of Telengana an autonomous state within Andhra Pradesh, the North-South lingual divide and the like are rampant in Indian Polity, thereby posing a positive threat to India's sovereignty and integrity.

Factors responsible for growth of regionalism are as follows:

Language Affinity

India is a multi-lingual state. Before independence nationalist appeals were made in various languages and various organizations were formed on the basis of languages. It was thought by the nationalist elites that it would promote patriotism. But post-independence period witnessed divisive tendencies around linguistic issues. There arose a controversy among the elite on whether the states should be re-organized on the linguistic basis or not. The question of official language also baffled the Indian elite. On the one hand, it was realized that the predominance of English language would keep the masses alienated, on the other hand, there could hardly emerge a consensus on the issue. On the language issue, the introduction of Hindi would annoy the people of South India. Under such circumstances, Hindi was made an official language but it was further stated that those who did not know Hindi, for them English would be used side by side as an official language along with Hindi. But members like Minoo Masani and T.T. Krishanamachari opposed this because they observed that it 'was designed to impose Hindi upon non-Hindi speaking people and their cultures'. Thus, language can easily be said to be the bases of regionalism.

Demand for secession from the Indian Union

Demand for secession from India constitutes the extreme dimensions of regionalism in India. Secessionist forces have been present in Jammu and Kashmir, Manipur, Nagaland, Mizoram and Tripura and infact in the whole of North-East India. For example,

(a) Demand for the creation of Khalistan as the home land of Sikhs between the year 1980–1992.
(b) Mizoram demand in Assam outside the Union of India.

(c) Demand for Nagaland outside the Indian Union.

(d) Demand for Jammu and Kashmir.

Demand for separate statehood within the Indian Union

After the 1956 reorganization of States within India, there continues to be demand for separate statehood in various parts of the country. The rise in the number of states of the Indian Union from 16 in 1956 to 25 in 1989, to 28 in 2000 to 29 in 2014 tends to validate this statement. In 1960, the bilingual state of Bombay was bifurcated into Maharashtra and Gujarat. In 1963, the State of Nagaland was carved out of Assam. In 1966, Punjab was reorganized into Punjabi speaking Punjab, Hindi speaking Haryana, and hilly areas into Himachal Pradesh and Chandigarh. In 1969, the state of Meghalaya was formed out of Assam. In 2000, the States of Jharkhand was created out of Bihar, Uttranchal out of Uttar Pradesh and Chhatisgarh out of Madhya Pradesh. The year 2014 has already witnessed the making of Telengana State. However, some more demands for the creation of separate states out of the existing states, still continue to be there. Like Swarashtra in Gujarat and Vidhrava in Maharashtra.

Demand for full statehood

The Union territories have been putting forward their demands for grant of full statehood. Most of such demands have already been accepted. In 1971, Himachal Pradesh got the status of a full state, and thereafter, Manipur, Tripura, Mizoram, Arunachal Pradesh (Former NEFA), Sikkim got full statehoods. Thus, the demand of full statehood reflect deep-rooted regionalism. However, it also reflects the policy of the government of India to please the people of these areas by satisfying their regional aspirations through the grant of statehoods.

Demand for Regional Autonomy within a State

In some of the states of the Indian Union, people belonging to various regions have been demanding recognition of their regional identity. These demands are now converting into the demands for the grant of statehood. Gorkhaland movement is a glaring example of it.

Cultural Pluralism

The presence of multi cultural, communal, lingual and caste group in India has greatly helped in the growth of regionalism.

Inter-state disputes as a manifestation of regionalism

Boundary disputes, water disputes and forest disputes between two states clearly reveals regionalism. Each state or region wants to win over and above the other states. For example, the boundary disputes between Maharashtra and Karnataka on Belgaun, between Karnataka and Kerala on Kasargod, between Assam and Nagaland on Rangma reserved forest in Rangapani area, between Assam and Meghalaya on Langpih, Hakumari and Jirigiran river area of Garo Gills, and between Assam and Arunachal Pradesh on Pasighat area are manifestations of regionalism. To this, we can add the Inter-state water disputes. For example, the disputes between Punjab and Haryana over the issue of distribution of Ravi-Beas and Sutlej waters, likewise the dispute between Gujarat, Rajasthan, Madhya Pradesh and Maharashtra on the issue of sharing of Narmada waters, among Karnataka, Kerala and Tamil Nadu over the distribution of Cauvery waters was again a case of regionalism.

Regional imbalance

Some regions have a high level of economic development and some are economically backward. The leaders of economically backward region instigatepeople living in that region and form regional parties for representing regional interest and for strengthening their power.

Religious factor

Akali Dal, Muslim League, Hindu Maha Sabha, Shiv Sena, Tamil Sena, anti-Hindi Sena are political parties which help in the growth of religious based regionalism.

Lingual Issues

The adoption of Hindi in Devanagari script as the official language of the Union by the Constituent Assembly could not solve the language problem forever.

The First Official Language Commission was appointed in 1955 with B.G. Kher as the Chairman. It submitted its report in 1956, which was presented to Parliament in 1957. A joint Parliamentary Committee examined the report and declared that English should be the principal language and Hindi the subsidiary official language till 1965. After 1965, when Hindi becomes the principal official language of the Union, English should continue as the subsidiary official language.

Although the Constituent Assembly had not favoured the idea of linguistic reorganization of States, soon after the commencement of the Constitution, violent movements started in various parts of the country for reorganization of States on linguistic basis.[39]

The creation of a separate linguistic state of Andhra Pradesh opened the floodgates of linguistic passions and demands for the creation of linguistic states were raised from all quarters. Consequently, the Central government announced on 29 December 1953 the appointment of a States' Reorganization Commission to examine the question of the reorganization of the States.[40]

In Madras, the DMK adopted a hostile attitude towards Hindi, and gave the issue a racial twist. They raised a slogan 'English ever Hindi never' and started with violent agitation and called it as North Indian Imperialism. The West Bengal Legislative Assembly passed a resolution in 1958 for the retention of English as the official language of the State. The Assam Government discarded both Hindi and English and declared Assamese as the official language of the State in 1960. In Punjab, the Akalis refused to accept Hindi as the official language.

Arnold Toynbee, the historian rightly remarked, "while linguistic nationalism is a disintegrative force, it is a fair price that India has to pay for the introduction of democracy. In a country of 440 millions, if we really want to reach these millions through administration and through education we have to give the fullest scope to these languages." The problem however is that, "Certain people tried to make language a clock for their ambitious designs in other fields notably in politics and employment."[41]

Union government convened in New Delhi in September–October, 1961 a national integration conference. The conference examined the language problem and recommended the adoption of a three-language formula for secondary education all over the country. The formula envisaged compulsory teaching of three languages in schools—the regional language, English and Hindi in non-Hindi States; and Hindi, English and a modern Indian language in Hindi States. The States did not respond favourably to the three-language formula and did not uniformly adhere to it.[42]

Eighth Schedule of the Indian Constitution dealing with official languages has also been exploited by social contractors and power mongers. Earlier there were fifteen languages now we have twenty two as a result of lingual agitation. It is unfortunate that the language problem, which is essentially a national issue, has been pushed into the quagmire of power politics.[43]

Remedies to Control Regionalism

1. Secession in every form needs to be checked by forceful implementation of the law and well designed socialisation process.
2. The policy of appeasement of the minorities by political parties for securing electoral gains always encourages negative regionalism. So, there should be an end of policy of appeasement.
3. By developing a common national official language and through reforms in the educational system, regionalism can be checked.
4. Socio-economic backwardness is the root cause of regionalism. To cope-up with these, it is important that there should be a proper and effective rural development, rapid industrial advancement along with sustainable development.
5. The centre should never try to act as a big brother of states. It should refrain from building up centralism in the name of national unity and try to work like a co-operative federalism.

CONCLUSION

National integration demands not only acknowledgement of multiple centres of culture but also non-discrimination and equal opportunities to all groups, including allowing them to continue and develop legitimate separate identities in their limited spheres. India's unity can be preserved and strengthened by encouraging the development of its diverse communities with relative autonomy and self-governing. This demands a determined struggle of all the oppressed and excluded sections against the reactionary forces, the so-called mainstream, and establishment of genuine federalism and democracy.[44]

Recently, new politics has also emerged with the growing demand of special status to the states like Bihar, Jharkhand and Odhisha. Regional leaders are making this as an election issue, national parties are also politicking on it. This issue is though related to the development of the area, but politicians are giving it a regional colour. It is surprising to note that politics and society is a dialectical concept, which can be comprehended or be distorted, but even those who are most vocal in condemning it cannot afford to ignore it. It requires a value free research to redefine it as it forms the basis of understanding political sociology as a discipline. It needs a new interpretation in order to regain its loosing utility and relevance. It is a basic premise of philosophy of science which will never be out of context or anachronistic.

Questions for Discussion

1. Critically examine the role of caste in determining the nature of Indian polity.
2. Religion is both integrative and divisive force. Comment.
3. Regionalism poses a major threat to national integration. Elucidate.
4. Write an essay on politics and society in the Indian parliamentary democracy.

References

1. Singh, M.P. and Saxena, Rekha (2011), *Indian Politics: Constitutional Foundations and Institutional Functioning*, Delhi, PHI Learning, Delhi, p. 38.
2. *Ibid.*, p. 40.
3. Das, Hari Hara and Choudhury, B.C. (1997), *Introduction to Political Sociology*, New Delhi, Vikas Publishing, pp. 210–231.
4. Barber, Bernard (1968), *Social Stratification: Introduction*; in David Sills (Ed.), *International Encyclopedia of Social Science*, New York, Macmillan Press. Refer: Satyabrata Chakraborty (Ed.) (2005), *Political Sociology*, New Delhi, Macmillan Press, p. 162.

5. Gupta, Dipankar (2003), *Social Stratification: Hierarchy, Difference and Social Mobility*, in V. Das (Ed.), Oxford India Companion to Sociology and Social Anthropology, Delhi, Oxford University Press, p. 162.
6. Das, Hari Hara and Choudhury, B.C. (1997), *op. cit.*, p. 222.
7. *Ibid.*, p. 224.
8. Sharma, L.N. and Ashraf, Ali (1983), *op. cit.*, p. 42.
9. Marx, K. and Engels, F. (1962), *Selected Works*, Vol. 2, Moscow, Progress Publishers, p. 65.
10. Bendix, R. and Lipset, S.M. (Eds.) (1953), *Class, Status and Power: Factions in American Society*, Glencoe, Illinois, Free Press, p. 29.
11. Key, V.O. (1961), *Public Opinion and American Democracy*, New York, Alfred A. Knopf, p. 138.
12. Sharma, L.N. and Ashraf, Ali (1983), *op. cit.*, p. 46.
13. Gerth and Mills (1958), *From Max Weber: Essays in Sociology*, New York, Oxford University Press, p. 181.
14. Chakraborty, Satyabrata (Ed.) (2005), *op. cit.*, p. 167.
15. Das, Hari Hara and Choudhury, B.C. (1997), *op. cit.*, pp. 275–276.
16. Sharma, L.N. and Ashraf, Ali (1983), *op. cit.*, p. 53.
17. Das, Hari Hara and Choudhury, B.C. (1997), *op. cit.*, p. 262.
18. Srinivas, M.N. (1952), *Religion and Society Among the Coorgs of South India*, London, Oxford University Press, Detailed in *Caste in Modern India and Other Essays*, Bombay, Asia Publishing House, p. 23.
19. *Ibid.*
20. Beteille, A. (1969), *Castes: Old and New*, Bombay, Asia Publishing House, p. 70.
21. Rudolph, Lloyd I. and Rudolph, Susanne H. (1967), *The Modernity of Tradition*, Chicago, University of Chicago Press.
22. Chakraborty, Satyabrata, (Ed.), *Political Sociology*, Anjan Ghosh, *Social Stratification and Politics*, Delhi, Macmillan India, pp. 173–174.
23. Arora, S.K. (1972), *Social Background of the Indian Cabinet, Economic and Political Weekly*, Vol. VII, No. 31–33, pp. 1523–1525.
24. Weiner, M. and Kothari, R. (1965), *Indian Voting Behaviour: Studies of the 1962 General Elections*, Calcutta.
25. *Ibid.*
26. Sheth, D.L. (1971), *Caste and Politics: A Trend Report, Political Science in India: A Trend Report*, Indian Council of Social Sciences Research, Delhi.
27. Das and Choudhury (1997), *op. cit.*, pp. 289–290.
28. *Ibid.*, p. 294.
29. Fadia, B.L., (2005), *Indian Government and Politics*, Agra, Sahitya Bhawan Publications, p. 877.

30. Chandra, Bipin (1984), *Communalism in Modern India*, New Delhi, Vikas Publishing, p. 2.

31. Engineer, Asghar Ali, (1989), *Socio-Economic Basis of Communalism* in Virendra Grover (Ed.), *Political System in India*, Vol. 7, New Delhi, pp. 335–345.

32. Fyzee, Asaf A.A., *The Muslim Minority in India*, Quest, Bombay, October–December, 1969, p. 22.

33. *Ibid.*

34. *The Indian Express*, 16 August, 1992.

35. Engineer, Asghar Ali, *Distorting Indian History*, *The Times of India*, Bombay, 11 March, 1975, p. 8.

36. Doctor, A.H., *Interest Groups in India*, Quest, Bombay, No. 53, April–June 1967, p. 39.

37. Chakraborty, Satyabrata (Ed.) (2005), Sanjeeb Mukherjee, *Nation and Nationalism*, *op. cit.*, p. 81.

38. Brass, Paul R. (1994), *The Politics of India Since Independence*, Cambridge, Cambridge University Press, p. 35.

39. Avasthi, A.P. (2001), *Indian Government and Politics*, Agra, Lakshmi Narain Agarwal, p. 651.

40. *Ibid.*

41. Banerjee, Sunanda (2002), *An Introduction to Political Sociology*, New Delhi, Janaki Prakashan, p. 126.

42. *Ibid.*, p. 653.

43. *Ibid.*, p. 656.

44. Nagla, B.K. (Ed.). (1999), *Political Sociology*, Jaipur, Rawat Publications, p. 233.

Suggested Reading

Hari Hara Das and B.C. Choudhury, *Introduction to Political Sociology*

A.P. Avasthi, *Indian Government and Politics*

Satyabrata Chakraborty (Ed.), *Political Sociology*

Manoranjan Mohanty (Ed.), *Class, Caste, Gender*

Web Links

www.sagepub.com/journals/journal200925.

www.en.wikipedia.org/wiki/Politics_%26_Society

Hyman, Herber: *Political Socialization, A Study in the Psychology of Political Behaviour*, Glencoe, Illinois, 1959.

Inkles, Alex: *What is Sociology*, Englewood Cliffs, New Jersey, 1964.

Johari, J.C.: *Comparative Politics*, New Delhi, Sterling Publishers, 1982.

John Losee: *A Historical Introduction to the Philosophy of Science*, 4th ed., USA, Oxford University Press, 1972.

Jones, R.E.: *The Functional Analysis of Politics*, Humanities Press, New York, 1967.

Kaplan, Morton A.: *System and Process in International Politics*, Wiley, New York, 1957.

Karl Popper: *The Logic of Scientific Discovery*, New York, Basic Books, 1959.

Khullar Mala (Ed.): *Writing the Women's Movement: A Reader, Zuban an Imprint of Kali for Women*, New Delhi, 2005.

Lane, Robert E.: *Political Life: Why People Get Involved in Politics*, Free Press, Illinois, 1959.

Lasswell, Harold D.: *The Analysis of Political Behaviour*, Routledge and Kegan Paul, London, 1948.

Lasswell, Harold D. and Kaplan, A.: *Power and Society: A Framework/or Political Inquiry*, Yale University Pres, New Haven, 1950.

Lerner, Daniel: *Passing of Traditional Societies*, The Free Press, Glencoe, III, 1985.

Lipset, Seymour Martin (Ed.), *Political Man*, Heinemann, London, 1969.

Mac Iver, R.M.: *Modern State*, Oxford University Press, New York 1955.

Mac Iver, R.M. and Page, C.H.: *Society*, Macmillan, London, 1959.

Madhav Gadgil: *Ecology and Equity*, Penguin, New Delhi, 1995.

Merton, R.K.: *Social Theory and Social Structure*, 2nd ed., Free Press, Glencoe, 1968.

Michael Haralambos: *Sociology: Themes and Perspectives*, Delhi, Oxford University Press, 1980.

Michael Rush and Philip Althoff: *An Introduction to Political Sociology*, London, Nelson, 1971.

Milbrathth, L.: *Political Participation*, Rand McNally, Chicago, 1965.

Mitchell, W.C.: *Sociological Analysis and Politics*, Englewood Cliffs, Prentice Hall, New Jersey, 1967.

Michels, Robert: *Political Parties*, Dover Publications, New York, 1959.

Mosca, Gaetano: *The Ruling Class*, McGraw-Hill, New York, 1939.

Motilal Shashi, Nanda Bijaya Laxmi (Ed.): *Understanding Social Inequality Concerns Human Rights, Gender and Environment*, Macmillan Publishers India, New Delhi, 2010.

Ogburn, W.F.: *Social Change*, Viking, 1928.

Oommen, T.K.: *Nation Civil Society and Social Movements Essays in Political Sociology*, Sage Publications, New Delhi, 2004.

Parsons, Talcott: *The Social System*, The Free Press, Glencoe, Illimos, 1951.

Polsby, Nelson W.: *Community Power and Political Theory*, Yale University Press, New Haven, 1963.

Pye, Lucian W. (Ed.): *Aspects of Political Development*, Little Brown and Co., Boston, 1966.

Pye, Lucian W. and Verba, Sidney (Eds.): *Political Culture and Political Development*, Princeton University Press, Princeton, 1965.

Rana G.S.: *Bureaucracy and Good Governance*, Alfa Publications, New Delhi, 2010.

Rangrajan Mahesh: *Environment Issues in India: A Reader*, Pearson Education, Singapore, 2007.

Swarankar, R.C.: *Political Elite: A Sociological Study of Legislators in Rajasthan*, Jaipur, Rawat Publications, 1988.

Schumpeter, Joseph A.: *Capitalism, Socialism and Democracy*, George Allen and Unwin, London, 1966.

Sethi Meera (Ed.): *Women and Development the Indian Experience*, Sage Publications, New Delhi, 2001.

Sharma L.N. and Ashraf Ali: *Political Sociology: A new grammar of politics*, Universities Press, Madras, 1983.

Sharma K.L.: *Power Elite in Rural India* in B.K. Nagla (Ed.) *Political Sociology* (1999) Jaipur, Rawat Publications, 1982.

Sharma Rashmi: *Women Development New Approaches and Innovations*, Rigal Publications, New Delhi, 2009.

Sherif, M. and Sherif C.W.: *An Outline of Social Psychology*, Harper and Brothers, New York, 1948.

Srinivas, M.N. (Ed.): *Caste in Modern India and Other Essays*, Prentice Hall, New Delhi, 1962.

Urmila Sharma and S.K. Sharma: *Principles and Theory of Political Science*, New Delhi, Atlantic Publishers, 2000.

Varma, S.P.: *Modern Political Theory*, Vikas Publishers, Delhi, 1975.

Verba, Sydney: *Small Groups and Political Behaviour*, Princeton, 1961.

Warher, W. Lloyod: *American Life*, University of Chicago Press, 1953.

Weber, Max: *Protestant Ethics and Spirit of Capitalism*, translated from German by Talcott Parsons, Unwin University Books, London, 1971.

Wiseman, H.V.: *Political Systems*, Routledge and Kegan Paul, London, 1966.

Wright Mills, C.: *The Power Elite*, Oxford, University Press, London, 1950.

Young, Oran R.: *Systems of Political Science*, Englewood Cliffs, New Jersey, Prentice-Hall, Inc. 1968.

Zoya Hasan (Ed.): *Politics and the State in India*, Sage Publications, New Delhi, 2000.

Key Terms and Purport

Affirmative action: Policy designed to correct past practices of discrimination against racial minorities, women, the disabled, and other historically disadvantaged groups.

Aggregation: This term refers to the conversion of political demands into alternative courses of action, usually by political parties.

Alienation: A state of mind reflecting man's estrangement from himself and from his social and natural environment. Rousseau used the concept to signify man's separation from his nature. Marx's distinctive contribution, however lie in the fact that he saw this state of alienation as associated with private property and technology which compels the division of labour, and the institution of the wage contract.

Anomie: It is rootlessness of values, a state of mind resulting from the loss of norms or guiding principles of life and social action due to a series of rapid traumatic changes and mental agony in one's life situation.

Apathy: An indifference to or lack of interest in or withdrawal from the socio-political process either due to extreme frustration or satisfaction.

Appeasement: A policy of acceding to hostile demands in order to gain peace.

Articulation: This term was used in the structural-functional approach to politics, referring to the formation of political demands.

Authority: A feature of a person, role, office or government which makes legitimate the acts and commands exercised in its name. Authority must be distinguished from power. Former essentially legitimate unlike latter.

Behaviour(al)ism: It is a protest movement in political science against traditional philosophy. It insists on analyzing the observable behaviour of political actors, through empirical method.

Bureaucracy: A rule by administrative officers. In a bureaucracy actual power is vested in those who are, from the legal point of view, administrative intermediaries between sovereign and subject.

Caste: The hereditary division of society in India. Traditionally, based on hierarchy and functional identity, members of a caste are supposed to follow the occupation, social customs and religious rites of their caste.

Charisma: A certain quality of individual's personality by virtue of which he is set apart from ordinary men and treated as endowed with supernatural or exceptional powers or qualities.

Civic culture: It is the citizens acceptance of the authority of the State and a firm belief in participation in civil duties.

Civil Society: The set of intermediate associations which are neither the state nor the (extended) family; civil society therefore, includes voluntary associations and firms and other corporate bodies.

Class: A general term subsuming all those distinctions between people which involve unequal, but systematic distribution of privileges, thus covering distinctions of rank, caste, estate, status or degree.

Cleavage: The splitting of a political system along ethnic, ideological lines or any other specific factor creating a gulf.

Communication: It is a transmission of information, ideas, emotions, values and attitudes. Political communication is a two way process, between the government and citizens, though the actual forms and degrees of communication vary with the political system.

Conflict: A social condition depicting a clash or opposition of ideas, views or interests. It plays a useful part in the articulation of diversity and reconciliation or consensus of a higher order.

Conflict resolution: The methods and process of negotiation, arbitration, and institution building which promote the peaceful ending of social conflict and war.

Culture: It depicts a way of life. It refers to the learned patterns of thought, behaviour and action that distinguishes one race from the other.

Cybernetics: A study of communication, control and internal governance of systems where the various operations interact reciprocally and systematically.

Demagogue: Like democracy, the idea of a demagogue has its roots in the ambiguous Greek word demos meaning 'the people', but in the sense of either 'the population' or 'the mob'.

Differentiation: Division of labour and specialization leading to differentiation of roles and structures whereby roles are separated and performed by different individuals and structures.

Discrimination: Originally act of noting differences, discrimination now denotes differentiation between people on grounds, such as gender, colour, sexuality, disability, or class.

Efficacy: A term describing the capacity and performance of the people and the government in a democratic set up. It forms the basis mass mobility and political leadership.

Elite: It is an active minority that represents higher status, excellence or power in society. Elitism advocates the belief that the special role of the Elite is both desirable and inevitable even in democracy.

Empirical method: The methodology used for making generalizations on the basis of sensory experience, observation and experiment.

Empowerment: It refers to increasing the economic, political, social, educational, gender or spiritual strength of individuals and communities.

Faction: Any group organized within a political party, institution or government, defined partly by its opposition to some rival group or leader, acting in personal or group interest.

Feedback: A technical term of systems theory or cybernetics, but is widely misused to indicate a response to a question, action or policy.

Feminism: It is a relatively a recent term for the protection of equal rights for women and to provide them dignified life without any forms of human rights violation.

Gender and politics: A series of contribution by feminists in the field of politics and political theory, to challenge the patriarchal dominance in political decision-making and sharing in power structure.

Glass ceiling: It is the invisible and unbreakable barrier which keeps minority and women from rising to the upper rungs of the corporate ladder, regardless of their qualifications or achievements.

Human rights: Human rights are a special sort of inalienable moral entitlement for human beings.

Institutionalization: A process by which a social pattern becomes a norm, enforced by sanction and social recurrence.

Integration: Diversity of any form, not affecting the oneness and belongingness of people. It is a way of identifying oneself with the nation.

Interest aggregation: It is the amalgamation and organizing of numerous views and opinions into larger issues so as to facilitate their conversion into viable policies and programmes in tune with public interest.

Interest articulation: It refers to the expression of ideas, views and interests—public or sectional, and to the formulation of issues with a view to win public support and governmental acceptance.

Interest group: A group, united by common interests, having sufficient identity of purpose to act on its own behalf and which therefore has some influence either on public opinion or on government.

Leadership: It signifies the role of providing guidance, direction and co-ordination to a group, organization or country. It also refers to the capacity to inspire confidence in the rightness of one's purpose, courage in their collective execution, and obedience in the threat of resistance.

Legitimacy: It is the popular support which provides both lawful and consensus binding to any act, order or action.

Masses: The body of common people in a society.

Mass media: The various agents of mass communication and entertainment: newspapers, magazines and other publications, television, radio, cinema and internet.

Modernization: A widely used term. It can be understood as the process of socioeconomic and cultural change from feudal to industrial, from rural to urban, and from community based on primary relationships to society based on secondary relationships.

New social movement: This is a term used to describe a diverse set of popular movements characterized by a departure from conventional methods of political organization and expression and a post-modern enlightened strategy.

Participation: It is the involvement of those affected by decisions in the process of decision-making. Involvement may include a right to elect representatives, to vote on issues, to campaign and canvass, to decide matters, to veto, etc.

Political culture: It is a set of values, norms and attitudes pertaining to politics and political processes. The assumption is that these values, norms and attitudes are predispositions that condition the style of political behaviour.

Political development: It is the capability of a political system to maintain its stability, to solve problems and meet demands, encourage popular participation and avoid disorder.

Political socialization: The process by which people come to acquire political attitudes and values. It is a life long learning process and a means of making a person into a citizen.

Political sociology: It is broadly conceived as the study of power and domination in social relationship.

Politicization: It is the process by which an activity or institution, seemingly non-political, is transformed into one that is consciously directed towards political ends.

Positive discrimination: An institutionalized way of enabling those historically disadvantaged by a political system to participate in public life.

Power: It is the ability to achieve the desired effect, to make people (or things) do what they would not otherwise have done, even in the face of resistance from others. It may be exercised either through persuasion or through force.

Pressure group: An interest group is the one which exerts sufficient influence on government to be able to put pressure on behalf of its interests.

Psephologist: A person who studies electoral behaviour, conducts pre-election and post-election opinion polls, analysis factors effecting voting behaviour and makes prophecy which may be correct or incorrect. But it has tremendous impact on the electorate.

Regionalism: The practice of or belief in regional government, as superior to the national interest thereby posing a positive threat to the sovereignty and integrity of a country.

Sanskritization: It is process where people from backward category immolates the culture of the forward class in order to move upward in the social hierarchy. Scared thread ceremony is one of its examples illustrated by psephologist M.N. Srinivas.

Secularization: It is the process by which man's orientation is changed from the mundane world to rational-spiritual world.

Sexism: It is a form of gender discrimination or prejudice based on a person's sex or gender. It is a practice that is supported in many different ways that are crucial to our socialization into our sex roles.

Social capital: It is the expected collective or economic benefits derived from the preferential treatment and co-operation between individuals and groups. It also refers to social networks, systems of reciprocal relations, set of norms, or levels of trust that individuals or groups may have, or to the resources arising from them.

Social mobility: It is the upward or downward movement of individual families and groups from one class or status group to another. It is often associated with uprising of underpriviledged.

Social mobilization: It is the process of deep social change that results the loss of roots and weakening of traditions.

Social stratification: It is a social division in the society based on Inequalities of wealth, power, influence, education, privilege and the like. It creates cleavage between higher and a lower order in the society.

Socialization: It refers to the process whereby the individual acquires the norms, roles and rules pertaining to social relations that enable him to be an effective member of society.

Stability: It implies the security of a regime from the threat of subversion, revolution, rebellion and eventual overthrow. Such security may be obtained on the basis of military or economic power but in the long run legitimacy and popular support are required to sustain it.

Structural functionalism: In this structure primarily refers to normative patterns of behaviour whilst function explains how such patterns operate as systems.

Value: It is under determinant of human behaviour. It varies from person to person and are different from norms which are set standards of society.

Westernization: It is an emulating pattern of the people of East without critically analyzing its impact on their oriental values and culture.

Source: *The Concise Oxford Dictionary of Politics* by Iain McLean and Alistair McMillan (Indian Edition), Oxford, Oxford University Press, 2004.

PROPOUNDERS

It is an alphabetical compilation of some important thinkers who have played a very significant role in evolving the discipline of political sociology, which is still in the process of making additional alterations.

Andre Beteille (1934–): India's leading sociologist who is famous for his contribution to caste system and of Indian politics particularly South India. He was awarded 'Padma-Bhushan' in the year 2005 for his scholarly contribution in Sociology. Some of his famous books are *The Backward Classes in Contemporary India* (1992); *Inequality and Social Change* (*1972*). He dynamically explains the contest between religion and secularism, between poverty and inequality and between caste and class.

Ashis Nandy (1937–): He is an Indian political psychologist, a social theorist and a contemporary cultural and political critic. His book *Alternative Sciences* (1980) gave him enough popularity. He has to his credit a lot number of books. He was graced with Fukuoka Asian Culture Award for his chief contribution in the field of culture and tolerance.

C.W. Mill (1916–1962): He was an American sociologist and a Professor of sociology at Columbia University. His books *The Power Elite* (1956); *The New Men of Power* (1948) *The Marxist* (1962) made him best known for his controversial critiques of both contemporary society and sociological practice.

Charles E. Merriam (1874–1953): He was a Professor of Political Science at the University of Chicago and was founder of Behaviourlist approach. He wrote many books. Some of them are *A History of American Political Theories* (1903); *Public and Private Government* (1944).

David Apter (1924–2010) was an American political scientist and sociologist. His major contribution is in the field of inter disciplinary study and research. He offers *The Politics of Modernization* (1965) was his most renowned work, for researchers.

David Easton (1917–2014): A Canadian Political Scientist who has authored several books *The Political System: An Inquiry into the State of Political Science* (1953); *A Framework for Political Analysis* (1965); *A Systems Analysis of Political Life* (1965); *Systems Analysis in Political Science Today* (1980). He introduced the input-output framework in systems analysis and talked about authoritative allocation of values.

Emile Durkheim (1858–1917) was a French sociologist and coined the term 'Anomie' which means rootlessness of values leading to suicide, riot, terrorism and many other impulsive sporadic outbursts which lucidly explains the process of change, revolution and political development. He is the author of many books like *The Division of Labour in Society* (1893); *Suicide* (1897); English edition (1951); *Bureaucracy and Political Development: A Paradoxical View* (1963).

Erich Fromm (1900–1980): He was German social psychologist and a champion of democratic governance. He is renowned for his critical analysis of human nature and freedom and its impact on the social psychology.

Fred W. Riggs (1917–2008): He was a political scientist and a pioneer in administrative model building and theory formulation, especially in developing countries, Riggs is known for his advocacy of understanding administration as part of the political process and of the need to integrate administration with political development or in other words, comparative Public Administration. He became popular with his book *Public Administration in Developing Countries* (1964).

Gabriel A. Almond (1911–2002): American Political scientist along with James Coleman edited *Politics of the Developing Areas* and wrote its famous Introduction (1960); authored with Sidney Verba, *The Civic Culture: Political Attitudes and Democracy in Five Nations* (1963); *Comparative Politics A Developmental Approach: An Analytic Study* (1972); *Comparative Politics: System, Process and Policy* (1978). He introduced a developmental approach to politics. His significant contributions to comparative politics include the identification of structures and styles of modern and traditional political systems and the introduction of three ideal types of political culture—subject, parochial and participant.

Gaetano Mosca (1858–1941): He was an Italian political scientist, journalist and public servant. He is credited with developing the theory of elitism and the doctrine of the political class. He wrote a book *The Ruling Class* (1939) English translation and is popularly known as democratic elitist thinker who mooted the idea of hereditary law in governance.

Giovanni Sartori (1924–): A thinker from Italy, who wrote books entitled *Democratic Theory* (1962); *From Sociology of Politics to Political Sociology* (1964). His major contribution lies in giving autonomous status to political sociology as a discipline, not necessarily bearing the marks of their parents.

Harold D. Lasswell (1902–1980), a political sociologist and psychologist from America who has authored many numbers of books. *Propaganda Technique in the World War* (1972); *Psychopathology and Politics* (1930); *Psychology of Hitlerism* (1933); *World Politics and Personal Insecurity* (1935); *Politics: Who Gets What, When and How* (1936); *Democracy through Public Opinion* (1941). His main focus was on some cherished values which makes a man influential.

Karl Marx (1818–1883): A great philosopher from Germany who became synonymous with the concept of class struggle. *The Economic and Philosophical Manuscripts of 1844* (1932, English edition 1953); *The German Ideology* (1845–1846); *The Poverty of Philosophy* (1847); *The Communist Manifesto* (1858); *Grudrisse, Foundations of the Critique of Political Economy* (1857–1858), German edition 1939–1941, English edition 1973); *A Critique of Political Economy* (1859); *Das Capital*, Vol. 1 (1867); *Selected Works* authored with Engels (1962). He is one of the greatest thinkers and a strong proponent of a revolutionary ideology and movement.

Karl Popper (1902–1994): He was an Austro British Philosopher of the 20th century. He is known for his monumental work *The Open Society and its Enemies* (1945). Through this work he tries to draw generalization based on empirical inquiry.

Karl W. Deutsch (1912–1992): A great thinker in the field of education has come out with many books—*Political Community at the International Level:*

Problems of Definition and Measurement (1954); *Political Analysis and the Nerves of Government: Models of Political Communication and Control* (1962). He has done path breaking work in the field of political communication, control and development. The application of cybernetics owes much to his ideas.

Lucian Pye (1921–2008): He was a Political Scientist, and a renowned thinker of Comparative Politics in United States of America. He was a Chinese thinker and specialised in *Political Culture and Political Development* which is also the title of one of his co-authored books (1965). His other books are often read by contemporary political researchers.

Max Weber (1864–1920): He hails from Germany. He championed the idea of bureaucracy as the most rationalized and legal type of rule or governance. He came up with many books like *The Methodology of the Social Sciences* (1949); *The Protestant Ethic and the Spirit of Capitalism* (1905, English edition 1970); *Wirtschaft and Gesellschaft* (*Economy and Society*) 3 vols. (1925). His basic contribution to political sociology is the introduction of the concept of ideal type of Rule.

Michael Rush (1937–): He retired as an Emeritus Professor of Politics in the year 2003. He was Associate Editor, *Journal of Legislative Studies*. He became popular with his work with Philip Althoff entitled *An Introduction to Political Sociology*, which came out in the year 1971. He also solely authored a book entitled *Politics and Society: An Introduction to Politial Sociology* in 1992.

Niccolo Machiavelli (1469–1527) is a great political scientist who has written a classic book entitled *The Prince* (1513); *The Discourses* (1518). His idea of fox like cunningness and lion like strength to be possessed by ruler has made him the father modern political science.

Oran R. Young (1941–): He is a Professor and Co-director of the programme on governance and environmental institutions. He came out with some famous works *Governance in World Affairs* (1999), *Compliance and Public Authority* (1979). He discussed the crucial points of communication in findings protection to environment in a stateless society.

Philip Althoff (1927–2013): He is a Professor of Political at Kansas State University.

Rajni Kothari (1928–2009): He was an Indian psephologist with a vast number of publications to his name, *Caste in Indian Politics: Politics in India* (1970); *Footstep into the Future: Diagnosis of the Present World and a Design for an Alternative* (1975). As a psephologist of the third world, Kothari has done original analysis of Indian politics and society and is well known for his interpretation of the Indian party system and the Congress system.

Raymond Aron (1905–1983) belonged to France. His works were: *The Opium of the Intellectuals* (English edition 1957); *Social Structure and the Ruling Class* (1966). As a sociologist, intellectual and journalist, Aron has written several widely read books on contemporary social and political issues.

Robert A. Dahl (1915–2014) is from America. He has written a book *Who Governs? Democracy and Power in an American City* (1961). Professor of politics at Yale University, Dahl is famous for his study of a university town, focusing on its power structure and the changing patterns of local Elites. This is not only a landmark in the study of community power structure but also a major contribution to the study of democratic theory.

Robert E. Lane (1931–): He is an American political scientist and political psychologist. He is the Professor Emeritus of Political Science in Yale University and he championed the cause of common people through Socialization in creating matured political culture. His book entitled *The Loss of Happiness in Market Democracies* (2000) is a work of great understanding and research.

Robert Merton (1910–2003) is from America. He has written a book named *Social Theory and Social Structure* (1949). He introduced the concept of dysfunctions and non-functions—indicating that some structures or institutions may produce consequences harmful to society if they fail to accommodate dysfunctions under justified conditions.

Robert Michels (1876–1936): He is an Italian political sociologist and economist noted for his formulation of the 'Iron law of Oligarchy'. He wrote many books—*Political Parties: A Sociological Study of the Oligarchical Tendencies of Modern Democracy* (1911); English edition (1915); *First Lectures in Political Sociology* (English edition 1949). His 'iron law of oligarchy' has far reaching consequences for the understanding of political process and reinforces the neo-Machiavellian projection of elitism.

Samuel Huntington (1927–2008): He was a conservative political scientist from USA who became popular with his meticulous work *Clash of Civilization and the Remaking of World Order* (1996); He also wrote a book titled *Culture Matters: How Values Shape Human Progress* (1997). He forwarded componential theory of political development.

Seymour Martin Lipset (1922–2006): American political scientist who has authored *Political Man* (1960); *The First New Nation: The US in Historical and Comparative Perspective* (1963). He is a prolific writer on the concept of political participation and the social basis of democracy.

Sidney Verba (1932–): He is an American political scientist and was Carl H. Pforzheimer University Professor Emeritus and Research Professor of Government in Harvard University. His book titled *The Civic Culture* (1963); *Voice and Equality* (1995); *Elites and the Idea of Equality* (1987) made him first rank democratic thinker. He designed political attitudes in democracy with the logic of comparative social enquiry.

T.B. Bottomore (1920–1992): He was a British Marxist thinker, a sociologist and strongly believed in the idea of equality. He, in his book *Sociology, Elites and Society* (1964) and *Dictionary of Marxist Thought* (1985), tried to prove that inequality is inevitable.

Talcott Parsons (1902–1979) was an American thinker. His Works are *The Structure of Social Action* (1937); *The Social System* (1951); with Shils *Toward a General Theory of Action* (1951). His identification of functional pre requisites (goal-attainment, adaptation, integration and pattern maintenance) and contrasting modes and styles of functions (universalistic-particularistic, specific-diffuse, achievement-ascriptive, affective-affective neutral and collectivity vs self-oriented) have been applied subsequently by scholars and have far reaching consequences.

Vilfredo Pareto (1848–1923): He is from Italy. His outstanding works gave him much name and fame. *Mind and Society: A Treatise on General Sociology*, 4 vols. (1916–1917) English edition (1935); *The Rise and Fall of the Elites* (1901), English edition (1935). His outstanding contribution to political sociology is his concept of logical and non-logical actions, residues and derivatives, and his theory of Elites and circulation of Elites.

Yogendra Yadav (1963–): He is an Indian sociologist. He is one of the founder members of the centre for the study of social systems and is renowned for his commendable work on modernization. Some of his famous works are *Essays on Modernization in India* (1978); *Social Change in India: Crisis and Resilience* (1993). At present he is senior leader in AAP.

Source: Sharma, L.N. and Ashraf, Ali, *Political Sociology: A New Grammar of Politics*, Universities Press, Madras, 1983.

Index